Obscuricon presents

'80s Teen Flick Festival

Guide Book

May 15 - 25, 2020

Raymond J. Regis Cinema
Raleigh, North Carolina

Curated by
Joseph Corey III

Guide Book Production by
Roger Becker

Josie Alma Press
Raleigh, NC

About the Curator:

Joseph Corey III has been a longtime contributor to InsidePulse and ASiteCalledFred entertainment websites. He served on the curating staff as researcher and programmer at the Moving Image Archive in Winston-Salem, NC. While in Raleigh, he was substitute host of the influential Cinema Overdrive film series. He is a graduate of North Carolina State University and the School of Filmmaking at the North Carolina School of the Arts. During the '80s, he was the main entertainment columnist in the Technician newspaper at NC State. He reviewed many of the films being showing at the '80s Teen Flick Festival upon their original theatrical release. He visited the Galleria in Sherman Oaks before the renovation. He didn't get to eat at Perry's Pizza Parlor.

Copyright 2020 by Joseph Corey III

All Rights Reserved

ISBN: 9798571614672

The *'80s Teen Flick Festival Guide Book* includes photos, stills, posters and soundtrack album cover for the purpose of criticism and documentation. All copyrights held by production companies, artists, authors and/or any copyright holders.

#80sTeenFlickFest

A Message From the Festival's Curator

On behalf of Obscuricon, the historic Ray Regis Cinema, the employees, the volunteers, the sponsors, the vendors and Carl the Janitor, we welcome you to our '80s Teen Flicks Festival. For the next 11 days allow yourself to be transported to a magical time before the internet, smart phones and reality TV. What did the teenagers of this historic time have in that distant time? Rubik's Cube, *The Official Preppy Handbook*, MTV with real VJs and dozens of movies starring teenagers that looked just like them.

The 33 films chosen for the festival represent an era when new faces appeared on the silver screen every weekend. This wave of talent can only be compared to the early '70s when movie producers discovered audiences in the inner cities wanted to see Pam Grier, Jim Brown and Fred Williamson on the marquee. When Hollywood realized teenagers were a big part of the box office, they had to find younger faces than Marlon Brando and Helen Hayes to play high schoolers. Producers went looking for fresh new faces for the '80s. Almost overnight new names began to appear above the title such as Molly Ringwald, Andrew McCarthy, Rob Lowe, Demi Moore, Jon Cryer, Matthew Modine and John Cusack. This wasn't a group of one and done disposable actors as they were cast in more and more films as the decade progressed. Teenagers watched their thespian peers grow up in public. John Cusack went from a pervy private school jerk in *Class* to holding a boombox over his head to profess true love in *Say Anything...* Molly Ringwald's plight went from a girl whose parents forgot her sixteenth birthday to a hooker in Kentucky. You never know how the roles would turn out for your favorite new actors except the certainty that James Spader's character would be creepy. You knew these kids better than anyone in your homeroom.

While a majority of the films screening are from major studios, we have dug into a few indie features that got into the teen flick business. Troma didn't do the usual high school flick when *Class of Nuke'Em High* melted down in theaters. Crown International did its best to create a high schooler's dream with *My Tutor*. Cinema Epoch delivered a high schooler's fantasy in *Private Lessons*. The small studios were willing to push the envelope of taste in order to get the teens wanting to sneak into the theater.

Since he's known as the King of Teen Flicks, all six of John Hughes' teenage films will be part of the festival. You'll get to see his progress as a director, screenwriter and producer from *Sixteen Candles* to *Some Kind of Wonderful*. Our offer still stands that if you buy tickets for the first five, we'll give you a free pass for *Some Kind of Wonderful*.

Amazingly enough after 11 days and 33 films, there's still so much more to this glorious time. You may ask about why we didn't pick certain films. Where is *Real Genius, Taps, Endless Love, Heathers, Nightmare on Elm Street* or *Footloose*? Rest assured that this will not be Obscuricon's final dive into the '80s if you pack all your friends into the Fiero, buy plenty of Old Style beer, pull up your Chic jeans, unite your colors of Benetton, strap on your most unique Swatch and enjoy the show. Just remember at the end of the night to put your drink cups and popcorn tubs in the trash or Carl the Janitor will reconsider welcoming you here.

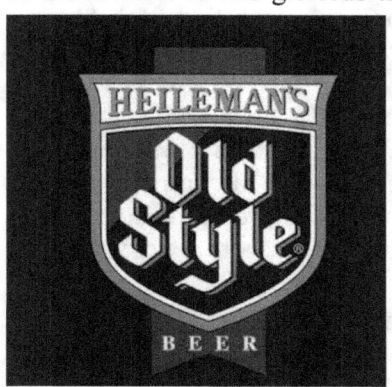

'80s Teen Flick Festival Schedule

Friday May 15, 2020
Foxes 7 p.m.
Fast Times At Ridgemont High 9:15

Saturday May 16
Sixteen Candles 2:00 p.m.
Breakfast Club 4:00 p.m.
Weird Science 7:00 p.m.
Pretty In Pink 9:30 p.m.
Some Kind of Wonderful Midnight

Sunday May 17
Private School 2:00 p.m.
Class 4:00 p.m.
Better Off Dead 7:00 p.m.
Risky Business 9:15 p.m.

Monday May 18
Youngblood 7:00 p.m.
Vision Quest 9:15 p.m.

Tuesday May 19
Red Dawn 7:00 p.m.
Lost Boys 9:15 p.m.

Wednesday May 20
My Tutor 7:00 p.m.
Private Lessons 9:15 p.m.

Thursday May 21
Class of Nuke 'Em High 7:00 p.m.
Class of 1984 9:15 p.m.

Friday May 22
No Small Affair 7:00 p.m.
One Crazy Summer 9:15 p.m.

Saturday May 23
Losin' It 2:00 p.m.
The Sure Thing 4:00 p.m.
Valley Girl 7:00 p.m.
Ferris Bueller's Day Off 9:30 p.m.
O.C. and Stiggs Midnight

Sunday May 24
The Pick-up Artist 2:00 p.m.
Fresh Horses 4:00 p.m.
St. Elmo's Fire 7:00 p.m.
Less Than Zero 9:15 p.m.

Monday May 25 (Memorial Day)
River's Edge 4:00 p.m.
Rachel Papers 7:00 p.m.
Say Anything... 9:00 p.m.

TICKET INFORMATION
Tickets are available in advance from the box office.

Cash Only!

$10 for an individual screening ticket
$40 for 5 tickets
$100 for a Weekend Pass
$200 for a Series Pass
Ask about our *Some Kind of Wonderful* Freebie Ticket.

We do not take reservations over the phone even if you're the **Sausage King of Chicago**. Our box office phone number is not listed here for exactly that reason.

How Teens of the '80s Watched Teen Flicks in the '80s

If you're under 50, you might not have a clue how teenagers watched the films we'll be showing over the next 11 nights at the festival. They didn't merely speak a title into their TV's remote control and have it instantly streamed to an internet connected HDTV in their bedroom. Nor did they watch them on their smartphone while sitting in the back seat of dad's electric SUV. Things were tricky back in the analog era when a teen wanted access to *Class* or *Risky Business*. The act of getting to watch movies improved as the decade proceeded, but in 1980 there were limited options when it came to R-rated films.

When you're a teenager in high school, the R-rated ones were the ones that counted. The films with the Restricted access rating were the ones you could summarize at lunch to get a crowd at your table instead of eating alone. They were the ones that promised more than an *ABC After School Special* could deliver. Telling the highlights of the film could make a freshman sound as sophisticated as a senior. The films were inspirational to a high schooler that craved a tale of a cinematic high schooler getting lucky with a female classmate, a teacher, a classmate's mother, a hooker or a classmate's sister. At some point characters were going to strip down and slide into bed to a soft rock tune or a female character was going to unfasten her bra to flash the camera. The ultimate film had a female locker room in full use just like a teen boy imagined the one at their school looked like on the other side of the shower head wall. If none of those scenes existed, the prudes at the MPAA would have given it a PG. The R-rated film knew its prime audience was hormonally charged freshmen in high school and they didn't want to tease that crowd. More tickets were sold when someone on the bus said, "I saw her breasts" than breaking down the subtext of the young hero's plight. Seeing as I entered high school in 1980, I'm typing from the experience of being there on that bus. The more pervy the plotline, the more we plotted to see the film.

How could a teenager under 17 get into an R-rated movie in the '80s? First way was to have cool parents who didn't mind taking their children to the theater. You'd hear rumors of kids whose parents would drive down, buy tickets for the R-rated teen film, purchase popcorn for everyone and sit far away from the teens during the film to give them a bit of privacy. Of course, these mythical cool parents were also the ones that allegedly let their teenagers flip through their *Playboy* magazines for the articles. The backup plan could be an older sibling sneaking them inside. But often the watchdog behind the box office glass would immediately point out that the sibling had to be 21 or over and considered a guardian to purchase a ticket for a teenager. Those were the MPAA fascist rules. The only good part in being busted was you could just fake ignorance and walk away in defeat. It didn't have the harsh consequences of attempting to buy beer at a Piggly Wiggly where the cops were immediately called and your name appeared in the local paper. There would be no small-town judgement stares or punishment for wanting to see *Foxes*.

Buying a ticket for an R-rated film so you could hang with the 11th and 12th graders got a little bit easier when the hot new craze in theaters arrived. Single screen theaters were suffering during the mid-70s. If they didn't book the right film or double feature, people didn't show up. There was a rush to turn them into Twin Theaters. How? By putting a wall in the middle of the theater and punching extra holes in the projector booth. Twice the offerings on half the screen size at least allowed owners to double the choice. However, this wasn't enough because viewers wanted more. The next stage arrived in the Megaplex phenomenon. These new buildings had four or more theaters and lurked near busy shopping malls instead of inside them. How did this help a teenager wanting to view the forbidden joy of an R-rated film? Since there were four films running at once,

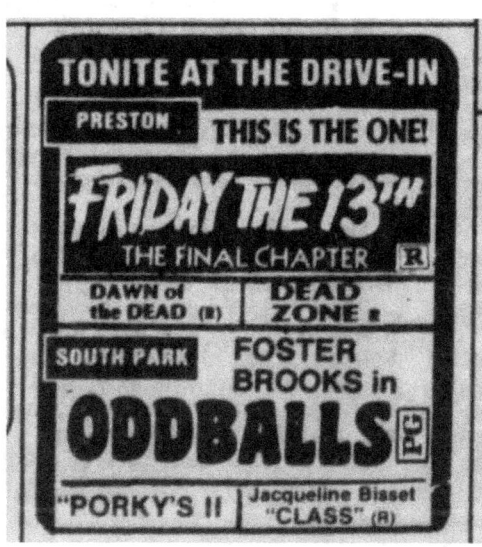

a clever patron could play theater switcheroo. The under 17 teenagers could buy a ticket for the PG-rated *ET: The Extra-Terrestrial* and sneak into the R-rated *Fast Times At Ridgemont High*. There were pitfalls to this plan. Certain theaters would try to look like they were enforcing the ratings by placing an usher at the doors to the R-rated film to make sure nobody was sneaking in. A lot of times this was being done because the show was a sell out and they didn't want to piss off people who bought tickets and couldn't find a seat because kids snuck inside. A lucky teenager would have a friend working as an usher or popcorn scooper at the concession stand so they'd know the prime time to slip inside without being hassled by an authoritative manager. Although there was a chance of still getting caught in the theater by an usher. Sometimes a jerk adult would tip off the manager that a bunch of teens didn't look like they belonged in the theater. This often happened when someone in the group started talking loudly about what they'd do to the female star. That's why lines needed to be practiced for when the usher arrived including "My mother told the person in the ticket booth that we had permission to see this film," "Dad's in the bathroom. He's not feeling good after his third burrito" and "You guys didn't clean up this floor very well. We found this five-dollar bill. Can you put this in lost and found?"

What if a teen missed the R-rated film in the theater because they couldn't sneak into the theater, ran out of allowance or were grounded

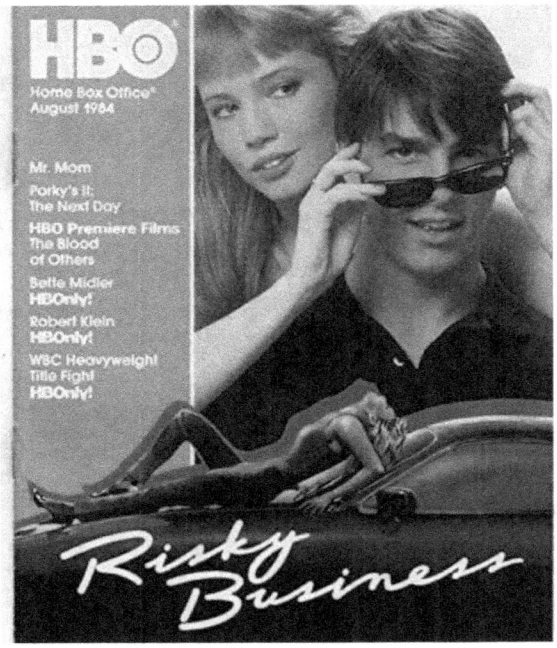

from the last time they tried this stunt? For a lucky number of students, there was a second chance when HBO, Showtime, Cinemax and the Movie Channel ran it. Not everyone had cable in the early '80s. My cousin's house in Boston didn't get cable on their street until the mid-80s. Those that were fortunate to have their city wired up, didn't get HBO and Showtime automatically. Talking parents into paying an extra $10 for one of the pay channels was a hard thing after the folks screamed about the cable bill being $20 for 13 channels. Those that had parents that wanted HBO still had the issue of attempting to watch R-rated films at home. This was a time when families didn't have a TV set in every room and the cable companies charged extra to wire up a bedroom. Most families only had a TV in the family room so the entire family could watch. This created a problem when a teen wanted to watch an R-rated film at home. This was before the invention of OnDemand and DVRs so the movie had to be watched at the time HBO was airing it. Younger siblings could easily narc out the teenager for watching those films the parents swore were forbidden. Some teens had to resort to sneaking out of bed in the middle of the night when everyone was supposed to be asleep to glimpse the movies. This could be trouble if mom or dad flicked on the light during *Fast Times at Ridgemont High* when Phoebe Cates was emerging from the pool and their teen son was impersonating Judge Reinhold kneeling in the bathroom. Quite often this nightmare bust led to the folks calling up Cablevision and having HBO yanked. The stigma of having parents cancel a pay cable channel couldn't be removed by Lava soap. Word eventually spread around high school about that kid that lost HBO. Rumors of what they did to cause such a drastic event would swell up like a tidal wave of embarrassment. These teens prayed their father would be transferred so they could gain a new identity at another high school in a different state that didn't get cable.

Eventually the R-rated films would appear late night on a broadcast TV channel. But at this point the forbidden cinema experience would be butchered with edits and dubbed lines to make all the naughtiness conform to family friendly entertainment. Pretty much everything that excited the teen when hearing about the movie in the lunchroom or the back of the bus would be excised. They'd be left with a child safe experience that would make them feel cheated out of the real deal. There would be no nudity. Odds are the R-rated cut wouldn't return to the local theater and HBO would quit running it after a few months. This less than PG version was all that was going to exist for the rest of their lives. That was so true until the explosion of home video.

Home Video Cassette Recorders (VCRs) finally started catching on in the mid-80s. While the machines were introduced in the '70s, they were rather pricey and only affordable to Bob Crane. In 1977 a VCR cost about over $1,000 after taxes. That's about $4,000 in today's dollars. That was more than a year of college tuition back then. The choice between paying for school or being able to tape *Quincy M.E.* made it an easy "no" for most families. The prices did drop so that by 1984, a good VCR was around $300 in either VHS or Beta format. Families liked the idea of being able to tape shows and be able to watch when they were ready to sit on the sofa. This meant a teenager could tape an R-rated film off HBO since their parents had them setting the timer to record everything else already. They could watch the tape with nude scenes and adult language intact while the folks were away. There was no chance of being caught appreciating the film as long as they could hear mom's station wagon pulling up in the driveway. But what about the films they missed? Studios were putting out prerecorded tapes of their older films, but the prices were outrageous. Luckily people came up with a remarkable solution with the invention of the Video Rental Club.

A Video Rental Club was the early version of the Video Rental Store. People would pay a fee to join the club so they could rent from the library of VHS and Beta video cassettes. This upfront money from new members was essential in being able to buy new stock. These were the legendary mom and pop operations that weren't franchises from huge deep pocket corporations. These were clubs named Videorama, Video Bar, Video Plaza and Dave's Videodrome. The brave new business-owners rented a slot at a strip mall, put up shelving units on the wall and ordered in tapes that might appeal to the local residents. And people came ready to rent uncut tapes including teenagers looking for that R-rated gold in a clamshell box. Teens with cool or oblivious parents could rent the tapes and take them home to see the carnal joys of cinematic high schoolers. But what if a teen's mom didn't sign off to let them

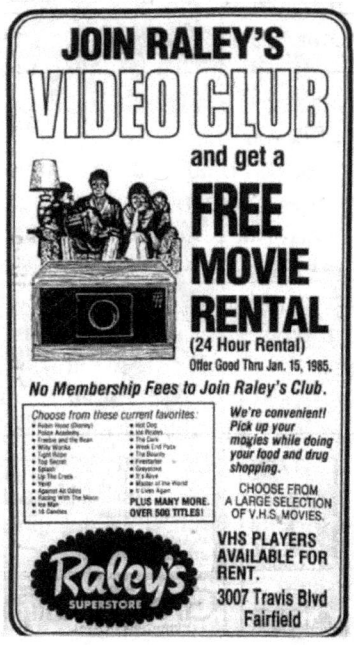

pick up R-rated tapes? There was a work around. If the teen had that friend that was over 17 with a membership, they could pick the tape off the shelf and check it out. The person behind the counter wouldn't give you the same interrogation like the movie theater employee in the box office. The video store clerk wasn't going to follow you home to make sure only people over 17 were on the family room sofa. Teens could take over the VCR on a summer afternoon when the parents were at work. There was no one to ruin the viewing experience. Since the fun was on tape, the teens could rewind and freeze frame the prime moments in the film. Showering scenes could go back and forth for hours. All the teens had to do was make sure they got the tapes back at the deadline and rewound. No one wanted to ring up a 50 cents rewind fee that would lead mom into knowing their beloved child checked out *Porky's*. Even more frightening was the video store clerk calling to remind mom to return that copy of *Goin' All the Way* or buy the tape for $75 and a reshelving fee.

There was a sense of risky business when a teenager wanted to see *Risky Business* or other classics of the time. Whether it be the ability to share the experience with classmates or merely see what everyone had been bragging about on the back of the school bus: the reward was so sweet. A teenager could lie and claim they saw it. But ultimately, they had to see that R-rated tale by any means necessary. Teenagers had to see what the adults wanted restricted from their eyes. It was all part of growing up in the '80s.

Brat Pack: Fact or Fiction?

Was the Brat Pack just a media creation or a real thing? The answer is both.

Writer David Blum coined the term in *New York* magazine when he did a profile on hot young actors Emilio Estevez, Rob Lowe and Judd Nelson. The title "Hollywood's Brat Pack" was a play on The Rat Pack that featured Frank Sinatra and Dean Martin or before that the Holmby Hills Rat Pack that was led by Humphrey Bogart, Sinatra and Judy Garland. Neither were an art movement, but more of a regular group of partiers. Membership in these clubs was pretty easy to determine. Was your name in the credits for the original *Ocean's Eleven*? Congratulations, you're in the Rat Pack. Did you wake up in Bogart's house under a pile of coats and no clue about the day or month? Then you're a member in good standing of the Holmby Hills Rat Pack. It also helped that all the members of these two groups were already major stars when they hooked up for nights of drinks and debauchery. The Brat Pack were the new kids that were just starting to land top billing in movies. The New York article came out after *The Breakfast Club* and right before *St. Elmo's Fire* when moviegoers sensed something was going on with this group of actors that seemed to be popping up at the multiplex in a new flick every Friday. But was there a real membership?

The article opens with what Blum considers the heart of the Brat Pack hanging at a table at the Hard Rock Cafe. Emilio Estevez, Rob Lowe, and Judd Nelson deal with women coming up to their table. Lowe is flirty. Nelson remains irritable. Estevez vanishes into the night with a Playboy Playmate. When we rejoin them it's just Nelson, Estevez, a Playmate and Jay McInerney, the author of *Bright Lights, Big City* which at the time was going to be directed by Joel Schumacher after *St. Elmo's Fire*. Every member of the Brat Pack was discussed for the two male leads. Years after the article, the film premiered with the stars being Michael J. Fox and Keifer Sutherland. James Bridges (*Urban Cowboy*) was in the director's chair. The film flopped and slid into obscurity.

The adventures of Estevez, Lowe and Nelson are rather pathetic as they keep hustling to get into movie theaters and nightclubs for free. They're upset when they get into a punk show for free and discover there's no roped off VIP section for them. It's shocking to read that the star of *Repo Man* can't grasp what punk rock means. I don't think Bogart needed a velvet rope during a Circle Jerks show.

Blum gives a Brat Pack membership list that includes Lowe, Estevez, Nelson, Tom Cruise, Timothy Hutton, Nicholas Cage, Matt Dillon and Sean Penn. He tags Kevin Bacon, Matthew Modine and Matthrew Broderick as "Not Quite There." There are no women mentioned since most of the actors worked on the mostly male casts of *Taps* and *The Outsiders*. Demi Moore gets blown off as Emilio's former girlfriend. Molly Ringwald is completely forgotten. The only older person that hangs with the young kids is Harry Dean Stanton and they drop by his house. He doesn't have to worry about getting a seat at the Hard Rock Cafe. Somehow, I find it hard to think that Tom Cruise and Sean Penn were spending much time with Judd Nelson at the Hard Rock having women climbing up to their elite table like the children on the cover of Led Zeppelin's *Houses of the Holy*.

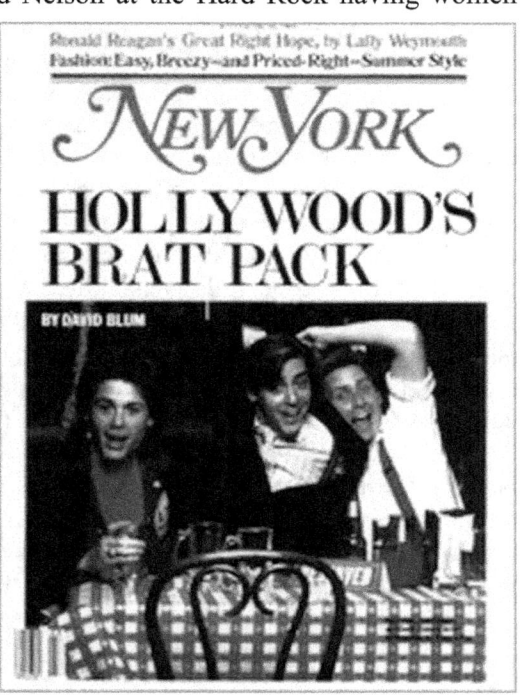

The major thing the Brat Packers have in common is they don't discuss their approach to the art of acting. None of the trio confess to the writer their desire to head over to RADA or Stella Adler Studio of Acting. This isn't a generation that were in the military and used their G.I. Bill cash to attend various acting schools in order to meet ladies. They don't talk about being on Broadway or Shakespeare in the Park. They didn't go to college because they just wanted to be movie stars. When it comes to Hutton, Estevez and Sean Penn, they grew up with fathers already established in the showbiz industry. They dream of becoming as big as their pal Tom Cruise who after the success of *Risky Business* is in complete control of his movies and doesn't have to read for the director. They want to be able to pick their scripts and directors. Estevez talks about his script he's written that John Hughes wants to produce and his Brat Pack buddies want to star in. Five years later the film would be released as *Men At Work* with Estevez directing and his younger brother Charlie Sheen being the star.

There's a telling moment when Timothy Hutton runs into Estevez. They have a short conversation about looking for Sean Penn. But Estevez makes him sound like a barely remembered acquaintance that he only met through Penn. One member of the group (that didn't want to be exposed) pointed out that Hutton might have won the Oscar for *Ordinary People*, but the actor is on a three movie cold streak after *Taps*. The Brat Packers don't want to be actors. They dream of transforming into movie stars with power like their pal Tom Cruise. Hutton would never be a guarantee of box office

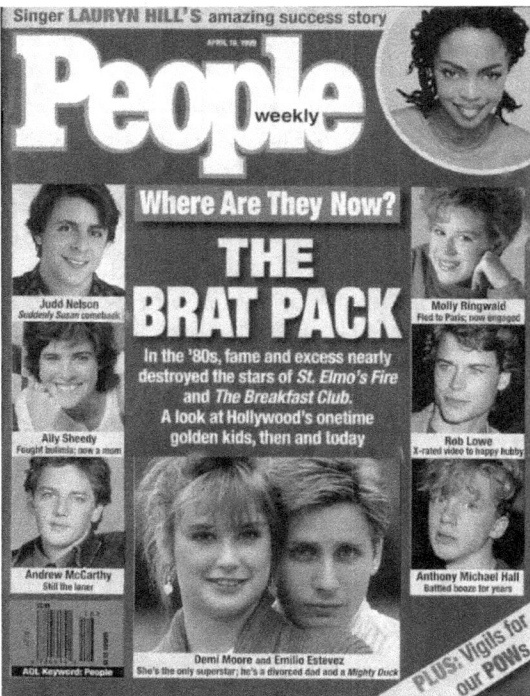

gold which is probably why you don't hear him called a Brat Packer anymore.

The article is extremely harsh on Andrew McCarthy. He's not even listed as a member even though he had made *Class* with Rob Lowe and is in *St. Elmo's Fire*. But his exemption becomes clear when an unnamed Brat Packer says that McCarthy plays his roles with the same intensity and won't last long. McCarthy had the last laugh on this group with his *Weekend at Bernie*'s being a bigger hit than *Men At Work*. As this festival will prove, Andrew McCarthy was a dominant force during the '80s.

Many people view the Brat Pack as being bigger than three guys drinking at the Hard Rock Cafe. For the longest time, the Brat Pack refers to any actor that appeared in John Hughes movies or *St. Elmo's Fire*. That's why Andrew McCarthy, Molly Ringwald and Demi Moore are immediately identified as "Former Brat Packers." The same goes for Ally Sheedy and Anthony Michael Hall. How can you leave off Robert Downey Jr, James Spader, Jami Gertz, Joan Cusack, John Cusack, Charlie Sheen and Jon Cryer. While Mare Winningham starred in *St. Elmo's Fire*, she's not really a Brat Packer since she didn't seem to star in any films with her old "Georgetown" alumni.

The Brat Pack originally were three drinking buddies who were able to market themselves in a magazine as an elite force in Hollywood. But they didn't turn out to be the only members of their thespian youth revolution. The Brat Pack is bigger than they imagined or cared to admit. Moviegoers determined the true membership of this group as the films came out in the '80s. There were so many members even if there wasn't an induction ceremony at that precious VIP table inside the Hard Rock Cafe. For the next 11 days, we celebrate their accomplishments.

Friday - May 15

Foxes 7:00 p.m.
Fast Times At Ridgemont High 9:30 p.m.

Growing Up Too Fast

While *Foxes* and *Fast Times At Ridgemont High* depict kids as growing up too fast, what truly separates them from the films of previous decades was the depiction of the adults. For the most part parents had previously been portrayed as either authoritative figures that had their lives together or oblivious to the kids and their hijinks. But things were changing. *Father Knows Best* never had a scene where Bud and Kitten walked in on dad crying his eyes out and letting them know that he has no clue how he ended up a parent. The '80s grown-ups feel like one night they went to bed after their final exam in high school and woke up with a job, a spouse, a house and two kids. The parents can't keep up the facade that allowed their parents to act like adults 24/7. Unlike their parents, they aren't too afraid of getting divorced instead of sticking it out until one of them dies so they can have a successful marriage. A few aren't even afraid of just vanishing to 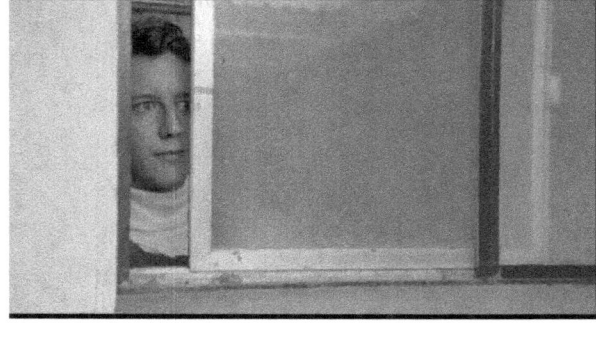 go find themselves through some radical therapy such as est or just joining a religious cult. What about the teenagers caught up in a world where the grown-ups aren't even giving the slightest pretension of stability and maturity? A few have to become adults to this generation of lost boys and girls. Both films about high schoolers in Los Angeles feature mature teenagers having to substitute for immature parents.

Foxes and *Fast Times* are also united in what can be described as "The Damone Saga." Actor Robert Romanus appears in both films as characters that are really into live music. *Foxes* has him as Scott, Jodie Foster's not quite boyfriend. Scott doesn't have many

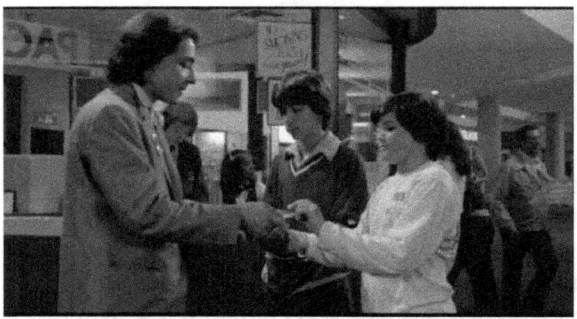

scenes, but he does end up at an Angel concert with Jodie and her group of gals. Fast forward a year to *Fast Times*, Romanus is Mark Damone, a high schooler scalping tickets to major rock concerts around Los Angeles. Sadly, nobody asks him for tickets to see Angel. While the films have completely different writers and directors, it's easy to imagine this is the same student. After things didn't work out with Jodie, he transferred schools and became fully engrossed in music. It should also be noted that later in the '80s, Romanus played Snake on *The Facts of Life*. On a historic night of television, his character "deflowered" Natalie. Damone knew how to sweet talk more than just a cutout of Debbie Harry.

Foxes

February 29, 1980

PolyGram Pictures

Directed by Adrian Lyne

Starring Jodie Foster, Scott Baio, Randy Quaid, Sally Kellerman, Cherie Currie, Marilyn Kagan, Kandice Stroh, Lois Smith, Laura Dern & Robert Romanus

Rated R - 106 minutes

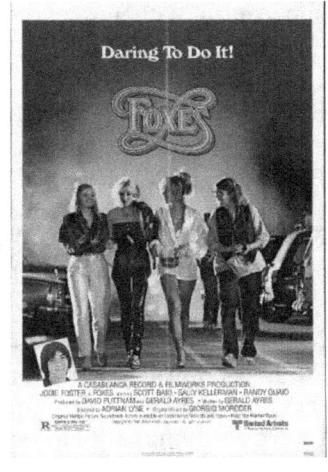

Jodie Foster was already a veteran of playing mature characters trapped in a teenage body long before *Foxes*. In 1976, Foster twice pulled off the feat in two completely different situations. First to come out right before Valentine's Day was *Taxi Driver*. Jodie played a 13-year-old girl forced into a life of prostitution by a pimp played by Harvey Keitel. She came off as more mature and savvier on the screen than Cybil Shepard. She gave a fearless performance in her scenes with Robert De Niro. Her junior high dropout character sounded like a graduate student of street smarts in a gritty R-rated universe and it got her an Oscar nomination. Just in time for Christmas, Jodie was back to being a grown up stuck in a 13-year-old body except this time she was in the Disney universe. *Freaky Friday* had her teenage daughter swapping bodies with her mother when they simultaneously declared, "I wish I could switch places with her for just one day." Jodie spends the movie acting as if Barbara Harris was trapped inside her. Harris gets to fake being a teenager which is a much easier gig. Adult actors were once children. But a kid hasn't various memories of what it was like when they were 45. Yet Jodie once more pulled off the switch flawlessly. Like *Taxi Driver*, *Freaky Friday* was a major hit and a cultural phenomenon although for nicer reasons. How many people in 1976 saw both movies in their local theater? Did the ticket taker at the Bijou recognize the same faces that enjoyed a bloody tale of vengeance showing up for the cheerful Disney frivolity? There must have been a few parents wanting to get out of the house during winter break that took the kids to a matinee. I haven't found any old newspaper ads for any Jerry Lewis Theater that offered the double feature of *Freaky Friday* and *Taxi Driver*. Imagine a parent watching *Freaky Friday* getting up to go to the bathroom, accidently returning to the *Taxi Driver* theater and thinking that Disney films are getting darker now that Walt's dead. In 1976, two distinct movie going audiences understood that Jodie Foster knew how to act way beyond her age.

Foxes was sold as a movie about four teen girls growing up too fast, being wild in Los Angeles and staying up way beyond a sensible bedtime. But people watching the trailer knew there must be at least one character that wouldn't completely end up in trouble with the law with Jodie Foster's name in the credits. Her Jeanie would be the nearly responsible character. The other three girls had to provide the R-rated trouble and possibly drag her down.

Deirdre (Kandice Stroh) is a massive flirt who is so boy crazy that she sometimes forgets that she has two dates for the same night. In her defense she lives in LA where people always overbook events since they figure a percentage of the people are going to bail at the

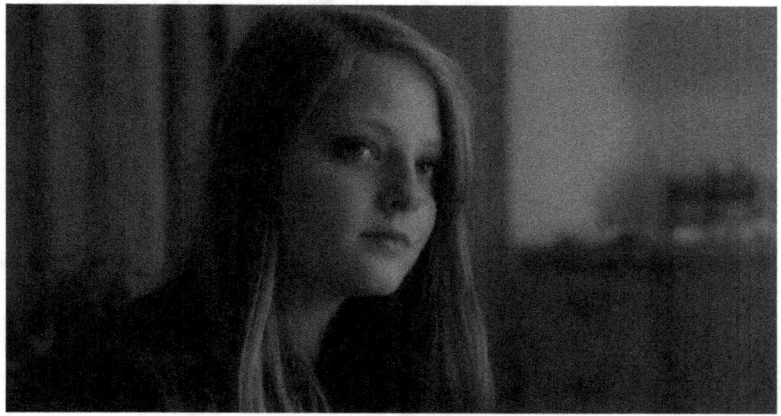

last minute. She seems to be the second most responsible member of the pioneering girl squad. Annie (Cherie Currie) was the most out of control as the troubled teen doing her best to escape her homelife. Her father is a brutal cop that has no problem chasing her down. She's a wild child who won't be tamed as she hits Hollywood Boulevard with a rough crowd. Jeanie has her hands full cruising around in her truck looking for Annie when she deep dives into booze, pills, weed and criminally minded guys. Can she really make Annie consider the consequences of her actions? Cherie Currie is perfectly cast since she was the lead singer of The Runaways. She does look like the kinda girl who would run away and raise hell all weekend long. And Jodie seems like the pal who would enter the seedy side of Tinseltown looking for her friend. Strangely enough Annie is not the most troubled of Jeanie's friends.

Back when *Foxes* came out, Madge (*The Violation of Sarah McDavid*'s Marilyn Kagan) seemed like one of the good girls. Forty years later she is every parent's nightmare. The high school senior isn't boy crazy like Annie and Deirdre. She has kept her virginity and only wants to lose it to her boyfriend so it can be special. This almost sounds noble until you realize that her boyfriend is a 30-year-old guy. And he's not just any guy...it's Randy Quaid. Remember how on *Saturday Night Live*'s Nerds sketch Lisa Loopner would declare that she's saving herself for Marvin Hamlisch? People would laugh at the line. But Marvin was a good-looking guy, won an Emmy, Grammy, Oscar and Tony for his musical compositions and was also around 30 when the sketches ran. If Lisa had said she was saving herself for Randy Quaid, the live audience would have started gagging and puking inside Studio 8H. Randy was about to play creepy Cousin Eddie in *National Lampoon's Vacation*. What parent wouldn't throw a fit knowing a naked Randy Quaid would soon be on top of their daughter. You might reconsider if it was his younger brother Dennis. Although Dennis Quaid (as of this writing) is engaged to a woman 39 years younger than him or three times what Randy's difference was with Madge. So perhaps neither Quaid brother is safe for a precious daughter. Ultimately Madge needs to be sent off to a rehab facility to be cured of this grotesque lustful desire.

Jeanie doesn't seem like she'd have an adult-like attitude towards life since her mother (*M*A*S*H**'s Sally Kellerman) is a bit of a mess. The divorced mother goes through guys at a rate that nearly matches Annie. She wants to find herself so badly that she vanishes from Jeanie's life for a while. It's Jeanie who has to be a mother to her own mom at certain points. Her traits of being mature and in charge comes from her father Bryan played by British pop star Adam Faith. We meet him when Jeanie treats her friends to a rock concert because her father is the road manager for headliner Angel. It's so easy to make a "like father like daughter" comparison since he has to deal with a bunch of out of control glamish musicians.

The band Angel is not a made-up group for the movie. They were rather real having been discovered by Gene Simmons of Kiss. When they hit the Shrine Auditorium for the movie, they'd released five albums. You might remember Angel from a song, but remarkably enough it's not a song they wrote or performed. Frank Zappa's "Punky's Whips" is about how his drummer Terry Bozzio finds a picture of the band Angel and unexpectedly falls deeply in lust with guitarist Punky Meadows. Narrating the song is legendary announcer Don Pardo who went from being the announcer on the original *Jeopardy* to being the voice of *Saturday Night Live* during the glory early seasons. Punky also gets mentioned in Zappa's "Titties and Beer." Coincidentally in the movie, Punky might be the member who puts a beer bottle near his crotch and acts like he's jerking off at

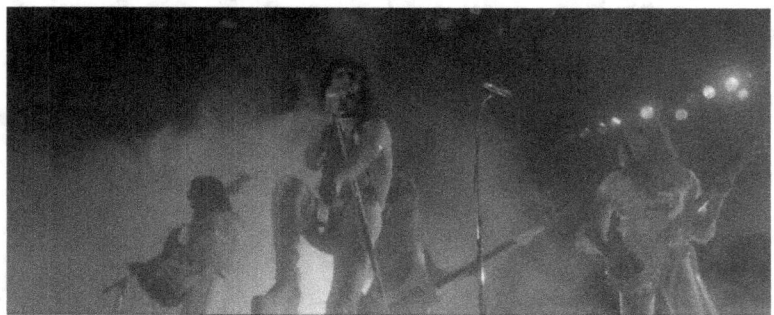

the crowd of screaming teenagers. He was so classy. Meadows and lead singer Frank DiMino would quit Angel after the movie came out. Their final single with the original line up was "20th Century Foxes." While the song played in the trailer and TV commercial, there was no MTV to make Angel the megastars with their soundtrack single. DiMino would have success later when director Adrian Lyne had one of his songs on the *Flashdance* soundtrack album.

While the other three girls are boy or Randy Quaid crazy, Jeanie isn't too concerned about hooking up. Scott (*Fast Times at Ridgemont High*'s Robert Romanus) has no clue if they're really dating anymore. And she treats Brad (*Happy Days*' Scott Baio) like a kid brother. There are hints that she might be more into her girlfriends since they're introduced all sleeping in a bed with the hazy smoke that director Adrian Lyne blew into every set. But 1980 wasn't a time to deal with bisexuality in high school so we can only speculate. Only thing that can't be speculated is that Jeanie had to grow up fast because nobody else seemed to want to be the responsible adult and Jodie Foster was once more perfect to play older than a teenager.

SOUNDTRACK NOTES: You'd imagine that Angel's "20th Century Foxes" would be the big song in the movie since it highlights the trailer. But it turns out that the song that keeps cropping up all over the film is Donna Summer's "On the Radio." Cher's "Bad Love" opens and closes the film. The score 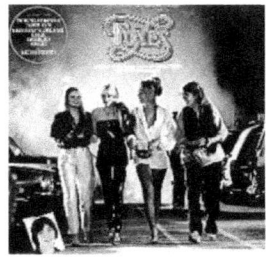 was composed by Disco synth icon Giorgio Moroder. This work would be overshadowed by his massively popular score for *American Gigolo* that came out four weeks before. Even though "On the Radio" hit number 5, the single was released nearly 3 months before the soundtrack's double album hit the Record Bar's racks. The vinyl wasn't a major hit and hasn't been upgraded to compact disc.

Fast Times At Ridgemont High

April 13, 1982

Universal Pictures

Directed by Amy Heckerling

Starring Sean Penn, Jennifer Jason Leigh, Judge Reinhold, Robert Romanus, Brian Backer, Phoebe Cates, Ray Walston, Vincent Schiavelli, Forest Whitaker, Kelli Maroney, Eric Stoltz, Anthony Edwards, Nicolas Cage and Taylor Negron.

Rated R - 90 minutes

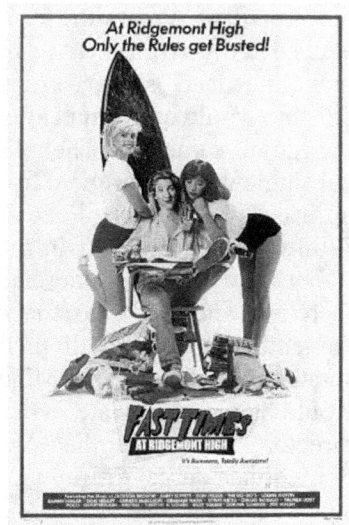

Early at film school, we had a class where the professor asked us what was the most memorable scene in cinema history. Most of the kids plucked out their favorite moment from the Star Wars trilogy or a major Steven Spielberg flick. A few tried to suck up by mentioning a classic black and white clip that often gets shown in Turner Classic Movies promos. When it was my turn, I forcefully answered, "When Phoebe Cates rose up from the swimming pool in Fast Times In Ridgemont High." There were a few snickers behind me since I was the only person to mention a scene that was R-rated. But I didn't say, "Just joking" and sputter on about Citizen Kane. I was serious that evening. Even now, decades later, there is no more blissful and memorable scene in cinema. Beyond being visually stunning, the scene mixes fantasy, desire and ultimately reality in such a potent blend that it hasn't been matched by any film since.

How does this scene fit into the film? Here's a little background to understand its potency. Brad Hamilton (Beverly Hill Cop's Judge Reinhold) starts the film with his life looking great. He's almost paid for a classic light blue 1960 Buick LeSabre. He's employee of the month at All-American Burger. Most importantly he has a cool girlfriend in Lisa (*A Nightmare on Elm Street*'s Amanda Wyss). He's ready to start the school year at the top of the world at Ridgemont High. And then things crumble fast. Being that he's a worldly senior, he needs to bust up with Lisa so he can explore all that's good about being a teenager with a car and steady income. As Brad tells himself in the fast-food men's room mirror, "I'm a single, successful guy." Mostly he needs to find a new girlfriend because after two years, Lisa still doesn't want to go to the Point and enjoy a sexual encounter in a little league dugout. But his timing on the break up doesn't go right. After days of planning how to gently let her down, she dumps him cold. Bad timing smacks Brad in the face once more when he does a favor for a co-worker needing a bathroom break. He takes over the cash register. This act of kindness gets Brad fired because of an unsatisfied breakfast customer. He doesn't stay unemployed long. He ends up stuck at a deep-fried seafood joint. This shouldn't be a step down in the fast-food industry ladder except Captain Hook's Fish and Chips makes him wear a pirate costume with a Blackbeard-esque hat. A part of him dies as he returns home in uniform looking like an escapee from a low wattage TV station's kiddie show. He mopes past the backyard pool and warns his sister Stacy (Jennifer Jason Leigh) and her friends to

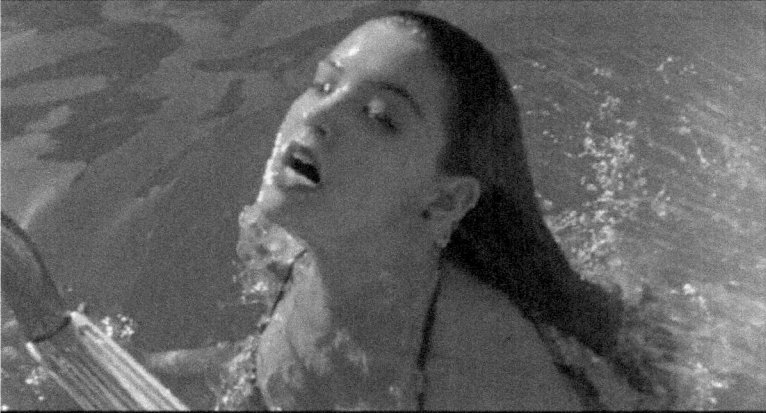

not mess up the pool before their parents get home. He's a broken teenager as he shuffles inside and goes to the bathroom. Instead of killing himself, Brad slides open the window and watches Linda sitting on the diving board. Even in the dreary overcast day and a bored look on her face, Linda deserves his full attention. She stands up on the edge of the springboard and adjusts her red bikini. The Cars' "Living In Stereo" kicks in on the soundtrack. Brad's imagination goes into overdrive and we get treated to the greatest moment in cinematic history.

The dreariness vanishes as sunlight sparkles on the pool and glistens in the airborne droplets from her diving splash. Linda emerges from the water with a look on her face that we all dream of receiving once in our life from someone. Her stare is filled with bliss and desire as she grabs the ladder and steps up. These four seconds of celluloid are so powerful in their beauty that they need to be looped at the National Portrait Gallery. When we talk about the look of love, Linda's face should be next to the definition in the dictionary. A generation of teenagers sitting in the dark theater learned that this is the expression their lovers must display to make the passion between them all real even if this vision was purely in Brad's imagination.

Brad is so overwhelmed with the image that he backs away from the window, kneels down, jerks off and keeps on dreaming. Linda's look is what makes Brad's fantasy so real because right off the bat he isn't thinking Linda naked and them humping. After all that's

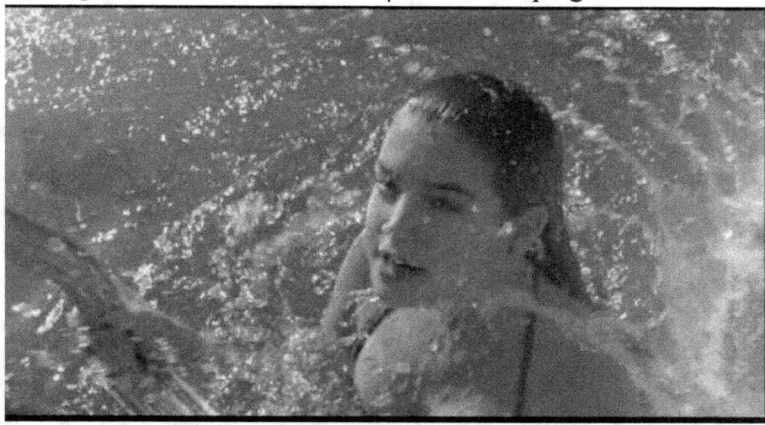

happened to Brad, he ultimately wants to be wanted by someone who isn't going to hold back or scream at him to get more tartar sauce. Of course, after Linda's look, Brad imagines her dropping her bikini top and embracing Brad. Even Brad upgrades himself in the fantasy. Instead of the dopey Captain Hook uniform, he's in a well-tailored suit. His erotic fantasy involves a woman that wants to be with him and a life that doesn't involve a deep fryer. He wants everything to be perfect in his erotic daydream that keeps him pumping that teen libido.

What sets *Fast Times At Ridgemont High* apart from so many goofy teen flicks is we also see the reality of this moment. While Brad jerks to his absolute smoking fantasy, we see what really happens when Linda dives into the pool. She rises up from the water and immediately complains about getting water in her ear. She runs into the house and charges into the bathroom. In a lesser teen sex romp, she'd stumble upon a kneeling Brad and take over from his busy hand. But in *Fast Times*, Brad's fantasy smashes into a brick wall. Linda's face doesn't go into bliss mode when she gets a look over Brad's shoulder to glimpse what he's doing. Her lips widen in a grotesque horror, she backs out of the bathroom and shuts the door. Brad can't catch a break.

I'm not sure what motivation Phoebe Cates used to achieve her look of love rising from the water. But her expression in the bathroom was reportedly all from a trick that Judge Reinhold played to bring out a genuine look of

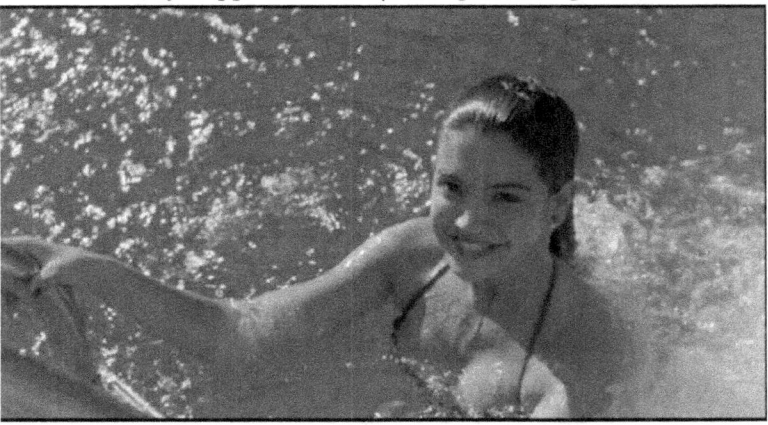

shock. Unbeknownst to her, Judge Reinhold snuck a large dildo into the bathroom. He knelt down on the floor and held the huge hunk of rubber between his knees as director Amy Heckerling declared, "Action!" The look of revulsion on Cates' face is purely from her initial thought that her co-star was deep into the scene and jerking off for real. Luckily, he was not exposing himself on the set. Instead, he was giving his co-star a device to ensure she was reacting to the moment and not merely acting. When Linda backs out of the bathroom, there's a true sense that she wants nothing to do with Brad and wasn't merely hitting her beats and marks.

While Brad is what appears to be the low part of his senior, he'd have a few more rungs to descend before Oingo Boingo's "Goodbye, Goodbye" plays. Even with this bad luck streak, Brad's not the true tragic hero of the film. That honor goes to someone who was floating in the swimming pool as Brad sank his Bismark. Why isn't it Brad? A viewer can't learn too much from his tumble in workplaces and loss of Lisa. The audience can only commiserate with his crappy part-time jobs trajectory with their own downward trajectory resume. Mike Damone (*Foxes'* Robert Romanus) is the tragic hero since we can learn four major lessons from him as he goes from hipster to the high school villain in 90 minutes.

Mike Damone in the movie is stitched together from two characters inside Cameron Crowe's original book like Frankenstein's monster. In the book Mike Damone is a friend of Mark "Rat" Ratner (*The*

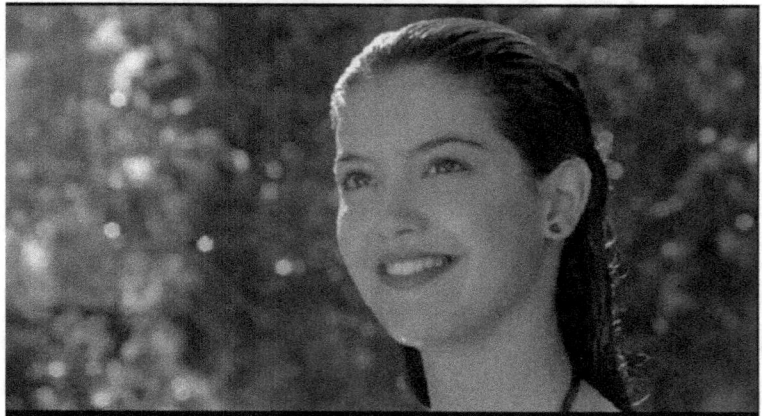

Burning's Brian Backer). The duo once worked together at a Sea World-like park. Damone in the book isn't a ticket scalper. That was Randy Eddo who was all about tickets and his love of music. Randy's not much of a character in the book so Crowe just merges him into Mike Damone to create a Super Damone. The composite character comes off a bit nicer than the Damone in the book, but still suffers the sad fate of being too fast and not there on time. The first big thing we learn from Damone is to never help a friend date someone. When we meet Damone, he's giving lessons in picking up the ladies to Ratner at the Sherman Oaks Galleria. Rat wants to take Stacy Hamilton out, but he hasn't got the nerve. Damone shares all his knowledge on wooing the ladies. He even guides his pal from his ticket taking gig at the movie theater to the Italian eatery where Stacy tosses out greasy pizza slices to shoppers. Damone breaks down what to do on the date including the right Led Zeppelin album side to play in the car. When the Rat forgets his wallet during dinner, Damone is willing to drive to the German restaurant and bail out his buddy so Stacy doesn't have to wash dishes in the back. The only thing he doesn't do is stand in the corner of the bedroom and inform the Rat how to make sweet love to Stacy. He needed to do that since the Rat has no clue how to get to first base with Stacy. The Rat can't even locate the warm up circle as Stacy aims to intentionally walk and wild pitch the guy to home plate. She's eager to get physical. She's already scored in the little league dugout at the Point with a stereo salesman. She's not ready to go at the clumsy and awkward Rat speed. Which is why when she hooks up with Damone. It's not really backstabbing a friend as being more attentive to Stacy's wants. But Damone was so helpful to the Rat, it feels like a betrayal. So, we learn to never be helpful when it comes to a friend's love life.

The second massive lesson from Damone's fall from grace is to always use a condom no matter how uneventful and short the sex is. Who knows why Damone doesn't last as long as the stereo salesman when he hooks up with Stacy. His quickie ending brings Jackson Browne's "Somebody's Baby" to a screeching

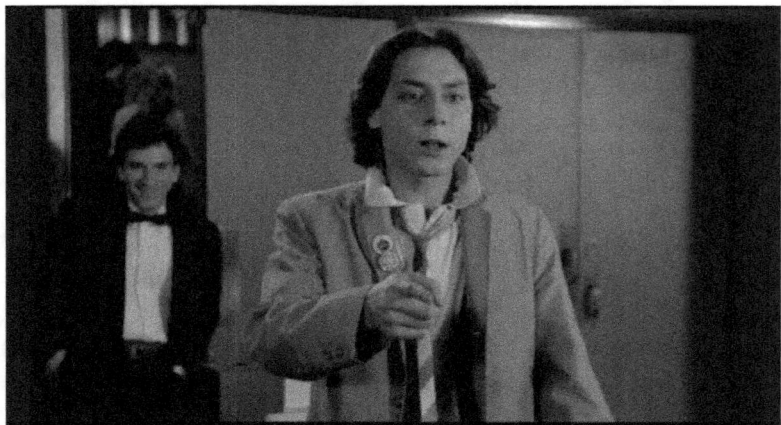

halt. This allows the audience to laugh at Damone's expense as if it were an erotic slapstick sketch on *The Benny Hill Show*. Five minutes later in the film, things get serious when Stacy informs Damone that she's pregnant and needs $75 to pay for an abortion at the free clinic. This is $200 in today's money. That's a lot more expensive than a condom costs. Sex education in the early '80s was under attack from the Reagan administration and Moral Majority. For many teenagers, *Fast Times* was the only sex education that spoke of the consequences of not being informed about various forms of protection. The movie didn't condemn sexual desires or tell you to be celibate. But there was a message of being sensible in this sequence.

This failure leads to the third lesson of Damone: Don't advance people any money without some form of collateral. Damone wants to do the right thing and pay his half of the abortion. But he doesn't have $75 on him because he'd been selling people the concert tickets without collecting the money. He ran too much of his business on a credit basis and calling up to collect debts proves fruitless. His biggest problem is that since the rock concerts had already happened, the people that owe him don't need to pay him back immediately. What's Damone going to do? Take away their memories of seeing Blue Oyster Cult at the Forum? Damone is screwed as he pleads for them to pay up. He has zero

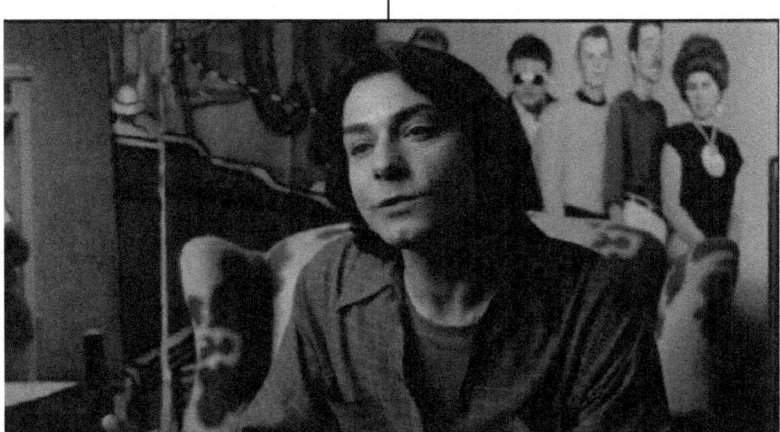

leverage over them. If you paid for a ticket for a friend to get into the theater to see *Fast Times*, you'd better hold onto your friend's jacket and refuse to give it back until the freeloader coughs up the cash for the ticket and their share of popcorn. Don't trust people to pay you back is a lesson a teenager rarely gets in high school economics class. The inability of Damone to collect on the moochers leads to him being too humiliated to pick up Stacy and take her to the free clinic which isn't that free. He is the villain at this point. Please note that in the book where Damone is not the ticket scalper, he refuses to take her to the Free Clinic on two occasions. She has the unwitting Rat drive her to the appointment. Later in the book, Damone ends up being the manager of Stacy's ice cream shop where he is a monster towards her. Film Damone is a tragic hero whose mistakes we learn from. Novel Damone is a giant asshole.

There's one final lesson we learn from film Damone: Cheap Trick isn't kid stuff. Damone initially gets dismissed by a girl in the bleachers during P.E. about buying tickets for the Rockland, Illinois legendary rockers. He does his best to sell her on the seats by singing their greatest hits including "Surrender," "I Want You To Want Me" and even "The Dream Police." Generations of teens have seen this moment and thought, "I need to get a copy of Cheap Trick at Budokan." What's strange is that Cheap Trick isn't featured on the soundtrack even with Damone's passionate praise. But their music is kept youthful by the film. When Cheap Trick was inducted into the Rock and Roll Hall of Fame, they didn't bring out Robert Romanus to repeat Damone's speech one more time. Instead, we got stuck with an opportunistic musical joke called Kid Rock yapping about Robin Zander and Rick Nielsen. It was such an anticlimactic snore. But if you've seen Cheap Trick live in the last four decades, you've heard Damone's words echo deep inside your mind right before the band hits the stage with "Hello There."

Fast Times At Ridgemont High was more educational than anything you remember from your high school classes. This wasn't another dumb teenage movie as some critics claimed upon initial release. Any student watching the film walked away with two important pieces of knowledge: Always use a rubber and make sure the bathroom lock is secured before you jerk off. This advice served millions of young minds better than Precalculus.

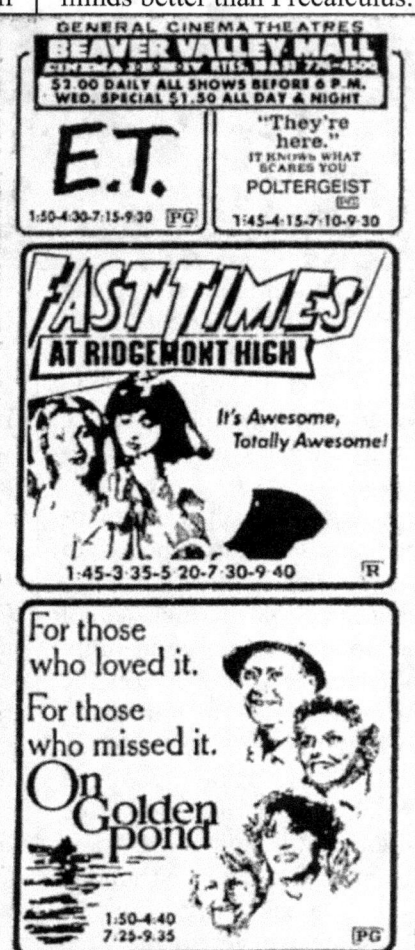

SOUNDTRACK NOTES: The music of *Fast Times* proved a mix of the old and the new that was taking hold of Southern California and playing in speakers around the shopping mall. There's quite a few members of the Laurel Canyon sound from the '70s on the tracks. Executive producer Irving Azoff brings 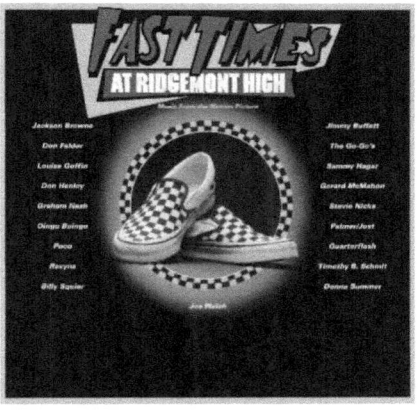 over his clients including Stevie Nicks and plenty of ex-Eagles such as Don Henley, Joe Walsh, Don Felder, Timothy B. Schmit. No word on why Glenn Frey wasn't part of the solo fun with "Party Town." The new sounds are represented by The Go-Gos, Oingo Boingo and Quarterflash. Jackson Browne wrote and recorded "Somebody's Baby" for the movie and it wasn't even nominated for an Oscar. The Academy members felt "If We Were In Love" from *Yes, Giorgio* was more worthy because the forgettable song had music written by John Williams. Strangely enough the breakout star of the soundtrack wasn't a singer, but the black and white checkerboard Vans sneakers that posed on the cover instead of any of the cast members. They became the must have footwear for those who viewed surfer Jeff Spicoli (Sean Penn) as their spiritual mentor. Even now after all these years, this model is a Vans top seller. And the young clerks know what you want when you say, "Do you have the *Fast Times* sneaker? The Spicolis?"

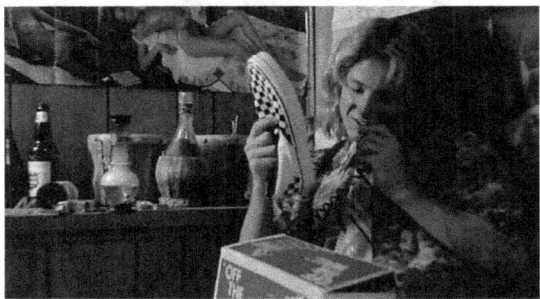

Saturday - May 16

Sixteen Candles 2:00 p.m.
Breakfast Club 4:00 p.m.
Weird Science 7:00 p.m.
Pretty In Pink 9:30 p.m.
Some Kind of Wonderful Midnight

John Hughes "King of the '80s Teens"

When we announced the festival, the first thing someone asked was "Are you going to show the John Hughes teen films?" This became a trend as the next 100 someones wanted to know how many of the John Hughes films we'd be screening. The only reason I'm not hearing it now is that my office door is locked as I type this introduction to the night. Our simple answer has always been "We're showing all of them!"

John Hughes might be the only director truly associated with this era. Even during the '80s his name was immediately associated with the teen genre. How big did he become? After making *Sixteen Candles* and *The Breakfast Club*, people seemed shocked that Hughes didn't write and direct *St. Elmo's Fire* when the movie came out. He owned the era. What's amazing about this PR success story is that Hughes didn't make his name dominate the

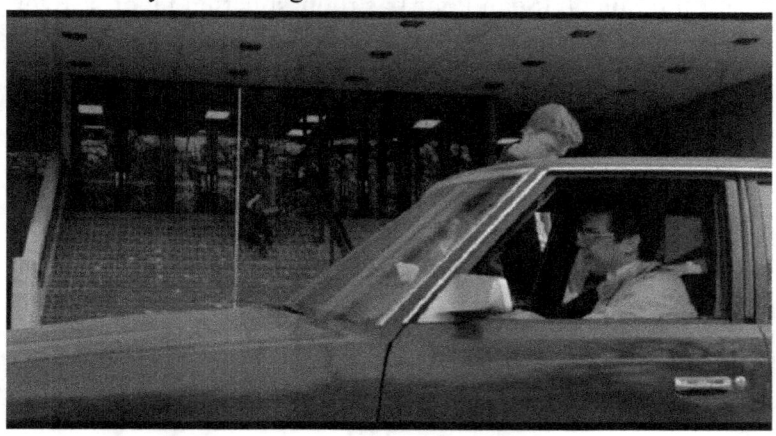

poster or the trailer like Michael Cimino. He did make sure the publicity photos had him hanging with his young cast like he was the hip uncle. He didn't want to look like the director holding a script and pointing. He rose to stardom as much as his teen actors that became the core of the Brat Pack.

Did any theater going teenagers care about who directed *Private School* or *Youngblood* at the time? Nope. Most of the directors weren't wanting to spend their career toiling in teenager films. It was a rite of passage like being a teenager. Once was enough. Even people who made more than one teen movie like Rob Reiner and Martha Coolridge weren't elevated to the status of Hughes during the '80s or over the decades. Hughes was on top of the teen mountain from Spring of 1984 until Thanksgiving of 1987 when he grew up with adult stars in *Planes, Trains and Automobiles*. He became so powerful that two movies that he wrote and produced are attributed to him and not the guy who really directed them. Nobody asked if we're showing both of Howard Deutch's teen films.

How did John Hughes become this cinematic poet to a generation? While he's been associated as a Chicago guy, he was born and grew up outside Detroit, Michigan. His family moved to the Windy City during his high school years. He was a big Detroit Red Wings fan which explains why Cameron was wearing a Gordie Howe jersey in *Ferris Bueller's Day Off*. There will be more about that fashion choice later in this guide. Hughes attended the University of Arizona, the school that also gave us Garry Shandling and Rob Gronkowski. Like Shandling, Hughes got into writing jokes for others including Rodney Dangerfield and Joan Rivers. Sadly, selling jokes isn't quite that lucrative and he had to get a day job. This is where things get interesting as John Hughes worked in the advertising business. His most memorable campaign involved proving how close your razor shaved by scraping a credit card against your cheeks. His biggest account was Virginia Slims cigarettes. Most biographies point out that during his trips to New York City to meet with the Phillip Morris folks, he'd also drop by the offices of the *National Lampoon* magazine in the late '70s. It was here where he hooked up with P.J. O'Rourke. The magazine by this point had been gutted with their legendary talents either going to *Saturday Night Live* or making big Hollywood productions in the wake of *National Lampoon's Animal House*. Hughes began writing for the magazine while holding down his day job at the advertising firm.

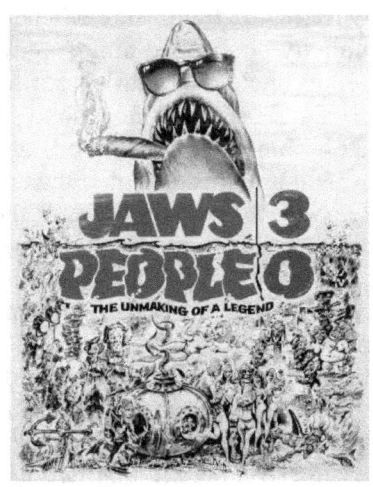

Hughes' most memorable pieces in the magazine were tinged with nostalgia, darkness and bite. He became part of the movie making element of the magazine which quickly taught him a few lessons about Hollywood. The first big project was the third installment of *Jaws* as the screenwriter. Instead of a serious third tale of the Great White Shark eating the citizens of Amity, he wrote an out-of-control spoof of Hollywood wanting to take one more bite out of the box office. Horrible things happen to horrible showbiz people in *Jaws 3 - People 0*. Even Steven Spielberg was eaten by his former aquatic star. They had landed Joe Dante (*Piranha*) to be the director. Things were looking good.

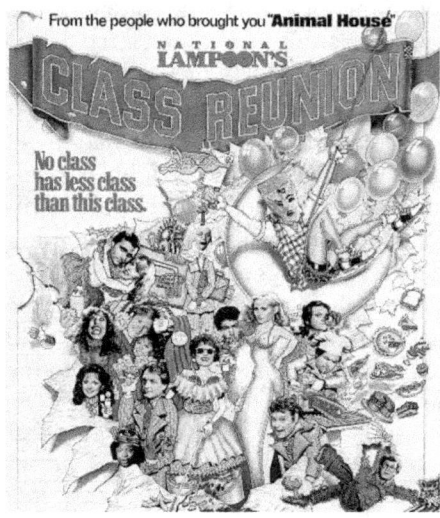

The rumor goes that Spielberg freaked out and had Universal red light the project. He couldn't ruin the legacy of his franchise. Yet somehow Spielberg gave his blessing to *Jaws in 3-D*. This failure must have given Hughes an understanding of how much bite you can put in a film script and still have people like it. His next big script for the magazine actually made it into production and release. Do you remember *National Lampoon's Class Reunion*? Probably not. It crashed and burned upon release. Hughes claimed the script he wrote wasn't what ended up on the screen. He understood the need to direct his own material. But he didn't have the clout for such a gig.

After two high profile disasters, Hughes' luck turned around and soared. He became a star in the summer of 1983 when two films that had him as the sole credited screenwriter became sensations. The first was *Mr. Mom* with Michael Keaton being a laid off husband who has to take care of the house and kids when his wife becomes the breadwinner. The second hit was even bigger as he adapted his short story "Vacation '58" from the magazine into *National Lampoon's Vacation*. The movie restored the name of *National Lampoon* and sadly extended the career of Chevy Chase. Hughes toned down the script so that it didn't end with the father shooting Walt Disney. That might have not been quite as hilarious as a comic hostage situation. Even more importantly Hughes flipped the successes into a three-movie deal with Universal Pictures that allowed him to be writer, director and producer. He hitched his future to Anthony Michael Hall, who played the son in *Vacation*.

Working in teen films made perfect sense since Hughes didn't want to be stuck in Los Angeles making movies on studio soundstages. With rather low budgets, Universal wouldn't mind him sneaking off to Chicago to make *Sixteen Candles, The Breakfast Club* and *Weird Science* at the fictional Shermer High

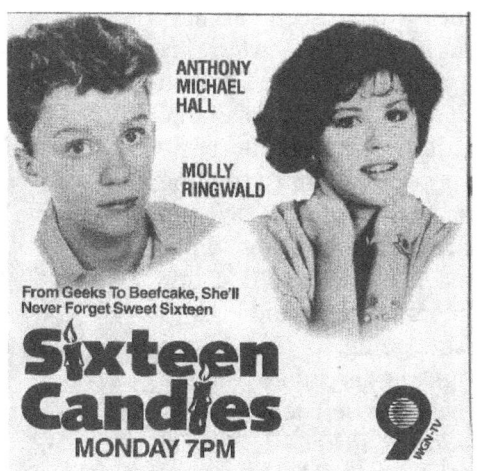

School. Amazing how low the budget can get when you're not having to pay and pamper Chevy Chase. Hughes avoided the interference of every creative executive in The Black Tower suffocating him with notes and set visits. Oddly enough Hughes was supposed to make *The Breakfast Club* first. When Molly Ringwald auditioned for the film, he was inspired to write a whole new script and changed up his production schedule. Because he was working so low to the bone with a three-picture deal, Universal didn't freak out at the switcheroo.

Neither one of the scripts were based on his two most popular teenage short stories published in *National Lampoon*'s April 1979 issue. "My Penis" and "My Vagina" both dealt with high schoolers waking up with a major bodily change. In "My Penis" it's a girl and "My Vagina" is a boy. Both stories showed how Hughes has an ear for how kids talk as they relate their tales. Both stories also show how Hughes had a very cutting sense of humor. Neither ends with a happy little joke. They are as dark and bleak as you'd expect in an issue of *National Lampoon*. The girl forces her boyfriend to suck her dick. The boy finds himself gang raped by his male friends and spends his Easter vacation getting an abortion. None of his six teen films come close to these disturbing endings. You read the two stories and ponder why Hughes abandoned his true sense of humor in the films. Or was it still there? Perhaps there's an unseen darkness in his movies. After his early failures, he learned that in order to play the Hollywood game, he has to cut out the most cutting parts of his ideas. What's funny in a shocking humor magazine that sells a few hundred thousand issues isn't going to get a green light in a studio picture meant to sell tens of millions of tickets. Universal Studio paid Hughes more than the *National Lampoon*. Did Hughes sell out or just learn how to edit to

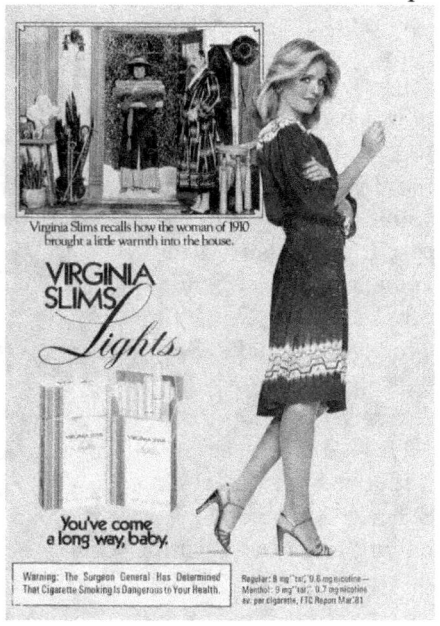

make his initial vision palatable to the studio bean counters and pinheads? What if Hughes maintained his outrageous vision, dialed the grotesque levels back and ended the script right before the soul crushing bleak ending that played in his head?

Do you wonder where Hughes got his sense of what a teenage girl was like? When he worked for Virginia Slims, part of his job was to fool young girls into taking up smoking their brand of cigarettes. The ads were supposed to appeal to women 18 - 35 although as we've learned over the years, big tobacco companies aimed younger. The average smoker picks up the addiction and brand identifies in high school. Most high school seniors are 18 so Hughes must have had plenty of exposure to research about what appeals to high school girls. He must have received extensive research from studies on how a teenage girl thinks and feels. His day job was to create a sophisticated fantasy that would allow a youthful reader to ignore the Surgeon General's warning that tobacco can cause health problems and lead to death. He was trained in the art of making people enjoy the pleasure of puffing away without letting them think about the consequences of being hooked up to an oxygen tank. The main magazine campaign for Virginia Slims was to make the slim sized cigarette a reward for women's liberation. "You've Come A Long Way, Baby" was the slogan. Vintage photos made fun of the way women were treated in the 1920s and 30s if they wanted to smoke a cigarette.

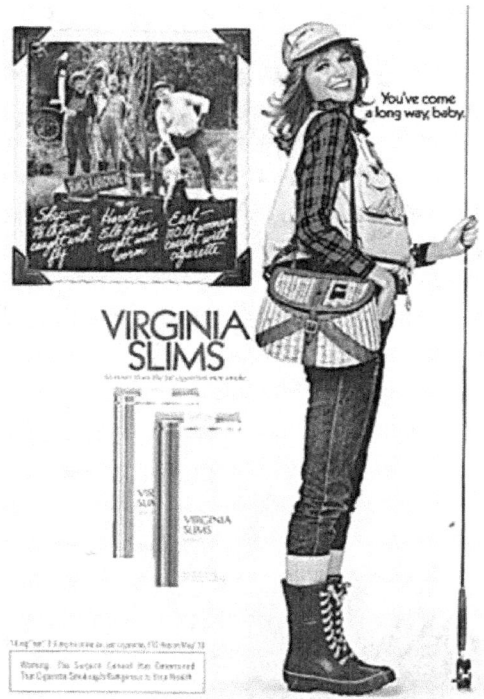

Men weren't tolerant of a lady puffing away. The ads made lighting up as an essential part of women's liberation as the right to vote, equal pay for equal work, access to birth control and protection from abusive husbands. The modern models in cutting edge fashions let readers know that Virginia Slims cigarettes will elevate you in womanhood. This was the original female empowerment program. The fashion and the comedic elements on the magazine page were geared towards impressionable young minds more than 35-year-old women. They were aimed at the same crowd that John Hughes needed to attract for his movies to be successful.

It's easy to view the teenage films of John Hughes as sweet and charming. Even the Wikipedia entry claims his films are a "more honest depiction of navigating adolescence and the social dynamics of high school life in stark contrast to the *Porky's*-inspired comedies made at the time." But were they that honest? Was Hughes able to stealthily continue his comic perspective found in his *National Lampoon* stories? Did he use his manipulative skills that were essential in pushing cigarettes on kids? Did he make us completely overlook how cancerous certain characters were? Were there hidden elements in the film that led to a grotesque ending in the original version he saw in his head? Was there a darkness to his Shermer High School students that audiences completely overlooked because of his ability to subliminally seduce? Think of this when you watch tonight instead of merely soaking in the nostalgia.

John Hughes knew how to tempt someone into accepting a horrible product as perfectly normal. Was that someone you?

Sixteen Candles

May 4, 1984

Universal Pictures

Directed by John Hughes

Starring Molly Ringwald, Anthony Michael Hall, Paul Dooley, Justin Henry, Michael Schoeffling, Haviland Morris, Gedde Watanabe, John Cusack, Joan Cusack, Brian Doyle-Murray, Jami Gertz, John Kapelos and Zelda Rubinstein.

Rated PG - 93 minutes

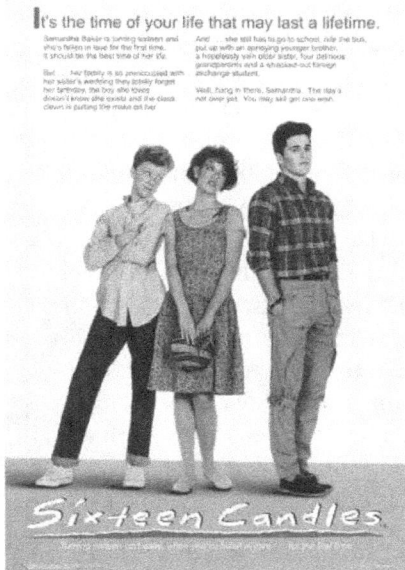

According to the back of the DVD, "*Sixteen Candles* is a warm-hearted coming of age comedy that helped define a generation." Universal Pictures' publicity department wants to frame the film as a sweet and sentimental cinematic masterpiece like a Christmas special. But what if I tell you that there is nothing "warm-hearted" at the core of this coming-of-age film. Writer-director John Hughes created a grotesque masterpiece that was able to be blatantly disgusting and pervy yet fooled people into thinking it's the anti-*Porky*'s. Even famed film critic Pauline Kael reviewed the film in *New Yorker* by saying, "It's less raucous in tone than most of the recent teen pictures; it's closer to the gentle English comedies of the forties and fifties." Hughes used every trick from his cigarette advertising days to fool viewers into not realizing they were being sold an extremely dark experience.

Hughes' prime misdirection dealt to the audience was to frame the film as a comedy about a girl who has her sixteenth birthday completely forgotten by her family. This could be a nightmare headline on the cover of *Sassy* magazine. The Sweet Sixteen birthday has become a serious birthday celebration thanks to the MTV show about young girls getting massive parties and outrageous cars from their rich and famous parents. The teenage girl at the center of *Sixteen Candles* won't be getting a Mercedes SUV from her dad after breakfast. Although she thinks her family's non-birthday wishes might be a hint of a big surprise party element. She played along with their game until she's shocked to realize this isn't a practical joke. This recalls the shock of Hughes' female character who wakes up with a dick in "My Penis." Except in this case Samantha "Sam" Baker (Molly Ringwald) wakes up Friday morning and has a shock to discover that nobody cares about her special day.

This is the prime misdirection employed by Hughes to hide the true element of the film in the early minutes. The immediate running concern for the film is if Sam's parents remember that their little girl is now 16. This issue makes the story seem so much more innocent than so many of the teen flicks of the time. Those other films are about teenage characters coming of age and wanting to get laid. Sam merely wants her folks to sing her "Happy birthday." Why are her parents oblivious to this most special date in their daughter's life? Turns out they are wrapped up in wedding plans for her older sister. It's a miracle they got Sam, her little brother and youngest sister out the door to school since the engaged sibling has become even more of a handful. Sam has become forgotten. Although she holds out that this might be a big practical joke that will be exposed later in the evening when her relatives arrive. This is what keeps her from yelling out that it's her birthday and throwing a tantrum. Sam is a good daughter. By making this look like the entire plot of the film, viewers think it's such a charming story like an illustrated children's book. When someone gets asked about the film, their immediate summary is "this girl wakes up and discovers everyone has forgotten it's her 16th birthday." He candy coated the ugliness at the core of the film so an audience can think his PG film has nothing in common with the R-rated high school sex comedy

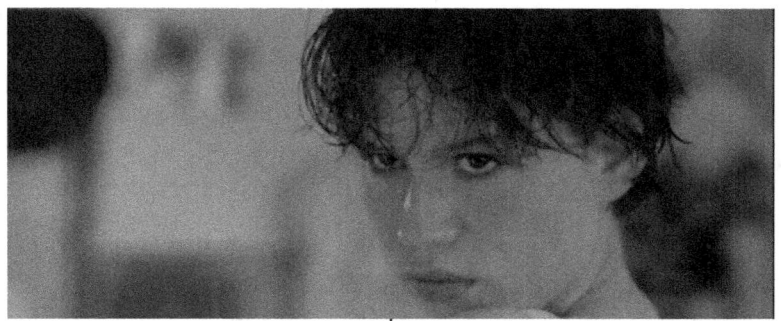

of *Porky's*. But when Sam gets to high school, we are treated to a scene that has something in common with *Porky's*. Both films give us a glimpse inside a girl's locker room with "teenage" nudity on display. There are two major differences in the approaches by the films. In *Porky's* the girls in the locker room nudity is the key to the advertising. The poster was a boy's eye peering through a hole as a girl's wet arm and leg were against the tile and adjusting the water. The trailer had the horny boys fighting to look through the peephole and the promise we'd see what's on the other side. *Sixteen Candles* didn't base their publicity campaign on getting to see Caroline Mulford (Haviland Morris) naked in the girls shower. Instead of a pack of lustful teenage boys ogling her, Mulford's nudity is examined by Sam and her friend. Turns out Caroline is dating Sam's dream boyfriend in Jake Ryan (*Vision Quest*'s Michael Schoeffling) Sam is jealous at how her classmate has the body of someone who had to skip 9 grades to be so physically mature. This is pretty much a true statement since actress Morris was around 25 when the film was shot. Ringwald was 15. Hughes does not get coy with the showering scene. He gives us a close up of Mulford's breasts and a second full body shot of her under the water with an angle that shows her ass and a breast. Hughes was able to make his shower scene classy by having it be about girls dealing with puberty. But the harsh reality is that a lot of junior high boys paid for a ticket to the PG rated film so they could see a naked woman without dealing with the R rating hurdles to get into *Porky's*.

The second part of the story is about Sam's crush on Jake Ryan and her avoiding the sexual bum rush of Farmer Ted (*Breakfast Club*'s Anthony Michael Hall). During an independent study "class," Sam's friend has her answer a sex quiz. Sam admits she's a virgin and wants to lose her virginity to Jake Ryan, who sits near her desk chair. We remember Jake as a rich handsome teenage boy with a great haircut. He's so dreamy with his smooth ways. On the other hand, during the bus ride home, Sam gets her personal space completely invaded by Farmer Ted. He creeps up on her and pounces onto her seat. His arms are positioned around her as if he's ready to squeeze the life out of her. He's so ready to hook up with her behind a nearby bush. He is supposed to be perceived as the opposite of sweet Jake. John Hughes' pitching tobacco to teens training comes into play again. In a cigarette ad, the brand compares itself to another smoking product as if you'll be better off. The ads never mention that you might be better off not smoking. That's what the pesky and ugly Surgeon General's warning does. And since it's jammed in the corner of the page, it's gleefully ignored as the kids focus on the middle of the action. An ad from John Hughes' time at Virginia Slims read, "121 brands of fat cigarettes fit me. Virginia Slims are made slimmer to fit you." Hughes gives us a film that leaves Sam with a similar Hobson's choice. Which of these two teenage boys would fit nicely in Sam's fingers? In the end, no matter which boy she chooses, she's getting the same thing. The filtered Jake or the unfiltered Farmer Ted are both cancer causing agents.

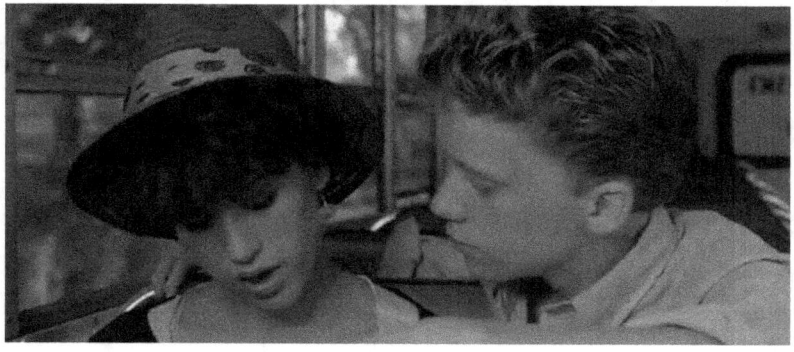

How can Jake be so bad when we remember him as so dreamy? Let's go back to that sex quiz. Sam thought her answers would be anonymous. But when she attempts to stealthily hand the paper back to her friend, it ends up in the hands of Jake. Since she's the only one to have answered so far, Jake knows exactly that Sam wants him to be her first. After he reads it, he asks a pal in gym class about her. Why does he want her? Does he feel something about her? It's pure narcissism. "I catch her lookin' at me a lot. It's kind a cool, the way she's always lookin' at me," Jake tells the pal. "She looks at me like she's in love with me." Jake is turned on by how she idolizes her. Since he knows how she wants to sleep with him, he's a bit of a predator at this point. The darker plot unveils at the Fresh Faces Dance back at Shermer High School's gym. Jake slow dances with Caroline, but checks out Sam. When their eyes meet, Sam isn't sure what to do. But before she can decide, Farmer Ted once more invades Sam's space. He spazzes out on the dancefloor next to her as Oingo Boingo blasts away. She finally runs off. Farmer Ted ends up having a bit of a talk with Jake while Caroline isn't around. The topic is Sam. Farmer Ted finds Sam sitting in a stripped car boy in the auto shop classroom. While they talk about her frustration of having her parents forget it's her birthday, Farmer Ted twice tries to dry hump her in the car. But all is forgiven when he has news that his pal Jake was asking about her. She's so excited she's willing to make a deal with Farmer Ted. Before this moment, Ted had made a bet with his nerd pals (including John Cusack from *The Sure Thing*) that he could score with Sam. He had to show them Sam's panties as proof of conquest or cough up a bunch of computer floppy disks. He only needs them for 10 minutes and Sam willingly pulls them off - all done off camera. While this part is on the fringe of cute, the next thing you know, boys are paying a dollar to see Sam's panties put on display like one of Elvis Presley's old jumpsuits. Ted and his pals are pantie pimps.

Here's an odd question: why was Sam able to gain entry into the auto shop classroom? In a real-world high school, the auto shop is locked up securely since students will steal tools and parts they can use on their car. How did she get in there? Shouldn't there at least be an adult in the hallway to make sure students stick to the gym during the dance? Is Shermer High security that lax? Or do they not care if wrenches go missing?

Caroline gets Jake to throw an after party at his mansion since his parents are away. This is where we get to see the cold narcissistic, predatory heart of Jake on full display. Even though we see Shermer High has minority students (in non-speaking roles), there's only white kids trashing the Ryan Estate. Was Jake so racist that he didn't even fake having one black friend at school? Caroline gets completely blotto on booze and who knows what else. Jake wants to track down Sam on the phone. In order to get privacy, he slams shut his door and traps Caroline's hair. He refuses to open up the door. He's too busy hunting down Sam. Caroline's equally messed up friends butcher her beautiful long locks to give her freedom. Is this the act of a dreamy boyfriend?

And Jake gets even worse after he discovers Farmer Ted in the wreckage of the party in the wee hours of the night. Farmer Ted starts downing shots as he talks to Jake about Sam. The two of them make a trade. Farmer Ted gives Sam's used panties to Jake and in return, Jake gives his new pal his parents' Rolls Royce, a six pack of Old Style beer and Caroline. The freshman is supposed to take the senior girl home. But early in the conversation Jake talks about how she's so inebriated. "I've got Caroline in the bedroom right now, passed

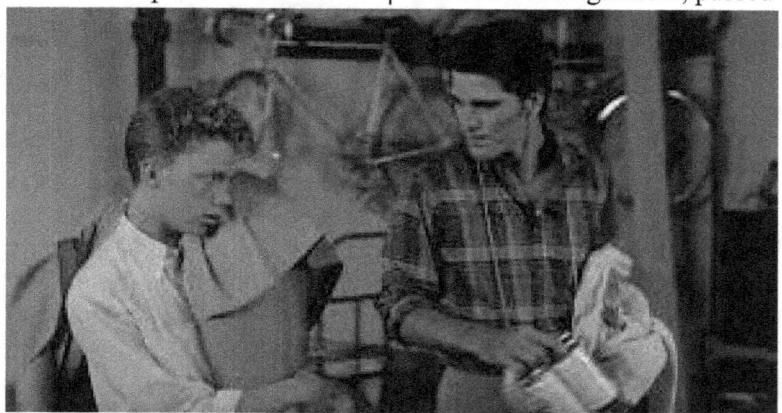

out cold. I could violate her ten different ways if I wanted to," he brags. Hughes immediately has Jake talk about how he wants a "serious girlfriend" and not a party girl like Caroline. Missing from his talk with Farmer Ted is the sex quiz. Jake knows he can violate Sam another 10 ways if he gives her a look.

Jake continues exposing himself as a horrible boyfriend as he lets Farmer Ted carry the unconscious Caroline into the garage and dump her in the Rolls. Ted has been downing liquor. He admits he doesn't have a driver's license. Jake doesn't care. He wants Ted to take her home. Even though Ted has a minor accident driving the expensive car out of the garage, Jake doesn't realize this is a bad idea. He even gives the kid more beer for the trip.

The drive is a bit of a nightmare with Farmer Ted smashing into everything on the road as the barely conscious Caroline hangs onto him and wants the party to keep going. Please note that in 1984, underaged drunk driving was a serious issue so this was not a "back in the day" thing. At one-point Farmer Ted takes his passed-out princess to his pals' house to prove he's a major stud. They take photographs of the teenage girl in compromising positions. Maybe Farmer Ted and the Nerds did more to her? When morning breaks, Ted didn't take her home. They're in a parking lot where a groggy Caroline realizes she had sex with the freshman. This is one of those moments where John Hughes practiced maximum restraint by not filming what exactly happened between Farmer Ted and Caroline. The audience has nothing to gauge what happened except by Caroline referring to it as "weird."

When Jake shows up to see what Farmer Ted has done to his parents' Rolls Royce and his girlfriend, it's a textbook of consequence free behavior. Jake does not tear into the kid for destroying an elite car or even assaulting Caroline. Jake's talk with Caroline is guilt-free. She doesn't go nuts that this man she loved had traded him for a pair of Sam's used panties. It's a rather calm exchange where she describes hooking up with Farmer Ted once more as "weird." Their chat includes her saying it's up to him if they want to still be together. This leads us to Jake showing up parked outside the church where Sam's sister is getting married. Since John Hughes cut away before Jake gave Caroline his answer, we've always assumed he told her that he wanted to be with Sam. What if he told Caroline that he wanted them to stay together, dumped her off at her own home to sleep off her hangover and snuck over to the church for a hook up with Sam? How can we really trust that Jake did the right thing? John Hughes did the right thing to make people overlook the extremely shocking elements of his teen flick. He once again turns on a sweetness overload. After a nightmarish wedding with her sister blitzed on painkillers taken because of her period, Sam is relieved to come out of the church and see Jake next to his flashy sports car. She blows off going to the wedding reception to be with Jake. Even her father (*O.C. and Stiggs'* Paul Dooley) approves with a big OK hand sign as his daughter speeds away with Jake. The final cutesy image is the high schoolers sitting on the dining room table as Sam finally gets her Sweet Sixteen birthday cake. There's nothing openly ominous to the scene that's neatly wrapped by the Thompson Twins' "If You Were Here." Jake says, "Happy Birthday, Samantha. Make a wish." Sam responds, "It already came true." And the film ends. This allows a viewer to think of the film as charming since it opens with a girl whose family forgets her sixteenth birthday and ends with her getting her ultimate birthday wish.

This final act of misdirection is an amazing marketing move by Hughes to get the audience to overlook the most unsavory elements of his film. People leaving the theater are as clueless as Sam's dad. They feel good that Sam ends up with Jake. There's no talk about how Jake is a horrifying rich kid. How he didn't have the guts to break up with Caroline. How he had no problem letting his parents' house and car get completely trashed. How he had no issue with letting Farmer Ted endanger, exploit and have his way with Caroline. How he knew that he wasn't going to get any resistance from Sam if he wanted to take her virginity. Would Sam's father have given an OK if he had a clue what Sam's dreamy boy had done over the last 24 hours and what Jake might be doing to his daughter

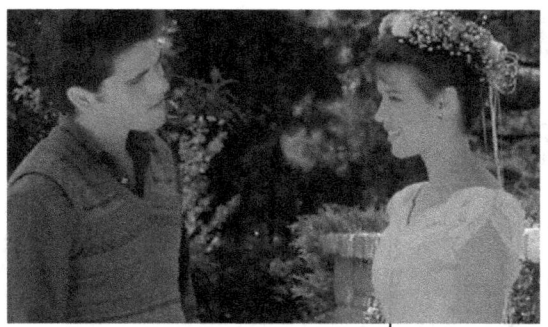

in the next few hours? Is *Sixteen Candles* really loftier than *Porky's*? Should we be showing this movie to our teenage daughters as a cute entertainment like an episode of *Small Wonder*? Some might imagine that after Sam blew out her candles that even more dreaminess occurred. But it's easy to imagine that *Sixteen Candles* was part of a trilogy with "My Penis" and "My Vagina." That Jake turns out to be the precursor to the Preppy Killer. Come Monday morning, Jake is back with Caroline and the cadaver dogs are being led around the Shermer High football field looking for Sam's shallow grave. This has all the earmarks of a disturbing and depressing European exploitation flick about the tragic death of a teen girl. "Everyone forgot her 16th birthday, but they'll remember the day she died!" would scream the exploitation poster. The film is disturbing and depressing for what happened to Caroline during the film. But Hughes keeps it light enough that we don't consider this the *ABC After School Special* about a popular girl trusting her dreamy boyfriend only to be part of a traumatic nightmare. But Hughes doesn't let Caroline suffer a trauma or feel pain and outrage. She just processes it all as just "weird." Are we really supposed to believe Sam isn't going to be Jake's next victim?

This reading of *Sixteen Candles* might seem a bit extreme as if I'm attempting to ruin your childhood. But even Molly Ringwald has come to terms that things weren't so "warm-hearted" in the film. She wrote in *New Yorker* (April 6, 2018) about realizing things were pretty dark in these films and the darkness wasn't addressed within the films. "What About the Breakfast Club?" has her examine John Hughes' teen characters and she's not too happy. She even reaches out to Haviland Morris to talk of Caroline's fate. It's a rather moving examination and not the usual "working with John Hughes was awesome" puff piece.

John Hughes establishes a teenage universe where there are no consequences or price to be paid for bad life choices. At no point in Sam's barely 40 hours of screen life does any adult say, "Why did you do that?" or "What were you thinking?" A cop doesn't pull over Farmer Ted for drunk and reckless driving. Jake doesn't worry about being grounded for life. Caroline doesn't fear she might be pregnant with Farmer Ted's baby. The kids don't have to answer for their actions so there's zero guilt attached to their behavior. No wonder Hughes quickly established himself as a favorite of the '80s teens.

Ultimately the film is the cinematic version of one of Hughes' Virginia Slims ads. We're supposed to believe Sam has come a long way, baby and ignore the Surgeon General's warning that this reality is dangerous to her health.

SOUNDTRACK NOTES: MCA records had little faith that *Sixteen Candles* was going to sell vinyl. Instead of a double album, the movie was given a five track "specially priced mini-album." Many of the musical moments were left off the EP including Spandau Ballet's "True," Altered Images' "Happy Birthday," The Vapors' 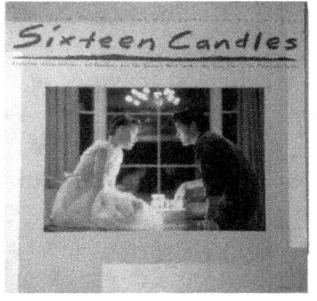 "Turning Japanese" and General Public's "Tenderness." On the plus side, you didn't have to lift the needle to skip over Oingo Boingo's "Wild Sex (In the Working Class)." The five tracks at least feature The Stray Cats' "Sixteen Candles" and The Thompson Twins' "If You Were Here." You do get the end tracks. Oddly enough "If You Were Here" wasn't released as a single. I have no idea why Patti Smith's "Gloria" was selected. I can't remember the scene where this played. The other two tracks are Annie Golden's "Hang Up the Phone" and Ira Newborn and the Geek's "Geek Boogie." It's a rather short affair.

The Breakfast Club

February 7, 1985

Universal Pictures

Directed by John Hughes

Starring Emilio Estevez, Paul Gleason, Judd Nelson, Anthony Michael Hall, Molly Ringwald, Ally Sheedy and John Kapelos

Rated R - 97 minutes

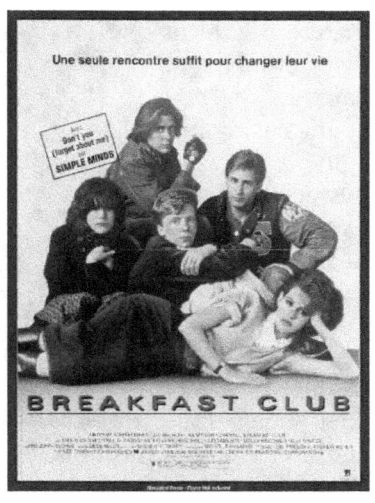

What's the first character you see in *The Breakfast Club*? The easy guess is the "Princess" Claire Standish (Molly Ringwald) as she sits in her dad's BMW and whines about having to waste a Saturday in detention. Does anyone else feel a little bit uncomfortable with a father who acts like her creepy older lover in that plaid scarf? Well Claire is the wrong answer.

The intellectual guess is Shermer High School since the educational institution in suburbs of Chicago plays a major role in what went on inside on Saturday March 24, 1984 starting around 7 a.m. Indeed, we get to learn a lot about the building where for a few decades, students have been molded into the adults of tomorrow. The opening of the film is a montage of various elements of the school that's now empty after a busy class week. The right answer is in the montage. Who do you see clearly before the Princess arrives? You might have to frame by frame the action to glimpse the answer.

Did you see Carl the Janitor? You probably didn't notice it the first time you saw the film in the theater back in 1985. Why? Because he was the middle face in the display for Shermer High's "Man of the Year" award. He won this award in 1969. He looks rather mature with a very professional haircut. You could easily imagine Carl as a business executive at Radio Shack or the top salesman at a Peugeot car dealership. How nearly 15 years later does Carl end up pushing a trash bucket around these same hallways? What's interesting is that this seems to be a throwaway joke. Think of the National Lampoon spoofs of high school yearbooks. Early in such a special edition they pay tribute to the honor student from a decade earlier and a dozen or so pages later have a picture of him cleaning the toilet in the boys room without tying the joke together.

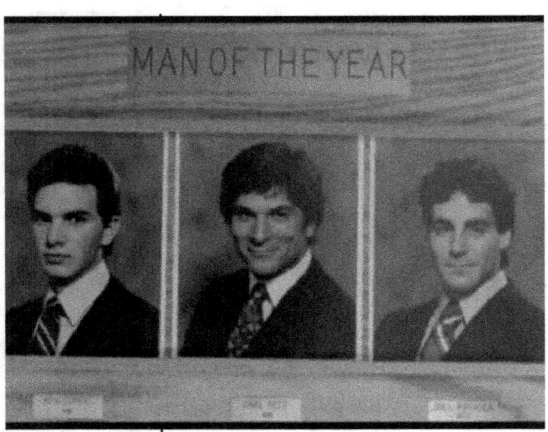

In the three scenes involving Carl, the subject of his honor is not brought up. When he enters the library, John Bender (*St. Elmo's Fire*'s Judd Nelson) jokes that Carl is the father of Brian (*Weird Science*'s Anthony Michael Hall). Later Bender asks Carl how he got to be a janitor since Andrew (*St. Elmo's Fire*'s Emilio Estevez) is interested in a career in the custodial arts. Carl doesn't give a real answer and gets a touch defensive that the kids think he's an untouchable peasant. He points out that he sees what they're saying and doing. "I am the eyes and ears of this institution my friends," he warns them. He then tells them that the clock is 20 minutes fast. Even though Bender seems to love to dig into everyone's soft spots, he doesn't scoff "Man of the Year" at Carl. Maybe he has zero clue that the handsome teenager in the display case is the rather beaten down janitor. This is hard to believe that by Bender's senior year, someone in the school had to put together that Carl Reed and Carl the Janitor are the same person. Bender doesn't use it as a parting shot at the end of the film when the released students walk past Carl as he mops the hallway floor near the exit door.

The second time we see Carl is when he pops up as Vernon illegally goes through the school's confidential records. Carl shakes him down for $50 to keep the secret. As the two adults pound down a six pack of Old Style beer, Carl says when he was a kid he wanted to be John Lennon. This is strange since Carl's Man of the Year photo doesn't look like he's going to be doing any Bed Peace with Yoko back in 1969. Vernon fears if these kids will take care of him when he's old. Carl jokes he wouldn't count on it. Vernon doesn't bring up the Man of the Year honor to Carl as proof that future generations are getting worse.

The third Carl moment is when the kids are dismissed and pass him in the hallway.

Ultimately, we have to ask the burning question of what the Hell happened to Carl so that he went from Man of the Year to stuck with the Saturday morning custodian shift at his old high school?

There had to be some trouble. At one point there was a rumor that Carl was a ghost forced to clean the halls for eternity. Except why would he want Vernon to give him $50? So there had to be a troubled history to Carl. Viewers had to pick through the few clues about him. His issues didn't lead him to becoming a born-again religious fanatic since the music on his Walkman headphones was E.G. Daily's "Waiting" and not Holy Roller preaching or Gospel Rock. (You can actually see E.G. Daily in *No Small Affair*, *Valley Girl* and *Better Off Dead* during the festival). Carl didn't see the light on the road to Damascus.

Normally the janitor stuck with Saturday morning is someone who needs a good reason to not party hard on Friday night. The shift at Shermer

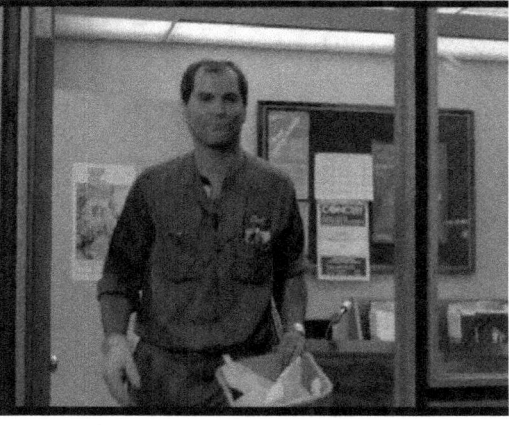

- Page 3 -

is rather solitary with no one else from the custodial staff in the building. We learn during the second visit that Carl isn't doing any 12 Step Program. He and Vernon pound down a six pack of Old Style beers in the room with the confidential files. They weren't in the room that long so the three beers each has given them both massive buzzes. John Hughes doesn't give us a clue where the beers came from. Was this private stock tucked away in a nearby teacher's lounge fridge? Or does Carl have a mini Igloo cooler hidden in his trash can so he can vanish into a chemistry lab, lock the door and take a party break? We know that Carl has no problem getting drunk on the clock.

When the kids are running around the school halls trying to avoid being seen by Assistant Principal Vernon, they never run into Carl. They are all over two floors in pursuit of a clean passage to the library. You'd imagine that on a Saturday with no classes that Carl would break out the floor buffer to scrub the tiles in the hallway. But all we ever see him barely use is a mop on the floor at the end. Maybe he was in the home economics kitchen getting pre-liquored up for a Saturday night?

For decades, it's been a mystery with plenty of speculation as to what Hell happened to Carl. We've all heard stories of former students returning to the school where they had won honors with the hopes of teaching the next generation to grasp success. But rarely have you heard of "The Man of the Year" mopping floors at his

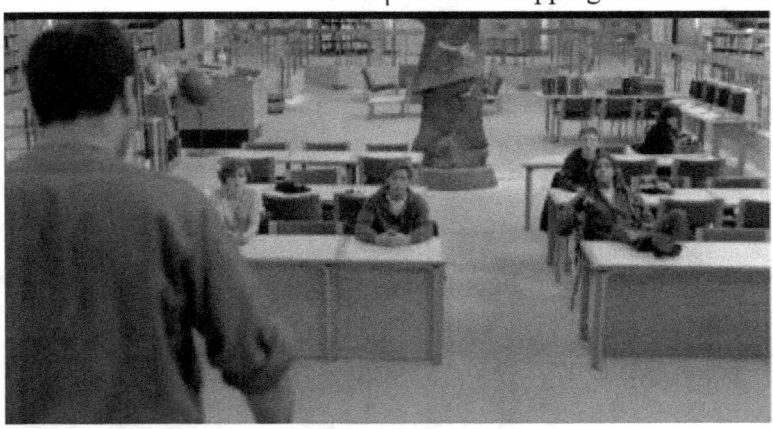

alma mater. When it was announced that a special 30th Anniversary edition of *The Breakfast Club* was coming to Blu-ray in 2015, there was a bit of publicity including the actors talking about their iconic roles.

John Kapelos shared with the Huffington Post website his biography of Carl and how he ended up a janitor at Shermer High. "You have to have your heart broken by your teenage sweetheart in your third year of university when you're doing a great football scholarship. Drop out. Lose her heart. Lose her affection. Make sure her father hates you even more and will never include you in his future plans. Even if you try to make up to her. And then you get a job at your old high school as a janitor, and you try to lick your wounds. That's how you become a janitor. That's Carl's pathetic backstory."

And for a while, it was felt like this was the truth about Carl that wasn't said on screen. He was merely a victim of a broken heart in college that derailed his high school potential. But it turns out there was a deeper truth and it wasn't merely an actor doing emotional history to inform his performance. There was film footage of Carl's journey to the custodial arts.

When the Criterion Collection released *The Breakfast Club* in 2018, they included nearly an hour of deleted scenes and extended scenes. The biggest revelation is what Carl really told the kids when he wheeled his trash bucket into the library. Turns out we only saw a third of Carl's lines. Sure, it starts with him saying hi to Brian and smart mouth Bender

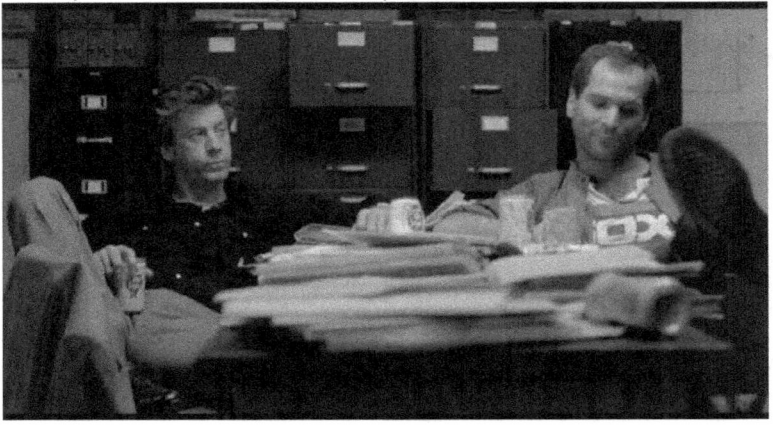

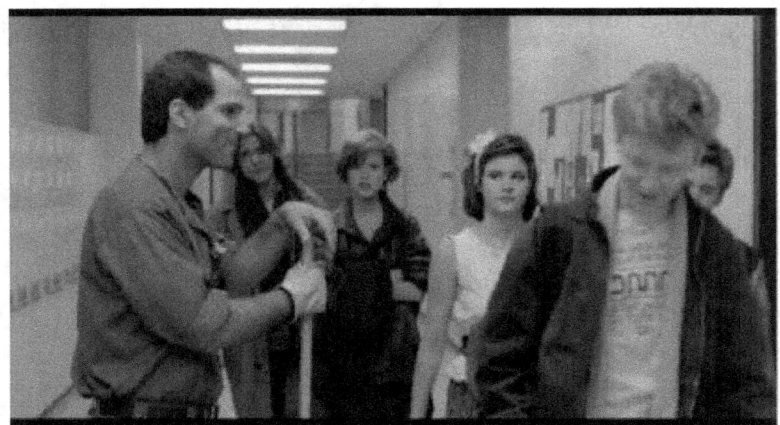

asking how you get to be a custodian for Andrew's sake. But in the outtake version, Carl has a darker time with the five kids. It was more than a broken heart that brought Carl back to Shermer High.

The road to being a janitor all started with Carl hooking up "with a broad named Maria Pegliania" and he uses hands to demonstrate large breasts. Something went wrong and Carl ended up living with his parents for about 8 years. Besides destroying the transmission in his father's car, Carl let them in on his other achievements. "Sold some hash, got busted," he confessed. But he speaks of being persistent in life. "Keep on fucking up. When you're tired of fucking up, fuck up some more. Fuck up as much as you like. When you stop doing that fucking up, come here and fill out an application with Kelly down in personnel and you'll be racking in $11.74 in no time."

Carl turned this detention into an episode of *Scared Straight*. Except Bender and the other four aren't too affected by his tale of bad personal life choices. Carl continues with a familiar line except the ending takes things to a fresh level of bleakness.

"I read your notes. I look through your letters. Go through your lockers. And I listen to your conversations. You don't know that. I am the eyes and ears of this institution my friends," Carl declares. But now he continues with "I know where you are now and I know where you'll be in the future." Carl stares down the five bad kids and gives them a crystal ball prediction that comes off like a gypsy curse. First he goes after Bender with "You have ten years max. That's right. Drugs, rundown trailer in west Texas. The whore bitch wife takes the kid, splits You shoot a fatal dose. Game over. Dogs eat your carcass before the cops arrive. They don't know who you are." He moves onto Brian's fate of having a series of heart attacks from being stressed out. He'll be dead before 40, but successful. He teases Allison Reynolds (*St. Elmo's Fire*'s Ally Sheedy) as a successful poet "which means nobody cares." He continues her sad plight by having three kids before she marries, stuck behind the wheel of a station wagon and the queen of the carpool lane. Andrew gets tagged as Muscle Butt. The future has him stuck as a district sales manager of a golf club manufacturer with a wife who gets fat on him. Finally, he holds up a mirror to Claire the homecoming queen to show off how she'll have "Six facelifts and two boob jobs by the time you're 40. And a husband with more girlfriends than anniversaries."

He wraps his predictions up with the familiar "Hey, but I'm just the janitor." He points out the clock being too fast and pushes the trash can out of the library door like we're used to seeing. But that extra few minutes turns cool Carl into a frightening character. He's more vicious than Vernon with the kids. He dumped that garbage can all over the five detainees while unloading his horrific past This is the type of speech you would expect delivered from that other '80s school janitor Freddy Krueger from the *Nightmare on Elm Street* horror flicks.

This outtake experience was more horrific for these kids than the ones in *Scared Straight* who were given a prison tour and a chat with the inmates. Because at the end of the film, they went back to school and had a chance to straighten themselves out. Carl will be roaming their hallways on Monday morning. He knows what they're doing. He's getting into their lockers. He might be swiping their drugs. No matter how tough Vernon and Bender imagine themselves, there is no one more frightening at Shermer High School than Carl.

At the end of Carl's visit, those five kids should have grabbed their pencils and written a college entry worthy essay about who they are with the answer being "someone who wants to graduate early so they can get away from Carl." Although Bender could also focus his essay on being a guy who doesn't want his face eaten off by wild dogs. What the Hell happened to Carl? Bad things and they might not be over.

SOUNDTRACK NOTES: The Breakfast Club soundtrack had the massive hit with Simple Minds' "Don't You (Forget About Me)." But it's a rather weak collection once you get past Wang Chung's "Fire In the Twilight." Keith Forsey who had just produced Billy Idol's *Rebel Yell* was in charge of the songs and wrote 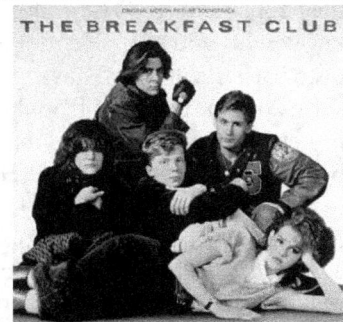 most of the tracks. He offered Billy Idol to sing the hit and was turned down. He also wrote E.G. Daily's "Waiting" so you can have something to listen to when mopping up like Carl the Janitor. Karla DeVito's teen anthem "We Are Not Alone" was co-written with Robbie Benson, her husband. You might remember Robbie as a teen star in the '70s with *Ode to Billy Joe* and *The Death of Richie*. The rest of the tracks are so-so. You do have "Reggae Song" in case you want to smoke up like Emilo Estevez. There are two other instrumentals from Forsey. This soundtrack could have been an EP instead of *Sixteen Candles*.

Weird Science

August 2, 1985

Universal Pictures

Directed by John Hughes

Starring Anthony Michael Hall, Ilan Mitchell-Smith, Kelly LeBrock, Bill Paxton, Robert Downey Jr, Robert Rusler, Jennifer Balgobin, Jeff Jensen, Vernon Wells, Michael Berryman and John Kapelos

Rated PG-13 - 96 minutes

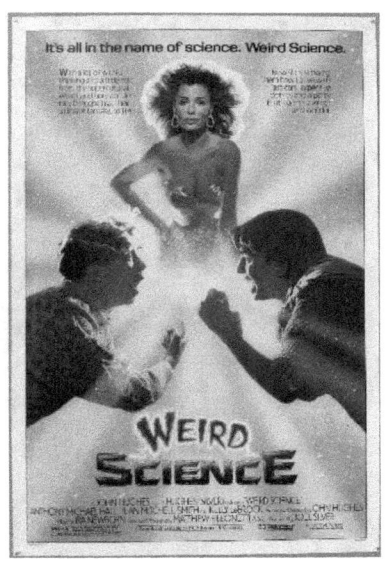

Was Anthony Michael Hall a creation of John Hughes? He got his first screen role as one of the thieving kids in Kenny Rogers' *Six Pack*. But when was the last time you saw that NASCAR film on cable? Realistically Hall didn't exist until he sat in the back of the Wagon Queen Family Truckster as Rusty Griswald in *National Lampoon's Vacation*. While he had to suffer playing Chevy Chase's son, he was rewarded by establishing a relationship with John Hughes. At the time Hughes was only the screenwriter having adapted his classic National Lampoon magazine piece "Vacation '58" about a middle American family's road trip to Disneyland that ends up with the father shooting Walt Disney. The story is a recollection from the son so in a sense, Rusty is John Hughes. Often when talking about this time, the focus is on how Molly Ringwald was Hughes' muse. But Anthony Michael Hall and him had a deeper connection. He was a teenage Marcello Mastroianni to Hughes' Federico Fellini. As fate would have it, Hughes was able to use his success to land a three-picture deal and he cast Hall as his Golden Geek

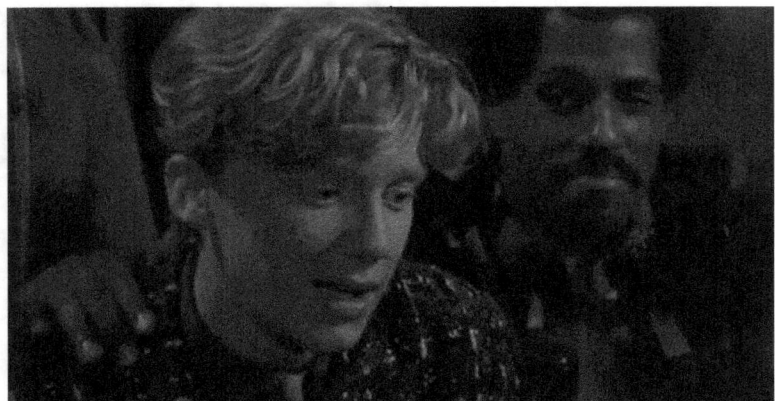

God for both *Sixteen Candles* and *The Breakfast Club*. Hall played two different kinds of geeks. He was wild in the first and frustrated in the second. Both had one thing in common: neither geek hooked up with Molly Ringwald at the end of the movie.

In reality, while making two back-to-back films together, Hall and Ringwald ended up dating. And this is where the partnership between Hughes, Hall and Ringwald began to fall apart. There seem to be a couple stories. At one-point Hughes envisioned being able to crank out more films with the duo like Andy Rooney-Judy Garland Pictures. He wanted them for *Pretty in Pink* with Molly as Annie and Hall as Duckie. Plus, they'd be the leads in *Ferris Bueller's Day Off* although who would be Cameron? He even wanted them back for *Some Kind of Wonderful* as...don't worry about those character names. The only one of his teen films they'd not both be in was *Weird Science*. And then their collaboration came to a bumpy end like a potholed downtown Chicago boulevard. Was he jealous that his homecoming queen and geek king were able to establish the relationship that he couldn't write and control?

It would be rather ironic that a man who once wrote of shooting Walt Disney had turned into the head of the *Mickey Mouse Club*. Walt wanted control over his prized Mouseketeer Annette Funicello. Did Hughes want to call the shots over Ringwald?

He did end up making one film each with the two actors although they weren't together on the screen. Ringwald was

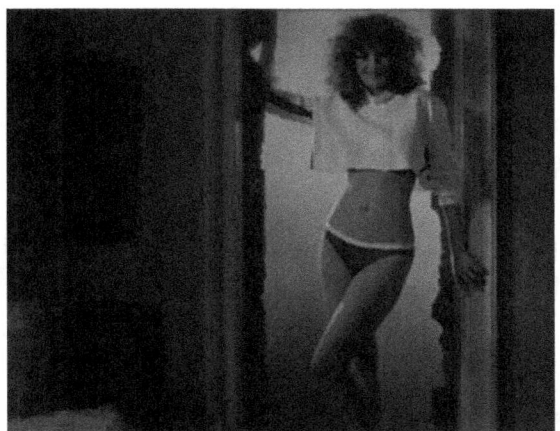

reportedly displeased when she discovered that after Hughes wrote *Pretty In Pink* for her, he hired a trailer editor to direct the film. It wasn't exactly the Muse treatment. *Weird Science* was promised to Hall early into the shoot of *The Breakfast Club*. Hall has spoken about being shocked when Hughes told him he'd already cranked out a third of the script overnight. If you've ever worked on a movie in a normal crew position, you don't have time to crank out a script. You barely have time to sleep. But somehow as a director, Hughes was able to take his mind off that library and type out a tale of two students having their pants yanked down in the girls gym at Shermer High. He was a fast writer.

Hall has said in interviews that he was offered all three of Hughes' upcoming teen films and said no. He was tired of playing the same role and stuck in high school. Instead of making another film in Hollywood or Chicago, Hall went to New York City to become part of the cast of *Saturday Night Live* on the 11th Season that featured his former co-stars Robert Downey Jr, Joan Cusack and Randy Quiad (from *National Lampoon's Vacation*). The season was a forgettable flop and not even an interesting disaster like season six when Charles Rocket and Gilbert Gottfried replaced the last of the original Not Ready For Primetime Players. The only thing of note from his time at Studio 8H was that Hall became the youngest cast member when he started at 17. He came back to Hollywood for two more teen films in the '80s including the college football recruiting comedy *Johnny Be Good* with Robert Downey Jr and Uma Thurman. He's acted steady over the decades and had a hit on USA Network with *The Dead Zone* TV adaptation. He was allowed to grow up by the viewing public. Hall and Hughes were tight when making their three films in less than two years. Hall was Hughes' on screen Mini-Me. Hughes was willing to play Hall's silent and disapproving father at the end of *The Breakfast Club*. Yet the director and actor went cold on each other for the rest of Hughes' life. You'd figure that at some point Hughes would have called up Hall's agent to offer him a role in one of his later non-teen movies. But nope. Guess there was not a perfect adult part for Hall in *Dutch* or *Curly Sue*.

Was Hughes upset that the Anthony Michael Hall that he created by pecking away on a keyboard didn't do exactly what his creator wanted? Could he not deal that his Mini-Me wanted to do more than be eternally stuck at Shermer High without the princess? Hughes took that answer to his grave.

SOUNDTRACK NOTES: The soundtrack album's notable track was Oingo Boingo's "Weird Science." The song played at the beginning and end of the film. They even revived Killing Joke's "Eighties." The rest of the tracks from bands such as Lords of the New Church, Wall of Voodoo and Kim Wilde have pretty much 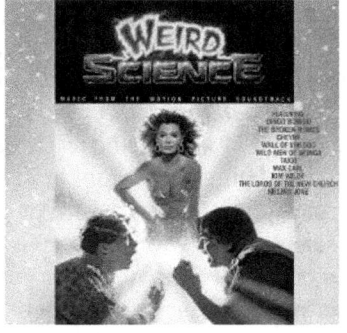 been obscured by time. There are a few bands that are completely forgotten including Taxxi, Cheyne, Max Carl and The Broken Homes. When is the last time you heard "Why Don't Pretty Girls Look at Me" by The Wild Men of Wonga? Perhaps the answer lies in you playing The Wild Men of Wonga too much. Ira and the Geeks returns from *Sixteen Candles* with "Geek Romance." The *Weird Science* soundtrack isn't formulated to make you the dance floor king at '80s Night outside of the theme song.

Pretty In Pink

February 28, 1986

Paramount Pictures

Directed by Howard Deutch

Starring Molly Ringwald, Jon Cryer, Andrew McCarthy, Harry Dean Stanton, Annie Potts, James Spader, Andrew Dice Clay, Dweezil Zappa and Gina Gershon.

Rated PG-13 - 96 minutes

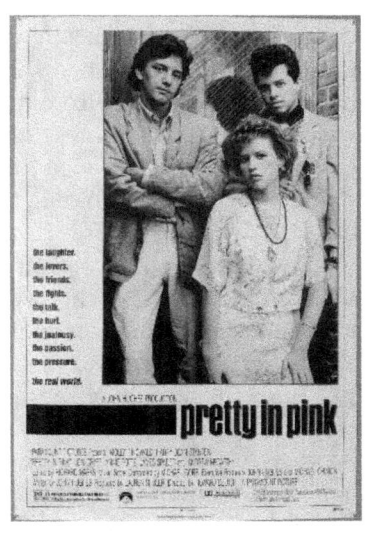

Whose film is Pretty in Pink? Under the normal rule of "A Film By," the credit goes to the director. But does anyone say, "You mean the film by Howard Deutch?" Everyone will immediately credit this film to John Hughes. But John was not sitting in the director's chair. He only wrote the script and assumed the duties of an executive producer. After wrapping up his three-picture deal with Universal, Hughes had set up a contract with Paramount. He had two films ready to roll: Pretty in Pink and Ferris Bueller's Day Off. He directed Ferris. Why didn't he direct both? Tak Fujimoto shot both so Hughes could have juggled them too. Perhaps he wasn't excited about making a film shot around Los Angeles and would rather focus on that Day Off in Chicago? Maybe he realized he didn't have to direct Pretty in Pink to be considered the key creative force of the film?

Over the course of a year, John Hughes had directed three teen movies. He had established his name as much as his teenage stars. A majority of the directors that had hits with low budget teen themed films immediately used their box office clout to work with grown up stars on at least medium budget films. Hughes having three straight hits was extremely unusual. Although to a certain degree, he must have known he'd established his name in the genre not from the success of *The Breakfast Club*, but how many reviews had to point out that he had nothing to do with *St. Elmo's Fire*. John Hughes hadn't merely gotten his name noticed by film critics. He had become a name that ticket buyers wanted to see like Stanley Kubrick or Martin Scorsese except for adolescent comedies. But with his new deal with Paramount, Hughes had his sights set on becoming like Steven Spielberg and receiving the credit for a movie without having to spend every day as the director.

Hughes put his mark on the film by writing the script specifically for Molly Ringwald. The question is what was the *National Lampoon*-version of the script conceived for Molly's character to endure before Hughes brightened up the story for the kids to enjoy instead of being horrified at the repulsive finale. *Sixteen Candles* he had her fall in love with a guy who let his girlfriend drive with a drunk teenager who eventually attacked her. In *The Breakfast Club* she fell in love with an abusive guy who sexually molested her under a table in the library. What horrifying fate was she going to endure this time? Most people want to think it was about the ending, but the nightmare at the core of the film is unspoken and takes place before the film rolls through the projector.

Andie and her father (Harry Dean Stanton) are coming to terms with the fact that her mother had just ran away three years before. They hadn't heard a thing from since her disappearance. It's almost like

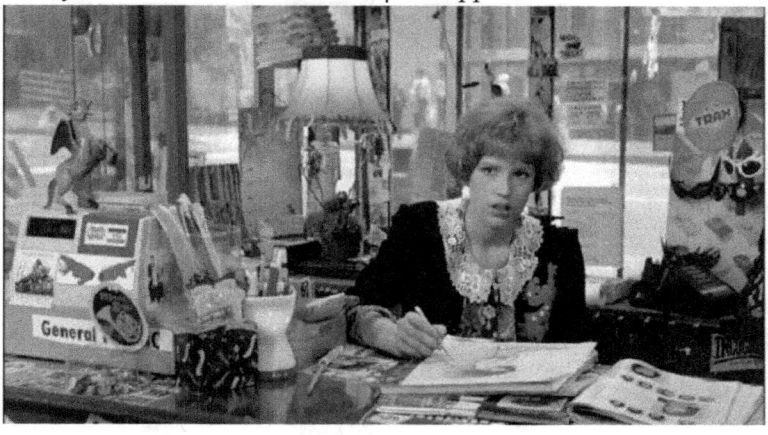

Paris, Texas II for Harry Dean. Except he doesn't track down his estranged wife this time. Andie's mom doesn't pop up before her daughter's prom. She didn't want to deal with her unemployed husband anymore, but why wouldn't she try to contact her daughter? Maybe because in the original idea that hit John Hughes had Andie's mother hiding in an unmarked grave? Wouldn't the John Hughes of the *National Lampoon* write a story about a girl who has two boys fighting for her affection be a lot darker. And here's the darkness to consider: what if three years earlier Blane (Andrew McCarthy) and Steff (James Spader) were driving around drunk when they ran over Andie's mother? The two bury the flattened woman in a grave behind the stable where Blane keeps his horses. It's a dangerous secret that bonds the two for life or at least until final exams. Since Blane was behind the wheel, Steff holds this truth as power over his friend. Now before the prom, the two boys want to see who can hook up with clueless Andie. They both have a warped fantasy to seduce the daughter of the mother they killed. Wouldn't this be the disturbing sweet ending a subscriber would read in the magazine back in 1979? Unlike the first two films, John couldn't stealthily hide this disturbing element on the screen with his Virginia Slim skills. There is a talk between Blane and Steff that openly dating Andie is dangerous, but it's supposedly because she's poor white trash and not a rich kid like them. The conversation is not quite as creepy as Farmer Ted and Jake Ryan in the trading panties moment. The scene is shot to obscure the fact that Steff is rolling a joint full of marijuana to avoid getting an R Rating from the MPAA for drug use. Far as your mother is concerned, Steff likes to hand roll his cigarettes. There's quite a bit being hidden in their exchange, but nothing that could get either indicted for homicide. Hughes not being the "real" director and not trusting Howard Deutch to handle his signature subterfuge makes such chats obscure without relying on visual misdirection to get away with horrific behavior between characters.

Who was Howard Deutch? At this point in his career, he had directed a few notable music videos including Billy Joel's "Keeping the Faith" and Billy

Idol's "Flesh for Fantasy." More importantly was a gig that had him cut trailers for movies including *Sixteen Candles* and *The Breakfast Club*. This is how he got to know Hughes and received an invitation to direct *Pretty In Pink* as he mentions on the behind the scenes documentary on the DVD. This was a smart move on Hughes' part since he knew the novice Deutch wasn't going to take control of the film. There would be zero chance that Deutch was going to explode on Hughes and remind him that he's merely the screenwriter. Deutch knew he could be fired in a heartbeat if Hughes was even mildly displeased. As much as your film school instructor will blather on about the director being the ultimate person in charge of a movie, this is a myth. There's plenty of Hollywood productions where the original director gets yanked and a new person finishes. Or they replace the director for a series of reshoots. A director's job isn't safe until after the movie is in the theater for a weekend.

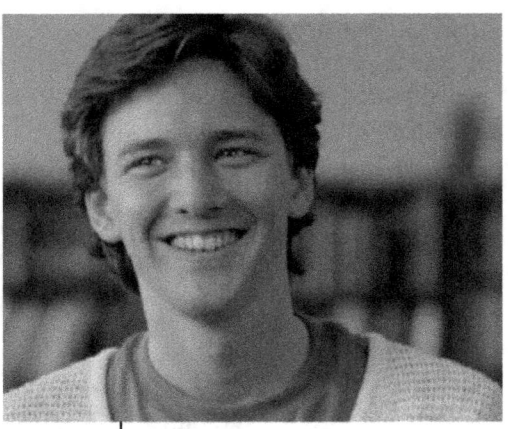

From watching Deutch in the vintage and more recent bonus features, he had zero intentions to butt heads with Hughes when things on the page didn't click on the set. He wanted the soundtrack to be mostly instrumental score music and John Hughes wanted New Wave hits. Guess who "lost" that battle?

This inability to take control of the story really shows up when judging the love connections between the characters. What was written on the page and ended up on the screen didn't add up and it's not merely who Andie chose to take to the prom. There's a lot of questions about the relationships in the movie.

The first big unexplained mystery of the film is why Blane is attracted to Andie. He's such a boring character. He gave her a stalker stare in the high school hallway that goes nowhere. The cute meet at her record store was just pathetic. He seriously wants to buy Steve Lawrence's *Take It Home* record and asks what she thinks of it. This moment touched me because at the time I had a massive crush on an employee of School Kids Records in Chapel Hill. I referred to her as St. Barbara. Whenever I'd drop by the store and she was behind the counter, I'd do my best to buy extraordinary albums to impress her with my taste. I wanted St. Barbara to smile as she rang up my purchases. And she did. But things never went beyond that. Watching Blane buy that

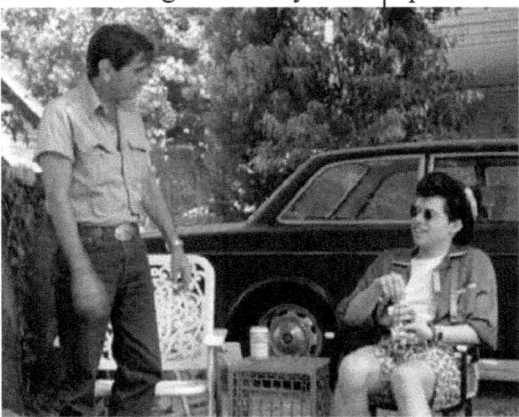

Steve Lawrence vinyl was horrific because it seemed like the kind of album he'd grab off the shelf since Perry Como was Devil Music in his mansion. Blane is so blah that if he explained that his family made their fortune inventing Miracle Whip and Wonder Bread, I'd believe it. He is a dull sweater vest mannequin. What would he want from Andie? It's not like he's a closet Alternateen who has to hide his love of Haircut 100 from Steff and the other rich kids. Having Andrew McCarthy playing him seems so wrong too. Barely 8 months before, he'd graduated from Georgetown and was screwing Ally Sheedy on top of a coffin in *St. Elmo's Fire*. Now he's back in high school being a take it slow senior at 24? Even more age out of place is 26-year-old James Spader lurking in the school staircase. His Steff looks like he ought to be getting staked out by Crockett and Tubbs on *Miami Vice*. When Steff wants to hook up with Andie, he ought to be busted by the cops for being a dirty old man. At least Steff makes Blane look younger. But Steff doesn't make Blane look any less bland. But would Deutch dare bring this up to Hughes that his rich boy romantic is dishwater dull especially when compared to Duckie (Jon Cryer)? This leads to the biggest relationship screw up in the film.

I'm not one of those people who think Andie should have ended up with Duckie. I do believe that Duckie gets completely screwed out of his real relationship in the film. He should have been shacking up with record store owner Iona (Annie Potts) at the end of the film. Did you see how Iona watches Duckie as he tries to impress Andie with a kinetic lip sync of Otis Redding's "Try A Little Tenderness" that uses every inch of her record store. Andie looks unimpressed as she waits for Blane to arrive for their big date at Steff's rich kid party. But Iona can't take her eyes off Duckie. Later she takes the brokenhearted Duckie to a nightclub and gives him the eye that seems to be the "will I sleep with him now or later" look. The moment is ruined when Andie drags Blane into the club. This gets Duckie's feathers ruffled that his crush wants to hump the heir to the lukewarm water fortune. It does end with Duckie proving he's moved on from Andie by giving a deep passionate kiss to Iona that startles and impresses her. Instead of her telling Duckie that he needs a mature woman in his life and forget Andie, she sells out big time to the Man. She dresses preppy and tells Andie that she's going out with a Yuppie and dreams of marriage in the near future. The Yuppie is as old as Steff and dull as Blane. He encapsulates the lameness of both sides of the rich guy world in one mediocre package. Both women settle for lame "safe" rich guys. Was the message of this movie to give up on being a Bohemian and embrace greed? Was this the element that Deutch brought to the film? Or was this merely John Hughes defending his new life as a multi-millionaire creator of non-edgy entertainment? Which of the duo were punching back at the Die Yuppie Scum crowd?

Back the original question: Whose film is *Pretty In Pink*? *Pretty In Pink* is not a Howard Deutch Film because there's ultimately nothing on the screen if we yank away all the parts that have John Hughes' fingerprints on them. For most people watching the film, they probably thought Hughes secretly directed the film and gave Deutch the credit like the rumors spread about Steven Spielberg directing *Poltergeist* instead of Tobe Hooper. Deutch didn't seem to care about the lack of recognition since he directed two more John Hughes Films

SOUNDTRACK NOTES: If you buy only one soundtrack album from a John Hughes' film, let it be *Pretty In Pink*. Right off the bat is Orchestral Manoeuvres in the Dark's "If You Leave." OMD finally scored a massive pop hit after being college radio sensations in 1980 with "Enola Gay." The version of the Psychedelic Furs' "Pretty In Pink" is a bit softer than the 1981 original from the band. New Order's "Shellshock" ought to get you dancing. They also squeeze in Echo and the Bunnymen's "Bring On the Dancing Horses." "Left of Center" brought together folkie sensation Suzanne Vega with New Wave superstar Joe Jackson. For some strange reason instead of Nik Kershaw's original version of "Wouldn't It Be Good," there's a cover version with ex-Three Dog Night's Danny Hutton Hitters. Before the needle picks up, The Smith's "Please, Please, Please, Let Me Get What I Want" sums up how I feel about the relationships in the film that just feel so wrong. While Dweezil Zappa (Frank Zappa's son) appears in the film and his *My Mother's A Space Cadet* record is the "Pick of the Week" at the record store, he's not on the soundtrack.

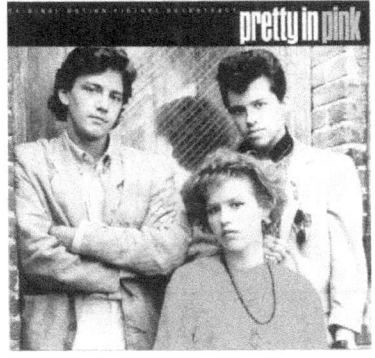

Some Kind of Wonderful

February 27, 1987

Paramount Pictures

Directed by Howard Deutch

Starring **Eric Stoltz, Mary Stuart Masterson, Lea Thompson, Craig Sheffer, Elias Koteas and Chynna Phillips.**

Rated PG-13 - 95 minutes

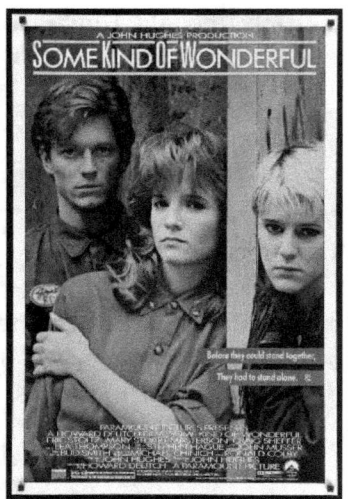

*A **Reminder**: If you purchase tickets for the previous four John Hughes movies on Saturday, you'll receive a free pass for the midnight screening of Some Kind of Wonderful. The ticket is not transferable or accepted for any other screening during the festival.*

Some Kind of Wonderful is the time that John Hughes ripped off a John Hughes movie. If I told you that Roger Corman produced this film, you might believe me since the plot is basically a reworking of *Pretty in Pink* with gender swapping. And not even some kind of gender swapping Hughes wrote in My Penis and My Vagina. The swap this time is a poor boy wanting to date a rich girl and his frustrated poor female friend. Doesn't that sound like the creation of a producer eager to cash in on the John Hughes money train? By this point, there was a simple John Hughes cinematic formula. Cast a bunch of hot teen actors. Fill the soundtrack with new wave hits. Give the movie a song title. Don't allow the kids to feel any consequences at the end of the movie. Clear off your driveway for when the money truck backs up to your garage. But it wasn't a low budget rip off operation that put *Some Kind of Wonderful* into theaters. This

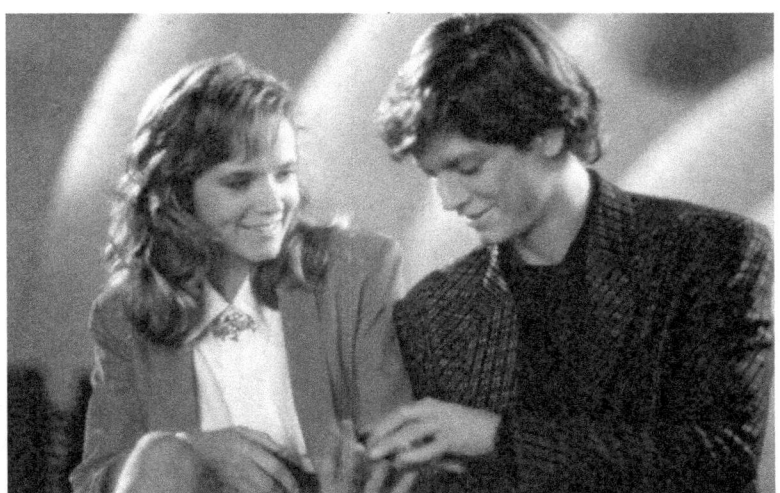

was the man who for five previous films had established himself as the adult who understood teens.
Even though Hughes was on a hot streak with the previous year's *Pretty in Pink* and *Ferris Bueller's Day Off*, there wasn't much buzz when *Some Kind of Wonderful* was announced. How could things have cooled off so much? The first thing that gave a bit of blah was the fact that Hughes wasn't directing. Like *Pretty in Pink*, Howard Deutsch was back in the director's chair with John Hughes writing and producing. Now there's tales of how Hughes originally hired Martha Coolridge to be the director. Unlike Deutch, Coolridge already had made *Valley Girl* and *Real Genius*.

While she wasn't a high school cafeteria name, her films were cool with the kids especially the girls who had crushes on Nicholas Cage and Val Kilmer. She was at least at a level that she'd be collaborating with Hughes and not merely following his instructions. The story goes that after *Pretty In Pink* became a hit, Hughes fired Coolridge and brought back Deutch into his world. There wouldn't be any arguments about who was the true behind the scenes genius on the set now. This would be John Hughes' film once more. The second big blah was the "what's it about" summary. A poor teenage boy (Eric Stoltz) who works after school as a car mechanic thinks he has a chance to hook up with the hot

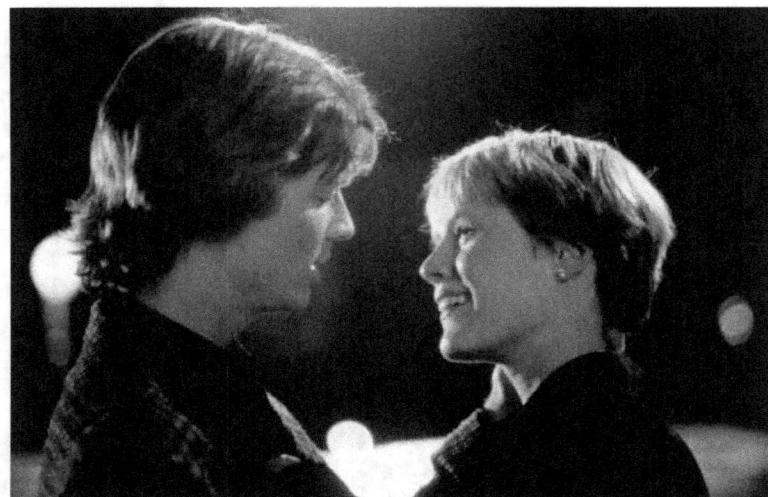

homecoming queen (Lea Thompson) that's broken up with her preppy boyfriend (Craig Sheffer). He gets a little help from his shorthaired drummer friend (Mary Stuart Masterson) on how to meet her. How does he plan on impressing the queen? By blowing his entire college fund on a pair of earrings. He's going to give them to her during their amazing first date that will drain everything out of his bank account. Hard to imagine someone getting into college that came up with this genius dating idea. After the serious excitement of *Ferris Bueller's Day Off*, the plot for *Some Kind of Wonderful* was a serious letdown. The trailer didn't make anything feel tempting.

When the film came out, nobody in my immediate circle was eager to see it even though I'd gone with pals to see Hughes' previous five films. I was working at my college's newspaper and no one requested a review. Months later, a group of us rented a bunch of VHS tapes and someone threw *Some Kind of Wonderful* onto the pile. About 20 minutes into the movie, I fell asleep. The unexciting film didn't keep me from nodding off after finishing my bottle of Boone's Farm Strawberry Hill. When I woke up, the action had picked up. The short haired blond friend was now being chased by the police and Peter Coyote. She was being helped by Keith Gordon to keep from being shot to death.

I wasn't sure what happened to Eric Stoltz, but his departure made things more entertaining. Turned out everyone had gotten bored of *Some Kind of Wonderful* and they had swapped out the tape for *The Legend of Billie Jean* (1985) during my slumber. The blond with short hair was Helen Slater (*Supergirl*) and not Mary Stewart Masterson. Maybe if we catch enough people napping during this midnight screening, we'll recreate this switcheroo experience for you?

Part of what makes this feel like a John Hughes knock off is there's no hidden plot in the high school action. There's nothing subversive or dark about the film. It's hard to imagine in the outtakes there being a "dogs eat your carcass before the cops arrive" coming from any of the characters. This film tries its best to be "warm-hearted" with all three main characters ending up in various degrees of happiness without there being an insidious quality. There's nothing on the screen that seems like it was watered down from John Hughes' *National Lampoon* sense of humor. There's not even a hint that the "real" ending of the film would have the drummer seduce the rich princess as the poor boy sits in the car alone and cries. It feels like it was the safe John Hughes film that everyone swore he was making all along.

The Brat Pack magic had worn off as none of the principals were tagged as the next generation bratters as their careers progressed. When is the last time anyone has asked Elias Koteas about his Brat Pack days? The cast here just felt like normal actors doing a gig for producer John Hughes. Lea Thompson escaped the disaster that was *Howard the Duck*. Stoltz was best known as the guy who was completely replaced by Michael J. Fox in *Back to the Future* and unrecognizable in *Mask*. Masterson had just been in *At Close Range* with Sean Penn and Christopher Walken. They weren't really discovered in this film by Hughes or the viewers.

Another reason why people didn't feel intrigued enough to come inside the theater was the poster. The image makes Stoltz, Thompson and Masterson look like they are pushing a cologne that works for either gender. The trio look so bored. Who wants to buy a ticket to watch a bunch of boring teens?

You can save $7 and just look in the bathroom mirror for 90 minutes. This sold itself as a date film if your other night out op-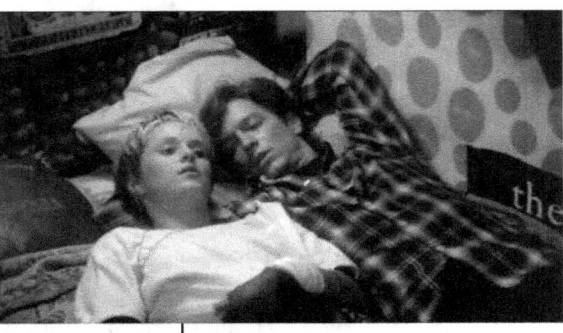
tion was going to a buffet with a C health grade.

There was a story that in the late '60s, Bob Dylan was getting tired of the worshipful praise of rock critics and fans. He couldn't bear the deification that was getting dumped on him. He schlocked out a double album called *Self Portrait* to scare the gushing crowd away from his doorstep. The collection of lesser tunes, covers and a few live tracks proved that everything he played wasn't genius. The record got the worst reviews of his career when it came out in 1970. It's such a mixed collection that if you consider yourself a Dylan fanatic and don't have a vinyl copy in your record cabinet, nobody calls you out as a poser. Maybe in the end that's what John Hughes wanted *Some Kind of Wonderful* to do to his career. He was ready to move into the world of adult comedies. He was lining up *Plane Trains and Automobiles* with big stars Steve Martin and John Candy. He had a budget that probably equaled all six of his first films combined. And not a drop of teen angst in the script. Maybe he didn't want to be held back by his audience who would keep hounding him to make another Molly Ringwald - Anthony Michael Hall high school hijinks flick. So, he created a mediocre film that wouldn't destroy his career, but gave his fans a sense that he's done all he can in the genre. This was Hughes doing a cover of John Hughes so he could be allowed to grow up to make comedies with adults. And after *Some Kind of Wonderful* vanished off the marquee, Hughes was able to do exactly that until he started cranking out kiddie films like *Curly Sue, Home Alone, Beethoven, Dennis the Menace,*

Baby's Day Out and Disney properties. He then quit Hollywood at the end of the '90s.

When people talk about John Hughes' movies, *Some Kind of Wonderful* is rarely mentioned unless you're deep diving for references. This is the film you have to buy if you want the discounted DVD boxset with *Pretty in Pink* and *Ferris Bueller's Day Off*. There's only two people who would declare *Some Kind of Wonderful* their favorite John Hughes film: Howard Deutch and Lea Thompson. Why? Because they got married a few years after the film was released.

SOUNDTRACK NOTES: Unlike previous John Hughes soundtracks that either scored Billboard hits or made established songs even bigger, *Some Kind of Wonderful: Music from the Motion Picture Soundtrack* wasn't a great seller. It had quite a few cool new wave groups that you'd hear on WKNC's Nightwave at 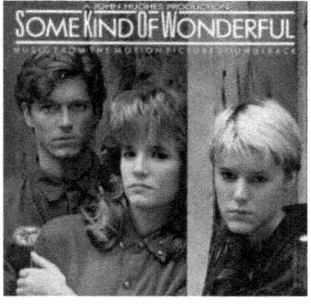 the time including Flesh For Lulu, Pete Shelley, Furniture, The Apartments, The Jesus and Mary Chain and Stephen Duffy. But it's like an obscure mixtape that your cousin would make you and not one for seducing the rich girl in your life. Lick the Tins' cover of Elvis Presley's "I Can't Help Falling In Love With You" was a smash in England long before the film came out and didn't help it gain traction in America. Strangely enough there's no version of Grand Funk Railroad's "Some Kind of Wonderful." We do get Charlie Sexton's "Beat So Lonely." Charlie currently tours as Bob Dylan's lead guitarist on his Neverending Tour. The songs aren't bad, but there's an obscurity to them. If you put this soundtrack on during your '80s themed party, nobody is going to guess the movie unless Howard Deutch was invited.

Sunday - May 17

Private School 2:00 p.m.
Class 4:00 p.m.
Better Off Dead 7:00 p.m.
Risky Business 9:15 p.m.

School Days

The whole point of movies is to escape from your humdrum life. That's why people push down the theater seat and strap up for a two-hour thrill ride starring the latest incarnation of James Bond. Or they seek to cringe from an undead monster wielding a chainsaw. But why would a teenager sit in the dark for 90 minutes to watch other teenagers stuck in a classroom?

Unless they were one of the popular kids or an established bully, there were times when a student wished they could transfer to a different school and be a new person. In the midst of geometry class while zoned out on a proof, they'd daydream about enrolling in an elite boarding school or posh prep school with cool classmates. When it came to a movie about high school, they wanted a film that let them see how their dream classmates existed. It was even better if their opposite sex dream classmates ended up naked on the big screen. There was a joy in not merely seeing a version of themselves on the screen, but a version of themselves willing to do those things that would get them in trouble with their parents, teachers, classmates and nuns. Some might get inspiration from the films and beg their parents to let them attend

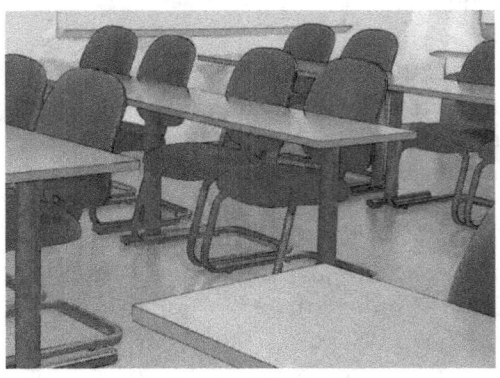

an elite boarding school. But others know that the odds were against them from living these high school fantasies processed through the Hollywood dream machine. What are the odds that their best friend's mom is that hot and ready to play? Or their girlfriend will have a rival who wants to seduce you. Or they have the skills to ski the K-12 without dying? Or they can afford a classy hooker? These movies let a teenager dream about what adventures awaited if they could only attend a different school. Those that did transfer schools learned that no matter where you go, you're still stuck with the same type of students. And you're pretty much the same person you always have been. But it's still good to dream and eat popcorn without worrying about stabbing yourself with a compass in the dark.

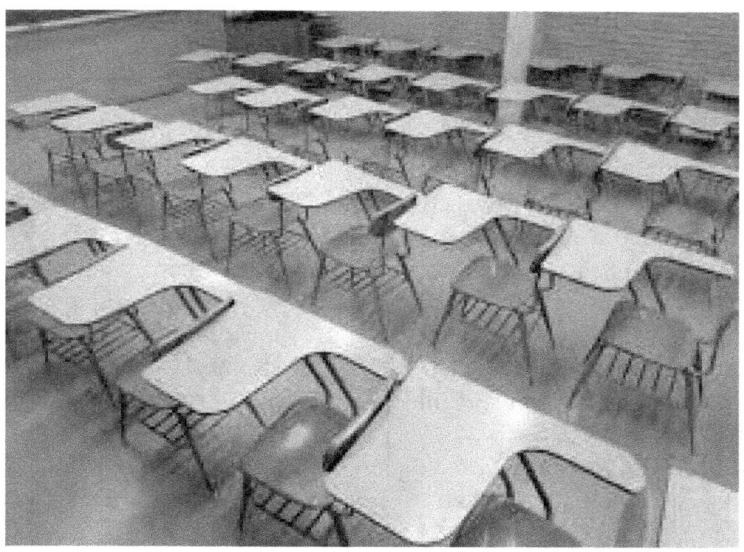

Private School

July 29, 1983

Universal Pictures

Directed by Noel Black

Starring Phoebe Cates, Betsy Russell, Matthew Modine, Michael Zorek, Fran Ryan, Kathleen Wilhoite, Ray Walston and Sylvia Kristel

Rated R - 88 minutes

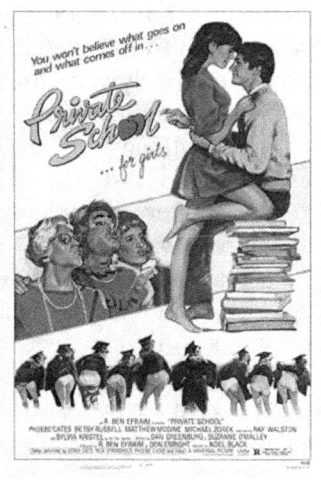

There are few places dreamier to a hormonally charged teenage boy than a private boarding school for girls. The basic fantasy is the teenage girls trapped inside the academic walls are eager for male attention. Remember that in the early '80s, bisexuality was not promoted in teenager aimed flicks so the young ladies weren't taking care of each other after lights out. There are fantasies about what goes on behind the walls of women prisons and convents, but those women will ultimately kill or convert you. Those are dangerous daydreams when compared to a finishing school loaded with girls in freshly pressed plaid skirts. A young boy in 1983 would imagine so much could happen if they found themselves inside her dorm room. Cherryvale Academy for Woman dips into those delirious daydreams. Right off the bat the teenage boy fantasy level is super charged since this is the same Tudor/Gothic style mansion used for Wayne Manor on the original *Batman* TV series. Imagine the rush of seeing an all-girls school with Phoebe Cates on top and the Batcave below? Popcorn buckets must have substituted for drool cups for boys with wide open mouths. This movie was based on a drawing in the margin of an Introduction to Biology textbook. What boy didn't want to be hooked up with Phoebe Cates and be Batman? The movie didn't feature Matthew Modine revealing himself as Batman although he did change his identity while inside Cherryvale.

What did a teenage boy imagine would happen behind the locked front door of a girls private boarding school? They dreamed of girls stripping down and showering. Back in the '80s, women group showering was practically an Olympic exhibition sport when it came to movies. If a woman showered alone, we knew she was going to be hacked to death. Females were only safe when showering together. *Private School* has so many moments of women showering together that it's almost a women's prison movie minus the shives. Nearly 40 years later, the movie still sparkles from the amount of lathering up shown on screen. Did they have to do any cleaning up of the negative when they made the high-definition transfer?

Private School wasn't a massive hit upon release. Why? Because the film came out during the summer, there weren't eager discussions about sneaking into a theater around the cafeteria lunch table. The guys you hung out with at the neighborhood pool might have expressed curiosity. But were they going to get out of the water to head to the movie theater when they can watch real gals diving? And who wanted to be reminded of school during the middle of summer vacation? When the bell for high school finally rang after Labor Day, *Private School* didn't get the same buzz as *Fast Times At*

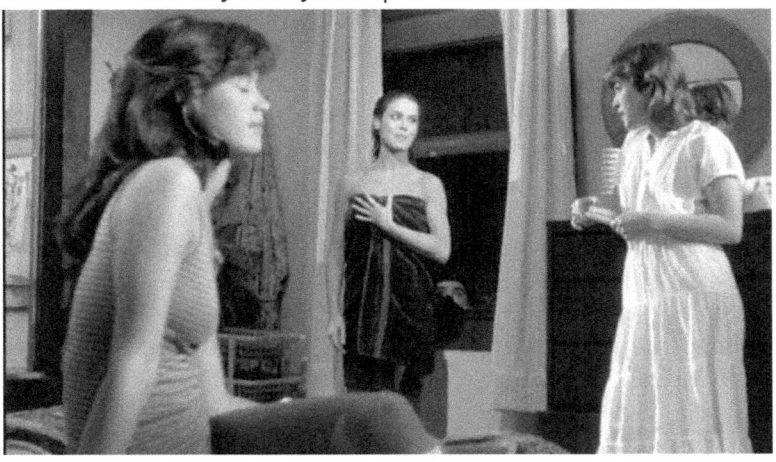

Ridgemont High. Even when it came out on home video, this was not quite the film you snuck into the pile under the excuse to your mother that you wanted to understand your educational options. How could an R rated film about a girl's private boarding school not be an overwhelming sensation?

Turns out there was a sense of disappointment that of all the female nudity in the film, none of it really belonged to Phoebe Cates. Curious teens were eager to see a continuation of her Linda character. Her character of Christine wasn't the worldly Linda eager to share her carnal knowledge of her time with her much older boyfriend Doug. Although Doug never showed up in the film. This time around Cates plays the girl who wants it just right for the first time. Christine wasn't going to hook up on a little league dugout bench. Linda was all about her older lover. Christine dates Jim (*Vision Quest*'s Matthew Modine) who attends the nearby Freemount Academy for Men. He's a teenager also on the verge of graduating. Although Modine was 24 when the movie came out and Phoebe had just turned 20. Perhaps Modine was cast to play Doug in *Fast Times*? In *Private School* Modine plays Jim as rather patient and eager to take things at Christine's speed with her stipulations.

While it seemed a letdown that Phoebe was playing a bit more prudish, the filmmakers introduced teen audiences to a potent Bad Girl. Jordan (*Avenging Angel* & *Tomboy*'s Betsy Russell) is the private school girl that public school boys thought only existed in their most extreme and lustful fantasies. She's a Cherryvale rival for Christine and would probably dethrone Linda back at Ridgemont High. Her ultimate bad girl attack on Christine is to steal Jim or at least hook up with the guy. Most teenage boys only thought about their one girl of their dreams. Very few perceived that they might get lucky as part of another girl's revenge sex plot. Jim is not exactly a devoted angel to Christine. He has no problem helping boost up his buddy Bubba (*Hot Moves*' Michael Zorek) to become a second floor Peeping Tom. Remember that this was back when such an action was considered "fun" and not an easy way to spend the rest of your life having to knock on new neighbors' doors to alert them to the fact

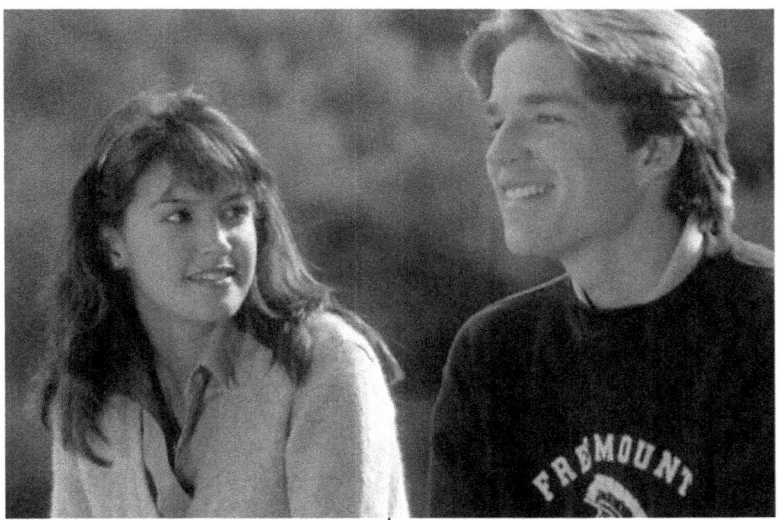

that you're a registered sex offender. This was a film that didn't quite deliver a lecture on the true consequences of bad teen behavior from the uptight adults. Although Sylvia Kristel (*Emmanuelle* & *Private Lessons*) does pop up in the film, she doesn't try to lecture the kids about what can go wrong if you end up in a seedy location in east Asia. These kids have only two things on their mind: getting naked and showering.

Let's get back to the concept of a bad girl wanting to seduce you before you can hook up with the love of your teenage life. This must have caused quite a few viewers to reassess their lives. Most teen boys are barely able to cope with the normal rejection of the dating scene. Nobody before this movie made the claim that when you begin going steady with the girl of your dreams, another girl is going to seduce you on the level of Jordan. Does Jim have the willpower to hold out for Christine? Jordan seems so bound to steal away Christine's love interest, it's a miracle they didn't come out with a special edition of *Fast Times* where Jordan pushes Linda off the diving board, busts into the bathroom and makes Brad change his lustful fantasy. Her intention to seduce could defy time, space and theater.

The money scene in the film involves the time Jim and his pals sneak into the girls dorm disguised as teenage girls. Jordan sees through his disguise, but acts like she's completely fooled. She lures the "new girl" into her dorm room and proceeds to arouse Jim to the point that you fear his senior year will end in a spontaneous combustion incident. In previous movies, the audience would sense that Jordan is just teasing him and then is going to embarrass her victim in a cruel fashion. But in *Private School*, Jordan seems ready to flip his wig and ravish his makeup and lipstick covered face in pure lust.

The battle for Jim will have a price for Jim. He can have immediate carnal gratification with Jordan. But is Jordan going to want Jim as boyfriend or merely a prize to wave under Christine's nose as a sign that she takes what she wants from her? Is Jim better off waiting for the right moment with Christine since she might want to still date him in college? If they wait, is there a chance their love might endure until freshman orientation? And the teenage boys in the audience must question why can't they be like Jim and have Phoebe Cates and Betsy Russell using them as a carnal tug of war rope?

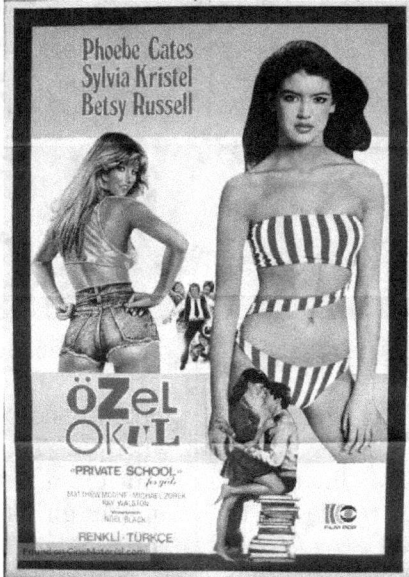

Private School did fine in theaters, but only made half the box office take as *Fast Times At Ridgemont High*. When it did come out on home video, the VCR was still gaining in popularity so it wasn't the hottest of titles on Beta. But the movie began to catch on with numerous repeats on the pay-channels. By this time, the lusty teens viewers were able to focus on the glory of Jordan's exploits and her classmates constantly showering.
.

SOUNDTRACK NOTES: The original soundtrack album for *Private School* is a bit of surprise since it features two songs from Phoebe Cates. This is rather shocking since her character doesn't sing in the film. "Just One Touch" and 'How Do I Let You Know" were released on a promo 45 for the film.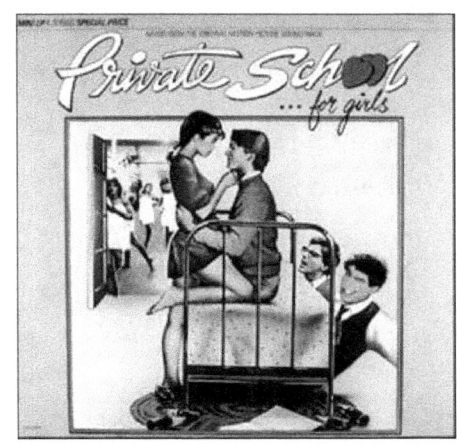
Phoebe Cates didn't become the next Irene Cara. Even more surprising was the soundtrack in America was only a mini-album so along with Phoebe's tracks was mainly songs by Bill Wray and Rick Springfield's "American Girl." Oddly enough the soundtrack did get a full album release in Japan with Phoebe on the cover. She was Godzilla size in Japan. The Japanese soundtrack's main additions were the Stray Cats' "Rock This Town" and Sam The Sham & The Pharaohs' "Li'l Red Riding Hood." Neither version includes Trio's "Da Da Da," Vanity 6's "Nasty Girl," Bow Wow Wow's "I Want Candy" or even Harry Nilsson's touching "You're Breaking My Heart." The main reason to track down the out-of-print vinyl is to enjoy the glory of Phoebe.

Class

July 6, 1983

Orion Pictures

Directed by Lewis John Carlino

Starring Jacqueline Bisset, Rob Lowe, Andrew McCarthy, Cliff Robertson, John Cusack, Alan Ruck, Virginia Madsen and Rodney Pearson

Rated R - 98 minutes

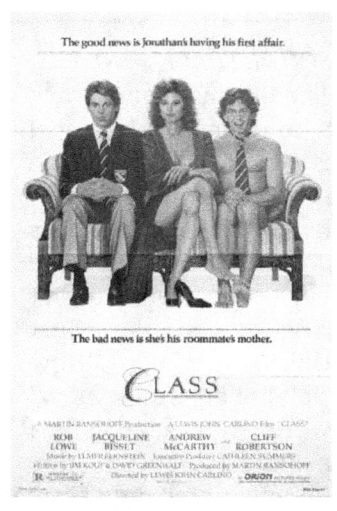

Contrary to popular belief, there were MILFs before *American Pie* debuted in 1999. Pop culture had dealt with the subject of "Mother I'd Like to Fuck" for a while. Soundgarden had a cult hit with "Full On Kevin's Mom" in 1989. Sadly, over the last two decades have allowed the concept of MILF to be watered down to mean any woman who is a mother. But this is completely wrong to a traditionalist who understands that the concept means the mother of a friend. A 24-year-old woman with a kid is not a MILF unless you're a five-year-old with the mind of a 30-year-old stuck inside your head for a kindergarten-based *Freaky Friday* sequel.

A few experts might point to *The Graduate* as MILF going mainstream in 1967. But that's wrong. Benjamin Braddock is around the same age as Elaine and does have sex with her mother Mrs. Robinson. But Ben hooks up with the Mom long before he encounters her daughter for the first disastrous date. If we must classify what happened here, Ben is on the cusp of the Mother-daughter combo as he sits in the back of the bus with Elaine. That's a totally different fetish or accomplishment depending on how you score life's little joys.

What was the first true MILF moment in pop culture? Eddie

Haskell in *Leave It To Beaver* was so ready to get freaky with Mrs. Cleaver. We think of him as insincere as he always complimented his pal Wally's mom. But while his words rang false, his eyes were all over Mrs. Cleaver's pearl necklace. Look at Eddie's smile. He wants to learn the secrets of the universe from June Cleaver. But since it was the '50s and broadcast TV, Wally would only dream along with an audience who were waiting for MILF to mainstream.

When *Class* arrived in 1983, it not openly explored the concept of MILF, but used it as a serious marketing element. There on the poster was Jacqueline Bisset sitting between a fully dressed Rob Lowe and a single necktie away from being totally nude Andrew McCarthy. She's falling out of her dress and playing footsie with Andrew. The poster blares: "The good news is, Jonathan's having his first affair. The bad news is, she's his roommate's mother." There's no mistaking that this film is enticing to the teenage crowd eager to see how *Class* earned its R Rating.

The movie doesn't go straight to the MILF action. The first part of the movie is about how Jonathan (McCarthy) a poor kid from Pittsburgh arrives at the posh Vernon Academy and shares a room with Skip Burroughs (Rob Lowe), the ultimate posh boy and douchebag. They don't get along together until they truly bond when on a trip to Foxfield School for Girls, Jonathan rips the blouse off Virginia Madsen (*Zombie High*). Since Jonathan is

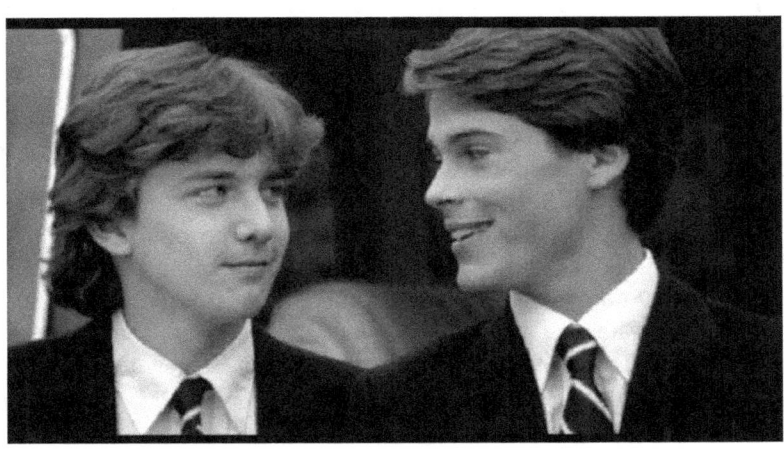

banned from attending the Halloween dance between the preppy schools, Skip gives him instructions on how to get to Chicago, go to the Free N Easy bar, pick up a woman and take her back to a certain hotel. Skip even funds this adventure by giving his roomie a bus ticket and $100 cash. This was the early '80s when a $100 could pay for a night out in Chi-Town and not merely cover cab fare. After a little debate about vanishing from school, Jonathan takes off on an awfully big adventure.

Free N Easy is what every young boy imagines when they hear about a singles bar where the drinks pour freely and the women are easy. Jonathan completely strikes out with the first two women. But then sits at the bar looking like a fool and becomes a target for Ellen (Bisset). The audience knows she's there to party. She'd already laid back on the bar to become a human margarita machine as they just poured the bottles straight into her mouth. She's an older woman who is on the prowl. None of the youngster's inept nature and clumsy nerves derail their encounter. She is what a high schooler dreams about hooking up when it comes to an older woman fantasy. And for high schoolers who had seen Bisset's extreme wet t-shirt action in *The Deep* on HBO, this was double fantasy.

Bisset was a Cougar before Cougar was beaten to death by everyone online. She sinks her claws into young Jonathan and drags him back to her hotel. He's as nervous as a teenage boy about to get his carnal dream. You might wonder why Ellen wants a piece of Jonathan? Perhaps the same reason that the unknown McCarthy landed this role after auditioning in New York City. He looks like a young David Hemmings. Who? Hemmings became iconic as the photographer in Michelangelo Antonioni's *Blowup*. He also appeared in cult films such as Dario Argento's *Deep Red* and Roger Vadim's *Barbarella*. Looking like Hemmings wasn't a bad thing when an older English woman cruises an '80s fern bar.

There's a bit of charm as Jonathan fumbles the seduction process. He isn't a horny teen trying to reproduce a Penthouse Forum letter like a name and address withheld horny teen from a private Midwestern school eager to get his rocks off. We can believe this

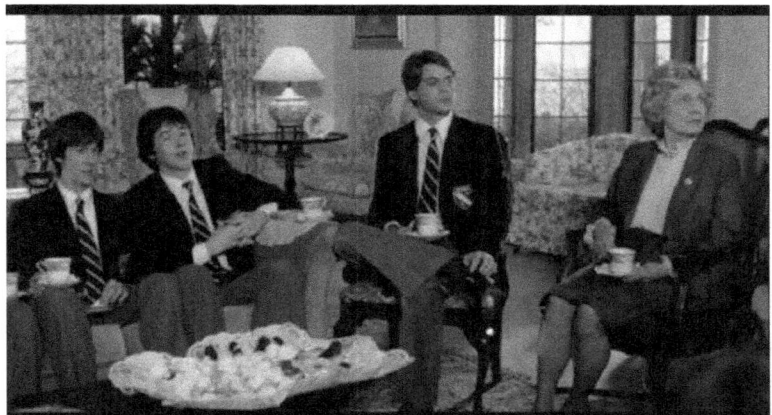

happened to him. His reluctance gives way when he gets hooked on being with Ellen. This quickly extends out from a one-night sexual rendezvous to an entire weekend of debauchery between the mature woman and her eager young lover. While he's a bit naive, he is at least smart enough to give her a great fake background story. He claims he's a doctoral student at a university. This cover allows him to complain about classes and have an excuse to not pick up the check at dinner. When he arrives back in his dorm room, Jonathan impresses Skip with wild times in the big city. He's now accepted by the rich kids in the hall that included Alan Ruck (*Ferris Bueller's Day Off*) and John Cusack (*Sixteen Candles*). And he keeps hooking up with his older woman on the weekends until his cover story is blown and she splits. But will he never see her again?

Skip invites his pal to his family's estate for part of his Christmas vacation. He gets to meet Skip's dad, the very cold and powerful Mr. Burroughs (*Star 80*'s Cliff Robertson) and more importantly, Skip's Mom. Guess who that is? This shocking turn of events makes this go from a Cougar film to a MILF movie. This is one of the greatest plot twists since *Chinatown* except Ellen doesn't turn out to be a sister/daughter. She's a Cougar/MILF. I can only imagine someone in the audience at the Crabtree Valley Twin screamed out at Jonathan, "Now you're a roommate's mother's fucker!" Of course, everyone should have known the plot twist since it's

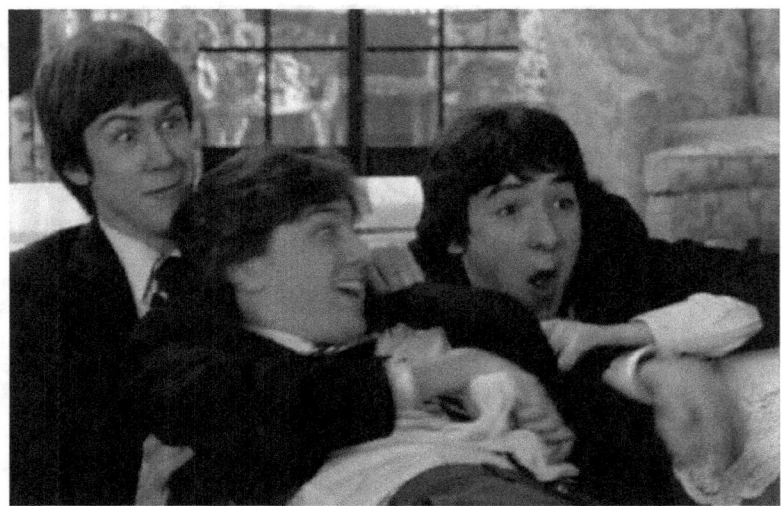

on the poster. The '80s were a time before people whined about "Spoiler Alerts." The bigger twist turns out to be that instead of a slapstick sex comedy you'd see on Cinemax After Dark, the film goes emotionally dark. Jonathan and Ellen aren't doing their best to keep screwing around the mansion behind Skip and Mr. Burroughs' back. There's a lot of soul searching instead of flesh baring.

There's an initial questioning of what are the odds that Jonathan shows up at a bar and hooks up with Skip's mom. The easy answer is that son and mother had somehow both heard of the Free N Easy being the easy hook up establishment of the Second City. Back in the '80s, *Playboy* magazine used to run a college issue that rated the party schools. One of the big things they'd list is the best spot for a one-night stand in each town. The fun joke one year was Brigham Young University's location was the departure gate at the airport. Maybe Free 'N' Easy was that special spot for the University of Chicago? Mother and son both knew this was the hot spot and Jonathan truly got lucky. This bar was where Ellen could drown herself in booze and no strings attached sex conquests.

Why did she need that escape room covered in ferns? Turns out Mr. Burroughs isn't a loving husband and expects Ellen to act a certain way when he's around her. He's got the idea that his family exists as if they're in an oil painting. It's hard to tell if he's secretly gay or just loves his family fortune more than his family. This lack of attention has turned Ellen into an alcoholic who sneaks into the city when he's away so she can live a second life. Bisset mentions there were more scenes of her in the original script that dealt with her issues. These character forming pages vanished during production outside of the one icy scene between Ellen and her husband. Why? Because the youthful audience that was going to sneak into the film weren't looking to be bummed out. Their fantasy was hooking up with an older woman who can snag the bar tab and teach them those special positions at a classy hotel. High school boys didn't want to witness damaged humans screaming for help between shots of Tequila and handjobs.

Class sold the fantasy of the MILF. The reality for most of us was that our friends' mothers looked like the ladies that worked in the lunchroom. They weren't serving up to the hotness of Ellen or Mrs. Cleaver.

How did Jonathan get into a Free N Easy bar so easy? As far as high schoolers drinking booze goes, quite a few states in 1983 had laws set up so kids 18 or 19 could buy beer or wine. But you had to be 21 to buy liquor. When we see Jonathan's student ID, his birthday is listed as November 29, 1964. When the film came out, the character was 18. Most of the audience would have just assumed he didn't need a fake ID to sneak inside. During the mid-80s, Ronald Reagan forced states to jack up the drinking age for all alcohol to 21. He blackmailed them with the threat of withholding highway funds. The states quickly jacked up the ages instead of fighting for a teenager's right to party. This happened in North Carolina without a grandfather clause in 1986. Thus, college kids who'd been legally buying Boone's Farm Strawberry Hill were forced to become inebriated outlaws until their 21st birthday. For those curious, the drinking age for the state of Illinois when *Class* was in production was 21 for both buying beer and wine as well as hard liquor. This had been true since 1980 for the downtrodden teenagers of Chicago. The boys of Vernon Academy needed a hook up to get all that Old Style beer into their dorm rooms. Somebody at the door of the Nice 'N' Easy did a pretty slack job at carding the underaged teens when Jonathan arrived. Or they had just paid off the cops so they knew they'd never be busted on selling liquor to a minor. At least by making Jonathan over 18, Ellen didn't get accused of statutory rape. She merely turned a teenager into a human margarita machine and a legitimate motherfucker.

SOUNDTRACK NOTES: There doesn't appear to be a soundtrack album for *Class*. Elmer Bernstein did the score which bonds the film a bit with *National Lampoon's Animal House*. Although this isn't quite a prep school version of his work that gave a lofty tone to John Belushi's college mayhem. The few songs used in the soundtrack includes The Dead Kennedy's "Holidays In Cambodia" to give a true touch of what the hip kids listened to in the dorms when mom could be outraged by the band's name and dad angered by the lyrics. Bryan Adams' "Hidin' From Love" came from his first album that wasn't a big hit. When Christmas hits, we are treated to "Little Drummer Boy" from Joan Jett and the Blackhearts. It's a rough and tumble take from the woman who loved rock n roll. It's a shame there wasn't a vinyl release so you can have something to play in the dorm when your roomie's mother dropped by for Parents Weekend.

Better Off Dead

August 23, 1985

Warner Brothers

Directed by Savage Steve Holland

Starring John Cusack, David Ogden Stiers, Diane Franklin, Kim Darby, Curtis Armstrong, Amanda Wyss, Aaron Dozie, Scooter Stevens, E.G. Daily & Taylor Negron

Rated PG - 97 minutes

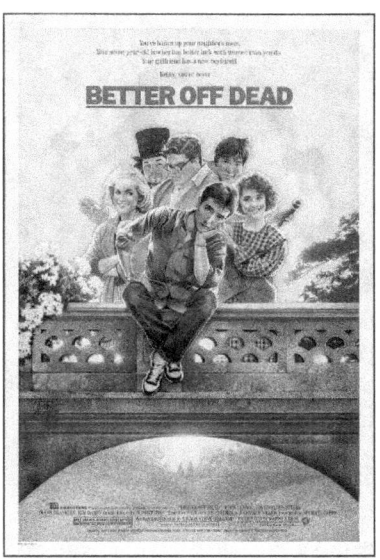

Most movies about high school romance have a similar formula: an awkward boy aspires to date the girl of their dreams. Everyone close to him senses she's out of his league because she's either rich, a cheerleader, belongs to a strange religion that bans dancing, dating the most important guy on campus or doesn't want to deal with someone she considers a putz. It was the '80s so being a lesbian was not an excuse option for the dream girl. Eventually the guy learns a suave trick and commits to something creative to get her attention and prove he's not merely a nerd/geek/loser/eunuch. They fall in love at a school dance and all the other students realize how wrong they were as the couple sway to a Spandau Ballet hit. The credits roll and every guy in the audience thinks maybe they have a chance with the girl of their dreams because that one guy made it happen.

But what if things went wrong with the relationship after the credits ended and the theater lights went up? What if their true love derailed before they arrived at the Shermer Hospice? These teenage movies never wanted to show us a scenario where the girl of his

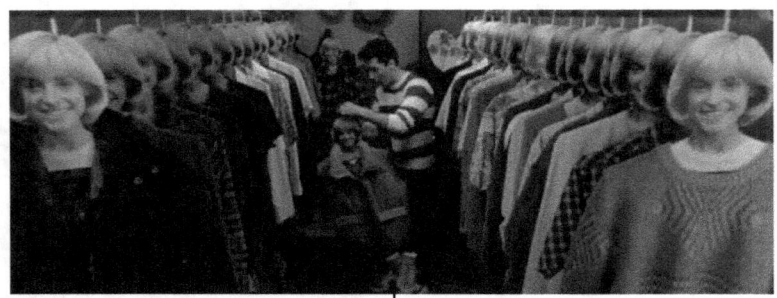

dreams dumps the guy cold in the middle of the school year. We were always sold the romantic dream with absolutely no warning of consequences. That all changed when Savage Steve Holland testified to the true savagery of what can go wrong in high school love. He was willing to share a painful moment in his own high school career with the world and figured out a way to make the audience laugh through the heartache.

Lane Myer (*The Sure Thing*'s John Cusack) might be a bit of a goofball with a messed-up family, a rather disturbed best friend in Charles De Mar (*Risky Business*'s Curtis Armstrong) and a drag racing rival whose brother speaks like Howard Cosell. But he's done one thing right in his life when he took a risk and introduced himself to Beth (*A Nightmare On Elm Street*'s Amanda Wyss) at the park. In spite of his awkward introduction, she went out with him and they even went all the way in the back of a station wagon. She was the girl of his dreams and the queen of his bedroom. Every inch of wall space was covered with pictures of her dreamy smile. Even the coat hangers in his closet had a unique way of reminding him of Beth. You'd almost think he was stalking her if he wasn't really dating her. Lane is completely devoted to Beth in an absurd yet understandable way. He's excited that both of them are trying out for their high school ski team. And that's when things went bad.

Lane's a good skier, but won't challenge the treacherous K-12 course. Why? Because it's a suicide descent for a merely good skier. The K-12 isn't so much a ski slope as just dropping off the side of a mountain cliff and seeing if you can land skis side down. There's one guy willing to tackle this extreme downhill and he's team captain Roy Stalin (Aaron Dozier). And that's where Lane's dream world gets shattered. Turns out Beth wants a man brave enough to tackle the K-12 and thus she dumps Lane colder than the ice-covered peak of the K-12. She wants some Stalin in her love life. In a shocking turn of events, Lane finds himself single in the middle of the school year before Christmas break.

High school is painful enough without watching your ex-lover sitting across the aisle from you during homeroom. The heart needs time to mend and there's no way you filter the pain through your system and deal with geometry. The cafeteria is more dramatic than any soap opera your mother can't stop watching. Everyone is staring at lonely old you and wondering who is going to be igniting your old flame at her table. Is she going to share her tater tots with Stalin? Every period bell is a mocking refrain at how you had the woman of your dreams and she's split.

Savage Steve exposes the cruelest thing that can happen to a man who has lost the heart of his woman: when people you thought were your friends ask if you'd be cool if they ask out your ex. Poor Lane gets everyone thinking they need his permission to date Beth. It doesn't matter if they're his teacher (*Fast Times At Ridgemont High*'s Vincent Schiavelli), postman (*Fast Times At Ridgemont High*'s Taylor Negron) or even a surprise celebrity (Not going to give it away, but they weren't in *Fast Times At Ridgemont High*). All of them tell Lane, "I've heard about you and Beth, and I was wondering, can I ask her out?" Sure, it seems like a funny gag in a movie, but this really happens

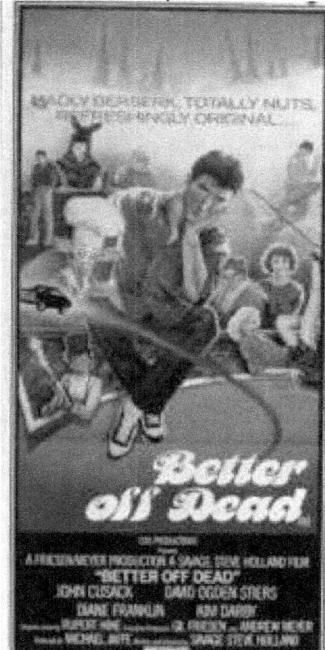

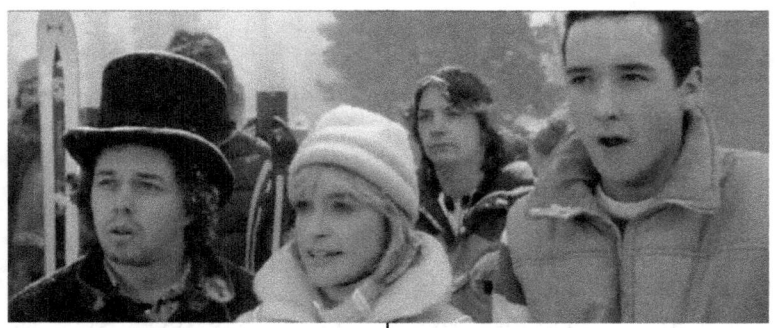

in real life. "Can I ask her out?" is a question that happens in a small social circle. Why? Because somehow your pal thinks this is going to make sure you don't get upset and cause a scene if they get lucky. There's only one reason anyone ever replies, "Sure, ask them out!" You weren't really that good of a friend with that person and you want your "friend" to receive the same soul crushing treatment that she gave you. You want your heartache to fade for a few moments as you laugh at that other guy's impending pain. Schadenfreude is a balm. But in *Better Off Dead*, Lane doesn't get this relief. Stalin doesn't give schadenfreude.

This emotion crush leads Lane to a series of halfheartedly attempts at suicide. Savage Steve turns what should be depressing moments into raw slapstick. When the film came out, major critics were a bit horrified at Lane failing at hanging himself, jumping off a bridge and setting himself on fire. But what did they expect Lane to do in such despair? This was during a time when the media didn't talk about breaking up. It's not like he could get help at school since the faculty was trying to hook up with Beth. Even his idea of winning her back by skiing the K-12 is pretty much death by ski slope. He's got nothing to live for in his mind. Being dumped in high school was the worst thing that could happen in your life in the non-fatality events category. It was being worse than not getting accepted at your safety school.

What's the ideal way to break up with your high school romance? The absolute perfect time to split up is right before you head off to your college's freshman orientation session if you're going to different universities. This way you've had an entire summer together to enjoy your new found adulthood. Then the night before you get a taste of your new life, you ease into a conversation that turns to "things are going to be different in college and I don't want us to feel like we need to deny what happens to us." You can use other wonderful excuses as long as they don't include the line, "I don't want to miss out on an upgrade from you." Always remember to throw in the sentiment of "if what we have is true and deep love, we'll be back together next Summer after the Spring semester is over." This way both of you can be happy and you have an excuse if you strike out as a pathetic freshman.

If you're both going to the same university, you're just emotionally doomed. But at least there's no homeroom.

Better Off Dead stood out from the cinematic crowd simply because we were finally shown the darker side of young love. Thankfully, Savage Steve Holland turned *Better Off Dead* into a slapstick comedy because otherwise audiences would be bawling their eyes out like they'd just seen *Love Story* again. Luckily the film does end with a brightness so the audience isn't contemplating doing anything drastic like overdosing on artificial butter. Some of you might notice Beth seems familiar when she rejects the love of Lane. Actress Amanda Wyss was already a high school heartbreaker with her role as Lisa in *Fast Times At Ridgemont High*. You might argue that when she dumped Brad (Judge Reinhold) early in their senior year that we'd already seen the heartbreak moment from *Better Off Dead*. Why is *Better Off Dead* different than *Fast Times*? Brad was looking to break up with her and was only beaten to the punch when

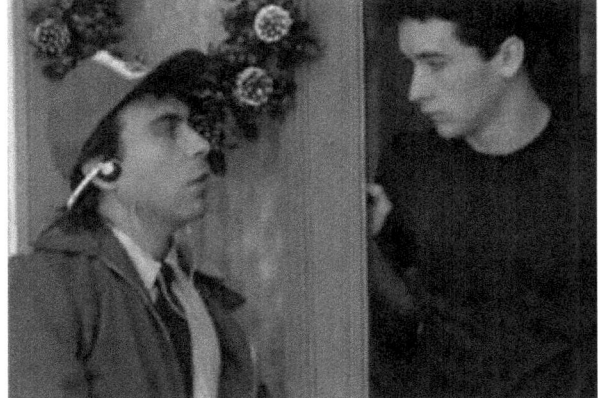

she cut off the relationship. This wasn't a massive emotional gut punch to Brad since he wanted to get serious action during his senior year from other girls. Lane wasn't looking to get frisky with French exchange student Monique Junet (*How I Got Into College*'s Diane Franklin) and needed his freedom for Beth. He wanted Beth to be his forever girl. The ultimate difference between the characters played by Wyss is that at no time did Mr. Vargas (also played by Vincent Schiavelli) drive off with Lisa after school like Beth does with Mr. Kerber. That's the biggest heartbreaker a high school student can ever experience. You might have a chance to win your girl back from a guy named Stalin, but there's no competing with a teacher.

SOUNDTRACK NOTES: The Better Off Dead soundtrack album is dominated by the work of Rupert Hine. The English musician and producer had first hit the charts in his home country working with Jon Pertwee on a *Doctor Who* single called "Who Is the Doctor." Hine would end up producing The 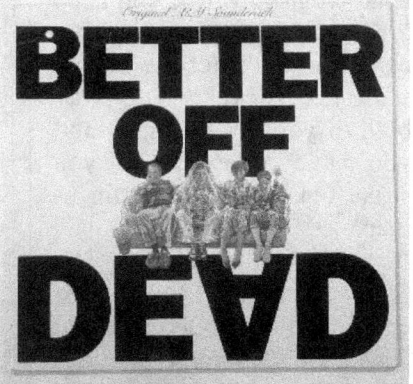 Fixx, Howard Jones, Rush, The Thompson Twins and Tina Turner's *Private Dancer* album. He brought a fine '80s sound to the screen. The opening track "With One Look (The Wildest Dream)" features Cy Curnin of The Fixx on lead vocals. Terri Nunn of Berlin joined him for "Dancing in Isolation." He was a one-man band for many of the instrumental tracks. The only two songs on the album that don't feature him are both from E.G. Daily. She performs at the high school dance in the film. You know Carl the Janitor from *The Breakfast Club* was loving this part of the film since E.G. Daily was his cleaning jam.

Risky Business

August 5, 1983

Warner Brothers

Directed by Paul Brickman

Starring **Tom Cruise, Rebecca De Mornay, Joe Pantoliano, Nicholas Pryor, Janet Carroll, Richard Masur, Bronson Pinchot & Curtis Armstrong**

Rated R - 99 minutes

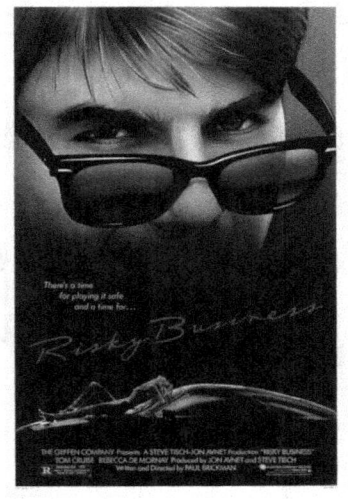

During the early '80s, theater goers were treated to a mini-sub-genre of white guys who accidentally ended up being pimps. The main three films appeared long after the pimp related films of the black action era had sadly ended in the '70s. *Night Shift* came out in the summer of 1982 with the Fonz (Henry Winkler) and future Batman (Michael Keaton) working at the city morgue and representing a group of prostitutes that includes Diane from *Cheers* (Shelley Long). *Doctor Detroit* arrived in the spring of 1983 with a nerdy professor Elwood Blues (Dan Ackyrod) stumbling into a pimp job when Dr. Johnny Fever (*Private Lesson*'s Howard Hessman) gets taken out of the game. Both of the films were slapstick comedies that sold themselves on being rather absurd. Then at the end of the summer of 1983, *Risky Business* arrived and elevated the "white guy as an accidental pimp" game with a cast of barely recognizable actors who'd become iconic.

Joel Goodson (*Losin' It*'s Tom Cruise) finds himself hanging out with a group of prostitutes when his parents go on a trip and leaves the high schooler without a babysitter for the first time. He has full use of the house, the keys to the dad's Porsche and no bedtime. They expect Joel to be a good son

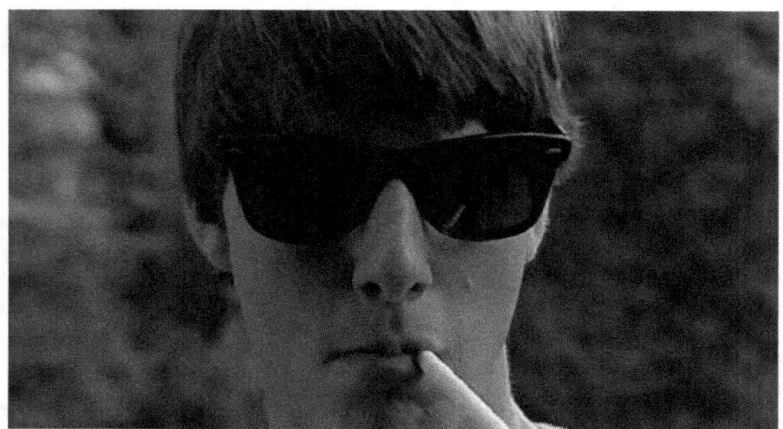

and focus on his Future Enterprisers project so he can get into Princeton. He does kick around project ideas with his pal Barry (*Beverly Hills Cop*'s Bronson Pinchot), but nothing seems like it will generate income or seem like the future of enterprise. Then his buddy Miles (*Better Off Dead*'s Curtis Armstrong) pushes him to discover the meaning of "what the fuck?" With the parents away, Miles arranges for a prostitute to drop by the house. This eventually leads to Joel meeting Lana (*The Slugger's Wife*'s Rebecca De Mornay) for a late-night tryst that turns into a lot more. Joel quickly learns two lessons when dealing with hookers: always negotiate the price in advance and get a hotel room. Since he does neither, he ends up with Lana in his house and holding a precious family object as collateral for his bill. She basically takes refuge with Joel to avoid Guido the Killer Pimp (*The Goonies*' Joe Pantoliano). This ultimately leads to Joel and his pals in the Future Enterprisers hosting a party with the prostitutes at his parent's house with his classmates burning all their birthday money to get lucky. They are rolling in dough compared to other groups that made lamps and other handy-dandy devices.

While this seems like a farfetched idea of high schoolers learning pimp skills to succeed, the future of enterprise would turn out to be about hustling humans. As the '80s progressed, major corporations got tired of having to deal with full time employees. They didn't want the burden of hiring a person, giving them health insurance, stock options, retirement plans and keeping them employed for an indefinite time. A corporation with a major project just wants people without putting real employees on their books. The solution arrived with the dawn of the contract employee. Instead of applying to a company, a worker sends their resume to a contracting company that's looking for certain skill sets. The contracting company hustles the worker to the various corporations that have certain needs. The corporation makes a deal with a contracting company to hire the worker. The contract could be for a few years, a few months or even a week or two. Most of the time the corporation pays the contracting company that pays the employee after taking their cut off the top. The contract company controls the worker which is what made it different from a headhunter who would find a worker for a corporation and get a bounty if the person's hired as an employee. The contract company prevents the company from hiring the employee outright without paying a huge fee during the contract. And there's a penalty if the company hires the worker within a certain period of the contract running out. The contract company doesn't want to miss out on getting paid. This is a modified version of the pimp, hooker and John relationship. The contracting company hustles their stable of workers. And the workers better please the corporations in a no-strings attached relationship that

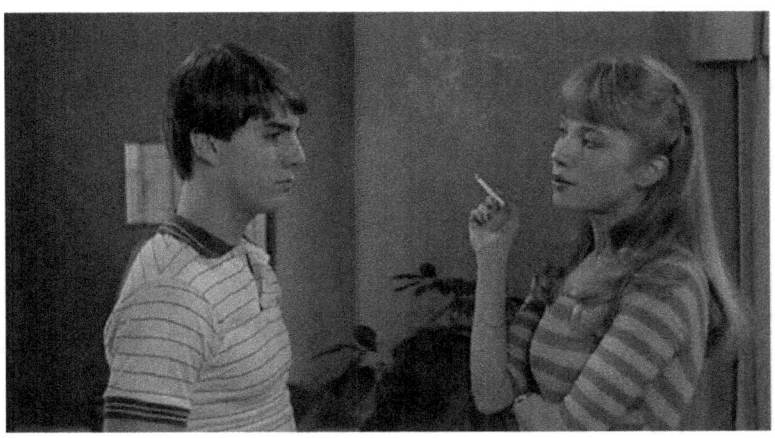

comes with an expiration date. Consider this the Employee Experience like the Girlfriend Experience offered at certain brothels.

Joel and his pals were on the cutting edge of success as they discovered the next frontier of big business was dealing in people. They didn't merely transform his parents' house into the greatest high school party ever held. They were getting a taste of the future and learning what it was going to take to be a success story.

During the Aughties, I found myself meeting up with a pimp for multiple interviews. Dennis Hof was America's most famous legal brothel owner as he ran the Moonlight Bunny Ranch outside of Reno, Nevada. He and the ladies he represented became famous as the stars of HBO's *Cathouse* series. In a sense too he had become a white guy that accidentally became a pimp. If I'm to believe the story he told me, he was doing well in the timeshare racket and hanging out with Andy Kaufman. The two of them would vanish to the Bunny Ranch on occasion. Dennis had saved up a bunch of cash that he was going to invest in a chain of Subway sandwich shops. But Subway was giving him the runaround on franchises. Kaufman suggested he use the money to buy the brothel. So instead of serving up BMT subs, Hof was offering Around the World with his all-female staff.

Part of what made Hof a success story was that he brought all the tools from when he managed timeshare sales staffs. He wasn't just applying

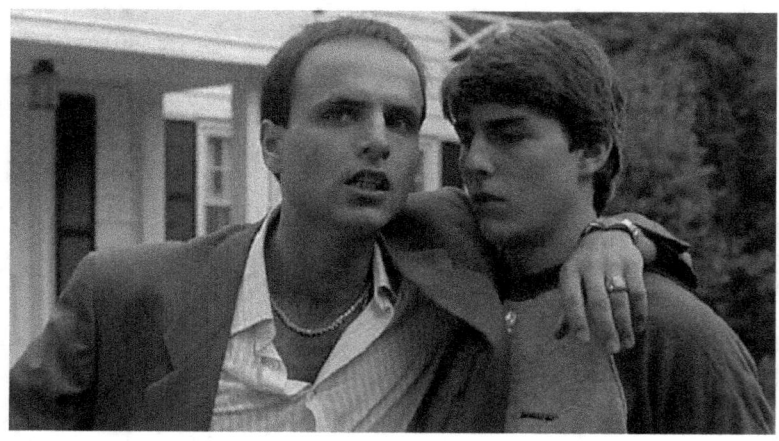

old school Pimpanomics and the lessons of the Game. Hof viewed his ladies as sales representatives who were ultimately selling themselves as the timeshare and not a one-bedroom apartment in Hilton Head. He would give the bunnies the same pep talks. He taught them to not merely sell what the customer wants, but get them to upgrade to all the other experiences on the party menu and buy a few toys to enhance the experience. Plus make sure they exit through the Bunny Ranch's gift shop and pick up a t-shirt. There was nothing to be ashamed about when it came to his brothel. This wasn't exactly that little brown house on the hill experience. Hof was the contracting company that would hook up corporations with workers willing to do a job without being a full-time employee.

Eventually Dennis Hof invited me out to his birthday party. And it truly felt like being a part of Joel's party. There was a strange feeling knowing that the woman you're flirting with will go all the way as long as you have manners, no noticeable open wounds and a credit card. Nobody was going to be teased and sent home with a phone number that was really for an OTB. This party was all about pleasure and what you fantasized about experiencing. Negotiating the after-party fun was limitless although it did involve the possibility of raiding the kid's college fund. What's wrong with sending the kid to the University of Wikipedia when you have a chance to score with AVN winner Sunny Lane and a few of her close friends?

Joel was getting a taste of the future of the business world from his time with Lana. Odds are that this was his big project at Princeton. His vision of "human fulfillment" easily goes from carnal to corporate. He can almost use the same banter to pimp a lady to a classmate as an IT Guy to a big Pharma company. They all just want no strings attached satisfaction and Joel could deliver. *Risky Business* ought to be taught in business classes at Princeton.

During the '70s, Paul Brickman was a screenwriter who gave us *The Bad News Bears in Breaking Training* with Jackie Earle Haley (*Losin' It*) and Jonathan Demme's *Citizen Band*. When Brickman wrote the script for *Risky Business*, he wanted to sit in the director's chair because he didn't want a lame director to ruin his script. He had a vision and after a lot of rejection, he got David Geffen's production company behind the film and taking a risk on him as the helmer. His clear vision led to Brickman using three different cinematographers during the shoot including Bruce Surtees (*Ladies and Gentlemen, The Fabulous Stains*) and Reynaldo Villalobos (*Blame It On Rio*). Brickman pushed the visuals of his tale. *Risky Business* was not going to be shot like a documentary about the reality of teenagers in the '80s. This was all about dream sequences as we go inside the libido and desires of Joel Goodson. The movie opens with Joel recounting his favorite sexual fantasy of parking his bike at a neighbor's house, sneaking inside and joining a strange woman in the shower. But the dream goes bad when things get too steamy and he finds himself blowing his college board test. The camera makes us feel the sexual fantasy devolve into a student nightmare. Brickman lets us know that he is going to give us a bit of an art house yet still give the teenagers a reason they snuck in the theater.

After having so much control and making his cut, Brickman found himself a victim of the film's ability to hook an audience. The audience got into the scene of Joel dancing in his underwear, falling into Lake Michigan with his dad's Porsche and being told to get off the babysitter by the cops. The comedy angle played big in the mind of the viewers when the film ran in previews. Brickman's original ending was dunked into Lake Michigan because it didn't leave them laughing. David Geffen wanted a cute and comic final scene between Joel and Lana. You still see most of Brickman's original ending in the film. Joel and Lana meet for dinner where Joel quizzes her

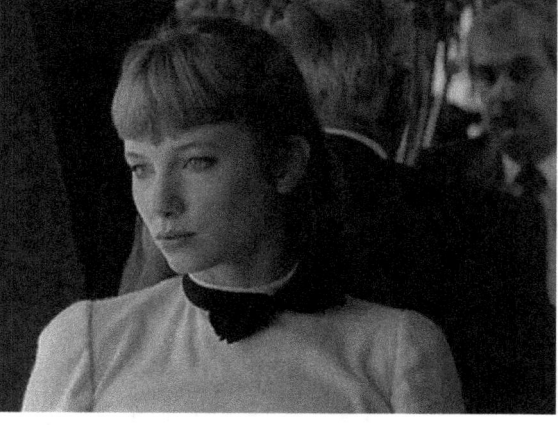

about why things happened. After he gets his answer, there's the montage of Joel discussing his Future Enterprisers' project followed by him and Lana walking through a park where they talk about hooking up again and Joel demanding to be paid this time. It's a cute sitcom kind of exchange. Brickman had something more powerful to wrap up his version.

Lana has been in control of the relationship, but the conversation at the table leaves her insecure. Tom has her come over to his chair. In front of all the other elegant diners, he has her sit on his lap as he holds her. As she nestles in his arms, the familiar voice over starts "My name is Joel Goodson. I deal in human fulfillment. I grossed over eight thousand dollars in one night." Instead of saying, "Time of your life, huh kid?" Joel wraps it up with "Isn't life grand." It's a colder ending. After she declared nobody owned her when she split with Guido, she was owned by Joel at the end. The high school student has become her master or as the case in the film, Joel is truly Lana's pimp.

Geffen made the right call for the box office as *Risky Business* grossed 10 times its budget and became a major video rental title for the '80s. The "cute" connected for the cineplex audience that wanted a fun date night film instead of a profound moment about the power dynamics and economics of sexual relationship. Even with a massive hit, Brickman went off the radar for the rest of the '80s. Reports had him feeling betrayed by having his ending brightened up. Brickman was finally able to restore the sliced away end footage for the Blu-ray release in 2008. Viewers saw how it should have ended all those years ago. It elevates the film because it shows Joel in a dream moment with Lana except now, he's in charge and not worried about missing his college boards. He's in control of his fantasies at the end. Nobody is telling him to get off the babysitter or the hooker to get off his lap.

We will be showing Paul Brickman's ending tonight. For those of you who have never seen *Risky Business*, you'll get to absorb the movie the director wanted you to see. After the credits we'll show Geffen's cutesy ending so you'll know what made couples in the '80s chuckle.

SOUNDTRACK NOTES: The soundtrack album is dominated by the German synth legends Tangerine Dream. Their electronic score adds to the dream state of Joel's fantasies. The slick and driving beat fits perfectly with a pair of Ray-Ban Wayfarers. The only bad part of the soundtrack is that all the Tangerine 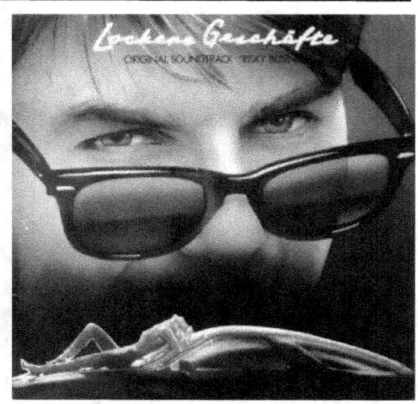 Dream songs weren't stuck on the same side of the vinyl so that you could drop the needle and let the love progress with your date that might not have a meter ticking. Maybe you want 20 minutes of Tangerine Dream for your next sexual encounter on the L? For some reason the first side of the album starts off with Bob Seager's "Old Time Rock N Roll." While this song is perfect for prancing around the living room in your underwear, it's not a song of seduction. After four Tangerine Dream tunes, the final track is a jolt of Muddy Waters slamming out "Mannish Boy." The second side gets you ready to cruise with Jeff Beck's "The Pump." You'll want to borrow your dad's Porsche and hit the road as Jeff hits those sweet notes. Prince's "D.S.M.R." and Journey's "After the Fall" take the notes deeper. Phil Collins drums away with "In The Air Tonight" followed by the final grooves being Tangerine Dream's "Love on a Real Train." Whomever arranged these tracks had no intention of ever getting laid like Joel. Songs used in the film, but not on the vinyl include "Every Breath You Take" by the Police, "Hungry Heart" by Bruce Springsteen, and "Swamp" by Talking Heads.

Monday May 18

Youngblood 7:00 p.m.
Vision Quest 9:15 p.m.

The Sporting Life

The '80s saw a major shift in sports. The "simple" times had started crumbling in the '70s with the introduction of the free agent. Players were finally in control of their own fate instead of traded around like baseball cards. The pro leagues began adding more franchises thus creating more opportunities for players. The NCAA men's basketball tournament was catching on with fans that began bracket bets in the office. Superstations began arriving on cable dials giving viewers in the middle of nowhere a big city sports feel on their TV. Atlanta's TBS brought Braves games, Chicago's WGN gave us the Cubs and New York's WOR featured the Mets.

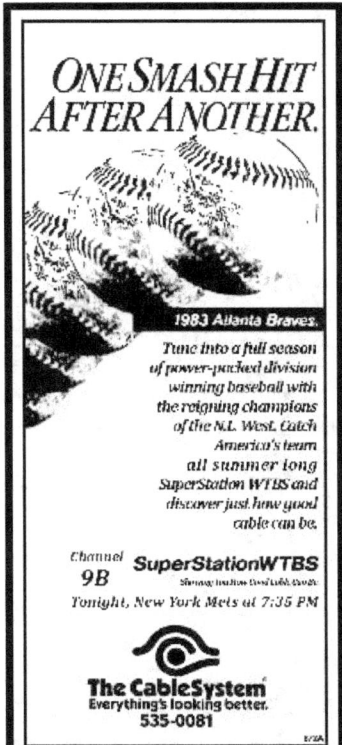

Even more importantly at the end of 1979 ESPN arrived and spent most of the early '80s creeping onto cable systems across the country. No longer was sports merely something that came on during the weekends or Monday Night. It was 24 hours a day even if part of those hours were spent in billiard tournaments and Australian Rules Football. Everybody was eager to have their highlights on the channels SportsCenter from pro teams, colleges and high school. Generations had been happy with a tiny photo and a

- Page 1 -

small write up in *Sports Illustrated*'s Faces In the Crowd feature. Now athletes now wanted their superstar athletic feats broadcasted across the nation.

The price of video camcorders was coming down every year. Any parent that swore their kid was a budding superstar sat in the front row videotaping their games. They'd edit the highlights and mail VHS tapes off to college programs or major prep schools. The lowlights would get hustled to *America's Funniest Home Videos* at the end of the decade.

The amount of revenue in sports was soaring. George Steinbreener only paid $8.7 million to buy the New York Yankees in 1973. In 1980, he paid $23 million for Dave Winfield to sign with his team. What truly changed in the '80s was mediocre pro players were finally making big dollars. While superstars always got paid with big contracts and large sponsorship deals, the middle of the pack players were living game check to game check. But by the '80s, a player riding the pine was doing well for themselves. No more would an NFL player worthy of a trading card list their off-season job along with their stats. Baseball pitchers that had losing records got signed by new teams for millions of dollars. The cash was flowing for playing a kid's game.

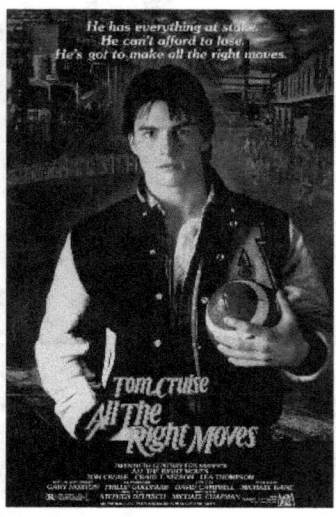

While previously kids would sit in the backyard and imagine themselves making the clutch play, they now dreamed of sitting in a press room and signing a fat contract. There was a seriousness to sports that went beyond just basic winning and losing. It was all about getting the attention of pro scouts for players and rich television contracts for teams. Teen flicks took note of the change in a few films.

Most teen films had sports being part of the high schooler's life. In

Class, Rob Lowe was part of the school's hockey team. *Better Off Dead* had a ski team at the center. *Fast Times at Ridgemont High* gave us a sense of how important football was to the school. *Teen Wolf* had a hairy Michael J. Fox dribbling the basketball for the big shot. But none of these films were focused on the sport since producers feared it limited their audience potential. Sports in the '80s was still perceived as a guy thing and not great date material. *American Anthem* was a tale of a football player (gold medal Olympic gymnast Mitch Gaylord) trying to join the US Olympic gymnastics team. Even with love interest Janet Jones (future wife of Wayne Gretzky), the film scored a 0.0. *The Boy In Blue* had Nicholas Cage as a competitive rower who experiences the dark side of sculling. The film sank on opening weekend. *Johnny Be Good* gave a comical look at the dirty business of college football recruiting. The producers united John Hughes superstars Anthony Michael Hall, Robert Downey Jr. and Paul Gleason. They even had Uma Thurman and Jennifer Tilly to keep it from being jock jams. The film didn't score a touchdown.

There were a few exceptions to this producer's perception. *The Karate Kid* was a date movie even with all the martial arts action. *All The Right Moves* scored with audiences because the tale of Tom Cruise as a high school quarterback needing a scholarship to escape poverty came out in the wake of *Risky Business*. *Oxford Blues* took Rob Lowe to England in pursuit of a woman and glory in rowing.

Both of tonight's films *Youngblood* and *Vision Quest* did well upon release with their tales of junior league hockey and high school wrestling. Both feature athletes taking their sports seriously. But only one of them features Madonna.

Youngblood

January 31, 1986

United Artists

Directed by Peter Markle

Starring **Rob Lowe, Patrick Swayze, Cynthia Gibb, Eric Nesterenko, Jim Youngs, Ed Lauter, George Finn and Keanu Reeves**

Rated R - 110 minutes

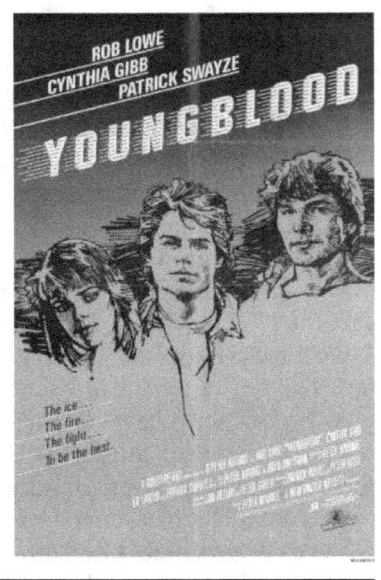

As you'll learn during this festival, a lot of the actors in this festival were in the running to star in different films. John Cusack was almost John Bender in *The Breakfast Club*. Anthony Michael Hall turned down *Ferris Bueller's Day Off*. Matthew Broderick was lined up for *No Small Affair*, but Jon Cryer his Broadway understudy had to step in. These swaps might not have made a big difference to the various films. You can see the other actor in the role. But when it comes to playing pacifist hockey player Dean Youngblood, there was only one right choice for the casting and Peter Markle nailed it.

Rob Lowe was Dean Youngblood!
Why?
Because in the '80s, no other young actor in Hollywood had a more punchable face. The first time Lowe showed up on the screen in *Class*, people hollered at the screen for Andrew McCarthy to take a swing at his preppy roomie. Nobody would have been upset if Billy Hicks had been bludgeoned in the kisser with his saxophone in *St. Elmo's Fire*. Somebody must have been furious that he didn't take about a dozen oars to his nose in *Oxford Blues*. Mother Teresa probably wanted to see Rob Lowe get force fed a knuckle sandwich

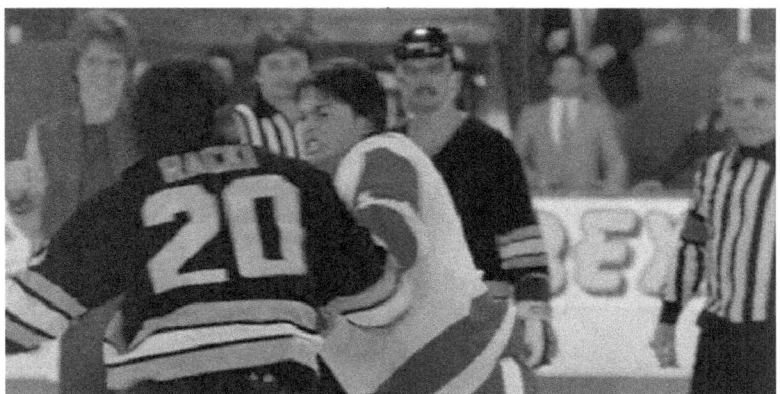

from Demi Moore during *About Last Night*.

If his teammates and co-stars Patrick Swayze (*Dirty Dancing*) or Keanu Reeves (*River's Edge*) had been hit in the face, audience members would be concerned why anyone would assault them. What could either of the future *Point Break* superstars have done to deserve a bout of unexpected violence? But Rob Lowe had played so many smug characters that the same popcorn eaters would have been shocked if his Dean Youngblood wasn't covered in blood while sent off the ice for a five for fighting in which he got in exactly zero blows against the rival team's goon. People knew he'd been up to something that deserved him to have sense slapped into his mug or punched for a disgusting self-centered scheme.

Rob Lowe's character was going to do something that would earn him a beating. And the crowds weren't going to defend his bad behavior like they did for misunderstood James Spader. They wanted to see him receive some Old Testament punishment and not sneak away with New Testament forgiveness. This is what they paid ticket money to witness and *Youngblood* delivered. Rob Lowe ended up with scars, blood and cracked teeth. Hockey is a bit of a rough and tumble sport. It's unusual for a player to not lose their teeth. There are several ways to get your chompers busted out of your mouth. The simple way is to get hit in the face with a hockey puck or another player's stick. The most common way to look like a Jack-O-Lantern is to get into a nasty fight with your opponent. Ever hear the old joke about a guy who went to a boxing match and a hockey game broke out? Well, it was true. Old school hockey was not a gentle thing of beauty. The legendary Gordie Howe joked that he played Biblical hockey since he'd rather do unto others before they do unto him. The argument against a guy who was a great skater and shooter was that they would always be a target to get yanked down on breakaways. If a player scored too much, they'd get beaten up after the red light was lit. For the longest time this scared away European players that knew they had the skills to play in the NHL, but not the right hook. The Olympics really didn't want the fights on ice to be more exciting than the medal round in the boxing ring. But in Canada, they loved it when the announcers could break into their prizefighting narration as the Goons dropped gloves.

That attitude was changing in the '80s as more European players were arriving on teams because coaches wanted goal scorers. Even Soviet players joined NHL teams at the end of the decade thanks to Glasnost. But the players that truly changed the approach to the game were homegrown. By 1986 when *Youngblood* opened, the two biggest stars on ice were Wayne Gretzky and Mario Lemieux. Both of the high scoring forwards were noted for not really being interested in dropping their gloves and belting out bloody noses against a goon from the checking line. That's not to say that they were Gandhis on Ice. Both also had tough players that were considered their bodyguards. Anyone that messed with Wayne or Mario were going to feel the pain of their protectors before they could swing a second punch.

Youngblood didn't reflect this new attitude on ice. This wasn't a story about how Dean Youngblood found a protective goon so they could both move up to the pro level. Dean was a solo act to stardom. The movie was a throwback as George Roy Hill's *Slap Shot* with Paul Newman making his team more violent to bring in the crowds. His star player Michael Ontkean (*Twin Peaks*) is a peaceful kind of guy who won't give into debasing his game by fighting. The films aren't carbon copies since *Youngblood* doesn't end with rebellion from the player in the big game. Dean Youngblood doesn't preach non-violence between the blue lines. He's returned to the team in order to secure a pro career and the fat paycheck. Instead of declaring finesse over fists, Dean faces off against the tough player from the beginning of the film in an epic sticks and knuckles beatdown that ends with missing teeth and enough blood to fill the elevator shaft in *The Shining*. *Youngblood* comes off as a defense of old school ice hockey that demands the brawling to keep the sport pure. This is like your drunken uncle screaming that designated hitter is a sham and pitchers need to pick up the bat in the American League.

The fight finale does prove to be an audience pleaser for both sides of the aisle. There are cheers from those who want to root for Dean Youngblood to toughen up his game and take out his nemesis. This is a rah-rah sports movie unlike *Slap Shot*. Those who want to see Rob Lowe lose a tooth because of what crimes he committed to the saxophone in *St. Elmo's Fire* will get to see him punched right in the face repeatedly. Everyone can root when the mayhem is unleashed. This is a pure definition of cinematic win-win.

During the early '90s, I covered the Raleigh IceCaps of the East Coast Hockey League for the *DailyFax*. It was a fax on demand magazine that was the cutting of technology before AOL smashed our primitive ways. Part of the gig was getting to talk to the players and

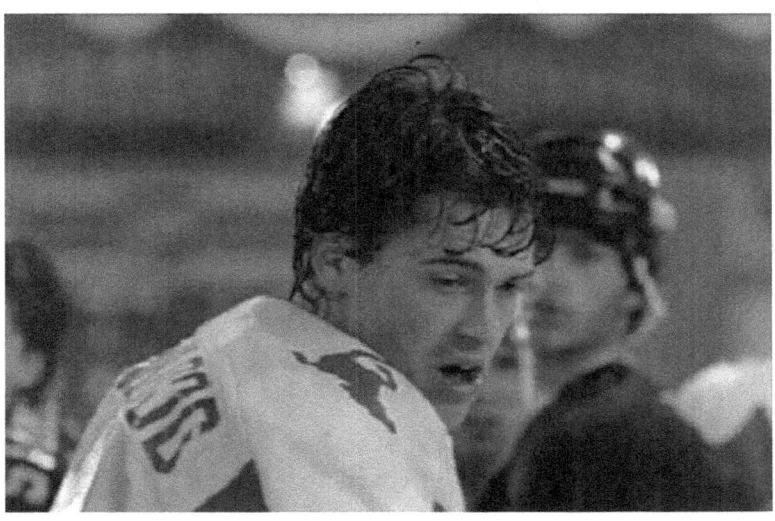

coaches. I never heard a coach complain that a new player suffered from Dean Youngblood syndrome. The only hockey movie mentioned was *Slap Shot*. Didn't hurt that the coach for the rival Johnston Chiefs was Jeff of the childish-goonish Hanson Brothers. Jeff Carlson ended up playing with both Gordie Howe and Wayne Gretzky during his career. He had not merely seen, but been a part of the end of Old Time hockey and the arrival of the New Game.

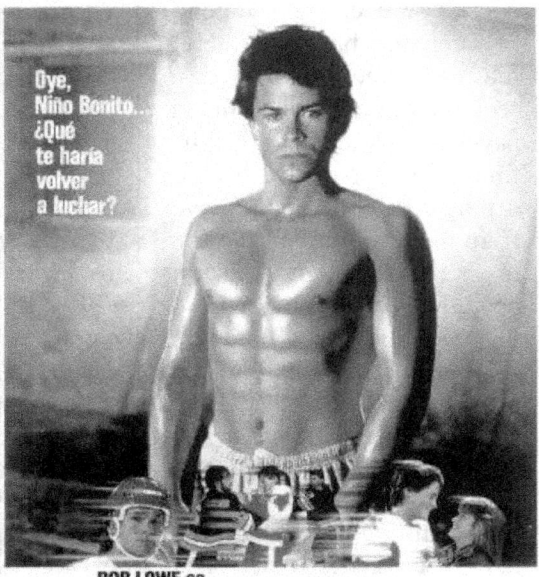

I was recently told by a former NHL star that over the years *Youngblood* has gained a cult following in the sport. Foreign players seem to like it since it shows what they believe is the junior league experience that they didn't quite receive in Europe. Overseas leagues have face mask rules so it's not as easy to unexpectedly bust a guy's nose up. They missed out on that element of the game. They also like the idea of the woman running the flophouse for players that trains them for groupie action.

Two years after making *Youngblood*, Rob Lowe was in Atlanta for the Democratic National Convention. During his visit he not only had sex with a 16-year-old female, but videotaped it. The girl's mother had him busted. He didn't get in trouble for having sex with a person under 18 because at the time the age of consent in Georgia was 14. He almost got busted for making a sex video with a partner under 18. But he made a deal with the local D.A. to merely perform 20 hours of community service and not go on trial. The incident became a selling point when promoting his 1990 film *Bad Influence* since his character makes a sex video involving James Spader. This crass marketing created a bit of outrage. There were plenty of people who were wanting to punch Rob Lowe in the face once more.

.

SOUNDTRACK NOTES: The original soundtrack to *Youngblood* was landmark in an infamous way. This was the first compact disc I ever found in the remainder bin at Camelot Music down at the mall. The long cardboard box was notched just like the vinyl to Queen's score to *Flash Gordon* and Neil 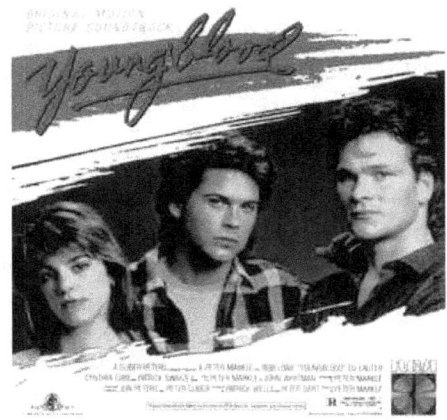 Young's *Re·ac·tor*. Even at a reduced price, the soundtrack didn't beg to be bought. They do include William Orbit's original score for the opening so you can get pumped up during skate around. Mickey Thomas does double duty with the solo track "Stand In the Fire" and Starship's "Cut You Down to Size." Mr. Mister didn't have a hit with "Something Real (Inside Me, Inside You)." It's probably a big seduction song in Winnipeg. Glenn Jones, Marc Jordan and Nick Gilder didn't bust out. Even John Hiatt's "I'm a Real Man" didn't get the traction from being in the film. Autograph's "Winning Is Everything" ought to be played at any hockey arena when they have a cheesy metal night or used for a montage of your kid's lil kickers soccer highlights.

Vision Quest

February 15, 1985

Warner Brothers

Directed by Harold Becker

Starring Matthew Modine, Linda Fiorentino, Michael Schoeffling, Ronny Cox, Frank Jasper, Harold Sylvester, Daphne Zuniga, Forest Whitaker and Madonna

Rated R - 107 minutes

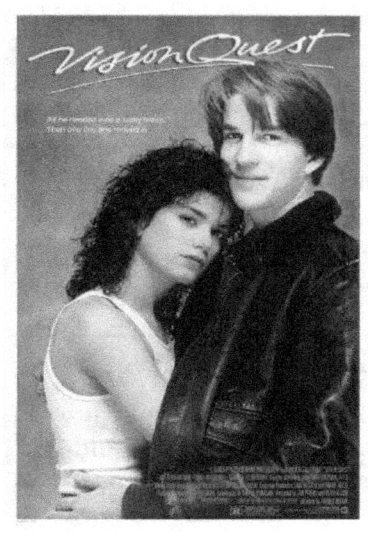

When the commercials began to run for *Vision Quest* on MTV, I had zero desire to see the film. No matter how many times Martha Quinn introduced the video for Madonna's "Crazy For You" or Linda Fiorentino gave those tempting looks, I wasn't buying a ticket. Why? It wasn't because of Matthew Modine since he was enjoyable in *Private School*. The reason was completely personal. Five years before in junior high, I suffered the endless abuse from a bully that was the school's star wrestler. I wasn't going to sit in the dark for two hours wanting to relate to a guy who could be based on my bully. I didn't want to feel an ounce of sympathy for a fictional version of my tormenter.

My wrestling bully was named Gary (REDACTED). He was a major talent on the team. The high school wrestling coach monitored his progress. He was eager to have the kid graduate up to his state championship team. Gary feathered up his dirty blond hair so he could look like pro wrestler Tommy "Wildfire" Rich. He also had a wispy mustache that wasn't going to fool any 7-Eleven clerk into not checking his ID for beer. He always wore a necklace with a "Freebird" pendant in honor of all those members of Lynyrd Skynyrd that had burned up in the plane wreck. Mostly I remember all the vileness that came out of his mouth when he decided that I was gay. I was not, but reality didn't stop Gary from his abuse. One day during gym class we were all sitting on the basketball court as the PE instructor was taking roll. She was the kind of woman that lived her life in tracksuits with a whistle around her neck. As I sat waiting for whatever crappy game was the lesson plan, Gary snuck up behind me and hit me with all his force into my back right between the shoulder blades. I let out a scream of pain that caused every head in the gym to turn except the PE instructor. She kept reading names and ignored the abuse. She wasn't going to call out the star athlete. Even when I took this abuse to the Vice Principal, he took Gary's side and made me sound like the tormentor. I was the troublemaker. Thanks to Gary getting away without any punishment, I became fair game for anyone that wanted to play Smear the Queer when I walked down the corridor to get to my locker. Luckily my parents were cool in sending me to the local Catholic High School. The nuns were a lot nicer than Gary.

If life was like an '80s teen flick, I would have worked out hard in the gym and become a leader on my own school's wrestling team. And in the State's championship, I would have had my chance to face off against Gary. This would end with my being disqualified for using an Atomic Drop. At the time the Catholic High School was rather small and we focused on basketball. There would be no faceoff between us in singlets.

Over the years I did wonder about what drove Gary to such violence and anger against me. My best guess is that he needed to display his hatred since his chosen sport was clothed gay sex. What percentage of the match involved Gary mashing and rubbing his crotch against another guy's ass? There is a history of wrestlers being molested by their coaches. The former Speaker of the House Dennis Hastert raped boys that he coached in high school before he rose to power in the US Congress. A college classmate gave up on his dreams of being a pro wrestler when he discovered that too many of the men in power expected to receive gay sex acts in order to move up in their organizations. Maybe Gary sensed that at some point in his wrestling career, he was going to have to do something that disgusts him for the sake of his career. Were these the dues he'd have to pay on the way to the title in his weight class? Or maybe he'd already been sexually aroused while clenching another school boy and pushing up against his buttocks in a struggle snuggle. Could his aggression against me be a ruse to cover his repressed feelings? Was his violence a cover? How could Gary be gay if he's into beating up the gay kid? This is not to rationalize away the abuse that Gary inflicted on me. Gary probably was just a hateful and abusive jock.

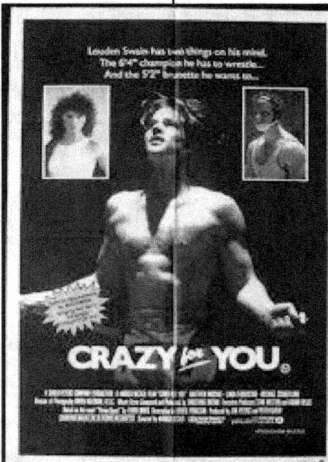

Because of Gary, I avoided *Vision Quest* when it came out in theaters. I did not want to sit there in the dark and think of Gary while watching Louden Swain (Modine) training hard for the wrestling match of his career. I didn't want to enjoy a film that might turn out to be Gary's favorite film with Louden Swain being Gary's role model. Eventually I saw it on cable and was pissed off because it would have been impossible for Gary to relate to Louden Swain.

Louden didn't terrorize anyone. Even in the scene where he delivers room service to the hotel room of a guy who attempts to seduce him, Louden doesn't flip out and beat up the guy. He's a good student. He's the type of guy I wish was part of my junior high experience. I can imagine Gary calling Louden a bunch of names before he stormed out of the theater so could shakedown the kids at the mall arcade. *Vision Quest* was not Gary's kind of movie. He was probably so pissed off that the psychotic Brian Shute (Frank Jasper) wasn't the real hero of the movie.

This is Louden's movie. He has the big dream of dropping two weight classes so he can

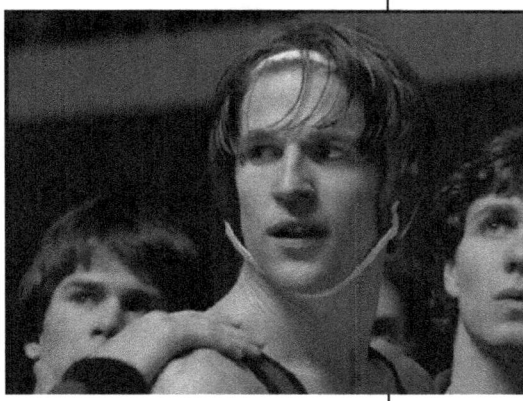

tangle with Shute. He does this not for money or fame, but the thought that when he looked back, he wanted to know that he took on the best there was. Louden does so much since he can't completely focus on wrestling. He has to go to school and keep up his grades. He also works at night at the hotel bringing up the room service meals. Then things get more interesting as his dad (*Deliverance*'s Ronny Cox) invites Carla (*The Last Seduction*'s Linda Fiorentino) to stay at her house when she runs into a bit of traveling trouble. As focused as Louden gets on losing the weight, he can't stop his libido from wanting to go a few rounds with Carla. He's got a lot of stuff going on including the occasional nose bleeds from dropping so much weight and constantly working out. He has quite a few visions in his quest.

As much as I hated amateur wrestling and still feeling the anger and pain from Gary's abuse, I didn't want to see both wrestlers choke each other out. I rooted for Louden, I didn't want him to merely survive their match, but to humiliate his destructive rival. If I couldn't take down Gary on the mat, I could witness an artistic tap out.

When the end credits rolled, I didn't hate all amateur wrestlers anymore. I didn't hate Louden or his buddy Kuch

(*Sixteen Candles*' Michael Schoeffling). The movie wasn't a balm to my trauma wounds. I still despised Gary because that anger will never go away. Only fictional wrestlers were fine in my life.

I did see Gary once after leaving that junior high. I was in a station wagon cutting through a neighborhood on the lame side of town. There was Gary on his front steps getting ready to go to his public high school prom. He had the same feathered hair and cheesy mustache. His mother was taking a photo of him. I wanted to roll down the window and scream something abusive at him. But I couldn't. His crushed baby blue tux was too garish for words. I knew that no matter what I screamed; nothing was going to haunt him more for the rest of his life than his prom photos.

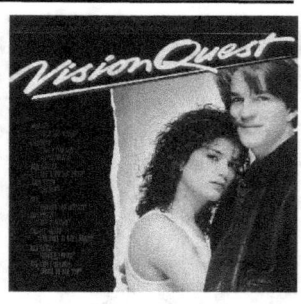

SOUNDTRACK NOTES: As mentioned, Madonna appears in the film, but not as an actress like in *Desperately Seeking Susan*. The Material Girl performs at a bar where Louden and Carla are chatting. She does "Crazy For You" and "Gambler." The singer became a massive sensation after her scene was shot. In a few countries the movie was released as *Crazy For You* to let people know that the Billboard #1 song was in the film. The soundtrack album was pushed up to #11. The record is a pretty good mix with the opening track of Journey's "Only the Young." This song was also a single hit and made #9. There's two AOR staples in the mix with Red Rider's "Lunatic Fringe" and Foreigner's "Hot Blooded." Sammy Hager's "I'll Never Fall in Love Again" was one of his better efforts before joining Van Halen. Naturally if you want to get pumped up, twist the knob for Dio's "Hungry for Heaven." *Vision Quest* gets a bit overlooked as far as prime soundtracks of the era, but it's a bit more than two songs by Madonna.

Tuesday - May 19

Red Dawn 7:00 p.m.
The Lost Boys 9:15 p.m.

A Great Place To Raise Kids

Nothing disheartens a kid like a real estate agent describing a neighborhood as "A great place to raise kids." This statement is followed with a list of boring wholesome activities that sound like a suburban update to *The Waltons*. Don't all kids don't want to learn square dancing at the city's rec center? They expect children to be excited about a weekend festival dedicated to wrapping foam rubber around dangerous coffee tables. A grown up's idea of a great place has a certain blandness and false security.

It's not that kids want to live in a dangerous place full of tetanus and bullets. The biggest fear is a safe place turns out to be a cover for something diabolical. This is the first thing you learn when you read Roald Dahl's kid books. Everything is a cover for something hideous. The biggest thing hyped for a great family place is all the churches in an area. Churches were a symbol of high moral fiber and a sense of decency. Back in the early '80s, jokes about priests molesting altar boys would get your parents upset. Turns out they weren't jokes. Ministers used their divine calling to commit serious crimes. Televangelists Jimmy Swaggart and Jim Bakker were exposed as sexual deviants at the end of the '80s. Swaggart was spending his flock's money on hookers and Bakker was jailed for illegally paying Jessica Hahn after he allegedly raped her. Church wasn't as safe of a place as advertised.

When I was growing up in a sweet suburban community, there was a rumor that the nearby picturesque pond was where a guy had been arrested. This wouldn't be that bad of a tale except the culprit was running around naked wearing a wrestling mask and holding a metal lunch box full of boys severed penises. Was this true? Did anyone else have this suburban myth circulating on their school bus?

At the end of the '70s, *Over The Edge* looked into the darkness of a "great place to raise kids." Families moved to the planned community of New Granada. They saw planned activities at a teen recreation center as a way that the youngsters can play while they dealt with adult things. It all seemed great. Except the teens rebelled against the sterile life as truth cracks the facade. This became a darker version of the ending to *Rock and Roll High School*. There's not much dancing as the school for New Granada burns. 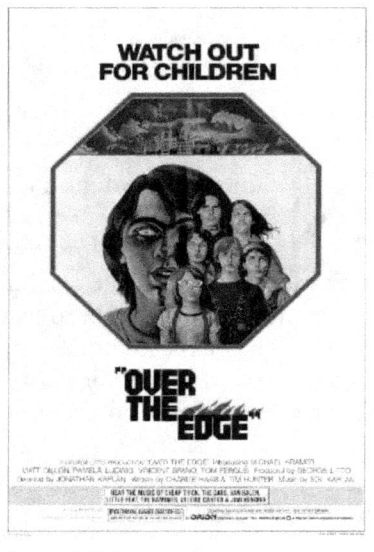 *Over The Edge* scared people and Warner Brothers yanked it out of theaters. We'd like to run it this weekend, but the film came out in the Spring of 1979 so it's not officially an '80s Teen Flick.

Tonight's double feature of *Red Dawn* and *The Lost Boys* is about two communities that people imagine are safe for kids. Calumet, Colorado and Santa Carla, California ought to be fine places that allow kids to grow up in a perfect way. The kids of Calumet enjoy the goodness of being close to nature in the Rockies. They grow up fishing and hunting with their parents. The youth learn the salt of the Earth stuff as if they grew up in a Sears catalog sporting goods section. A childhood in Santa Carla must be sold as a place to get in tune with nature at the beach. You can imagine both Chambers of Commerce selling those blissful lives in the town brochures to parents eager for that safe place. Neither town would point out that there might be an issue with an invading communist army or bloodsucking vampires.

Red Dawn

August 10, 1984

MGM/United Artists

Directed by John Milius

Starring **Patrick Swayze, Charlie Sheen, C. Thomas Howell, Lea Thompson, Jennifer Grey, Ben Johnson, Harry Dean Stanton, William Smith, Ron O'Neal, & Powers Boothe**

Rated PG-13 - 114 minutes

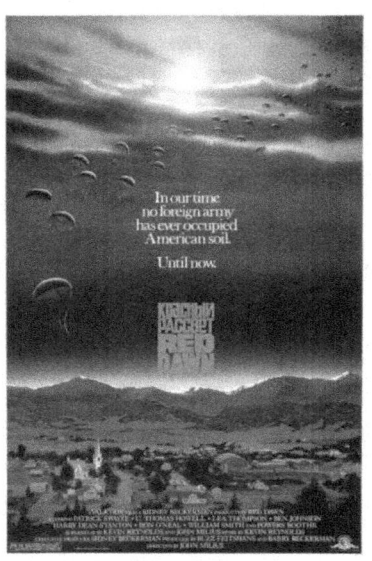

Kids today grow up fearing a country called Russia. Mostly they fear that government sponsored cyber hackers are going to get into their cellphones and steal all their discreet photos and post them on their Instagram account for all to see. Back in the '80s, we had to deal with the Soviet Union which was also called the USSR (Union of Soviet Socialist Republics) like in the Beatles song "Back in the USSR." The Soviet Union was a hardcore communist state that was determined to take over the world. Whether it be by persuasion or invasion, they were eager to spread the word of Lenin and Stalin.

Hollywood quickly embraced the Soviet Union as the bad guys after the defeat of Nazi Germany. They were the perfect villains because they existed to destroy the American way of life. It didn't hurt that the Soviet Union was not a big market for American made feature films and television shows. When you needed a plot against America, someone was going to be speaking Russian when they're exposed by the FBI.

Dragnet's Jack Webb made the propaganda film *Red*

Nightmare (1957) about what would happen to Americans if the Soviets took over. A regular Joe wakes up to not only find his town occupied by the commies, but his wife and children have been fully indoctrinated. He learns the harsh lessons of what it's like to live in a Soviet state instead of a sweet as apple pie American town. His job at the factory now demands he meet a quota every day even if it means working through his lunch break and staying late. That would never happen in America...although now it does. He gets forced against his will to give a speech about being a father...although now we call that a TED talk. The film swears the Russians will create their own TV channel to broadcast into America which predicts the RT (formerly Russia Today) on your cable box. The film is a massive piece of propaganda, but not so much against Russia. Jack Webb gives a list of freedoms that supposedly all Americans enjoy except in 1957 minorities weren't allowed to live where they wanted, attend any college, vote without issues or see *Red Nightmare* without being herded into the Blacks Only balcony at the movie theater. But there was no need to look inward about such issues because what really mattered was hating on those Commie Pinko Soviets.

During the summer of 1984, the Cold War was in full effect. The Olympics were taking place in Los Angeles. The Soviet Union was still pissed off that Jimmy Carter had boycotted the 1980 Olympics in

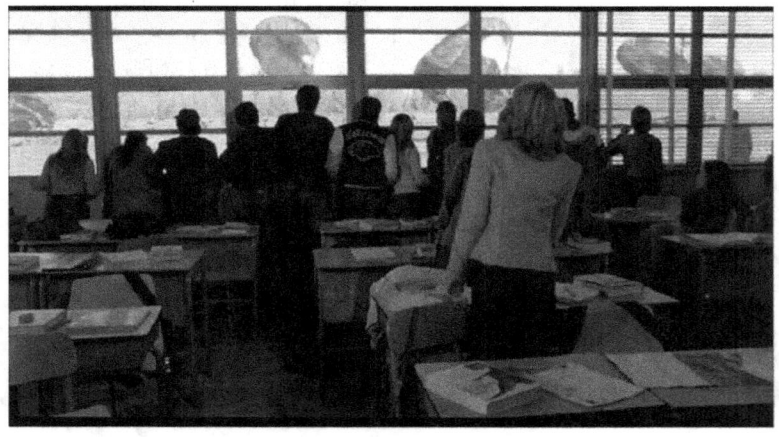

Moscow because of the invasion of Afghanistan. So not only did the Soviet Union not send their top athletes to Southern California, but many of their fellow communist countries said "Nyet!" The promise of the USA vs USSR was gone from the television screens. This was really bad for McDonalds that had a promotion where customers would get a scratch card that would reveal an Olympic sport. If the USA won the Bronze medal, the customer got a free regular soft drink. The silver meant a regular serving of French fries. The Gold was a Big Mac. And if the USA won 2 or 3 of the medals, you got the corresponding items. Without the Soviets and their commie pals on the fields, courts, rings and pools, the USA team went nuts on the medal count winning 174 medals including 83 Gold. That's a lot of Big Macs. People were getting free meals at McDonalds by the millions. The lack of the USSR made Americans bored of the Olympics. There was no one to root against. It's hard to scream at the TV that the judges were favoring the Swedes or Trinidad and Tobago. People got a Big Mac, but their hunger to yank Olympic glory from those Commie Pinko Soviets went unsatisfied.

Hollywood provided the satisfaction on the final weekend of the summer Olympics. Your local multiplex provided the clash between the USSR and USA that wasn't going to be provided on the basketball court or balance beam. *Red Dawn* was like the *Miracle on Ice* with automatic weapons instead of skates. People were ready to cheer for a group of American teenagers fighting back against the invading Soviet army that brought along

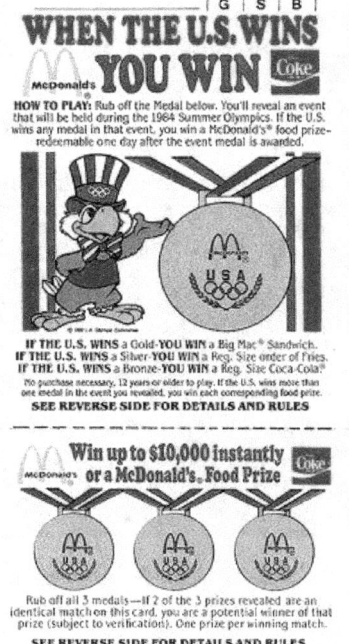

Cubans and Nicaraguans to occupy the town of Calumet, Colorado. This was the nightmare people had imagined ever since the Berlin Wall or the missiles were blocked from going to Cuba. This was World War III without it being symbolic on a hockey rink when a bunch of US kids had to take on the older Soviet military players.

Red Dawn quickly became proof to people that the threat was real. People would argue that the government shouldn't keep track of gun sales and registration because that's what the Soviets used against the citizens in the movie. Placing the action in Calumet played into a bit of paranoia since it's not an obvious first strike military target. Any town could be invaded by the Red Threat. Thus, it was fine for people to stock up on weapons because your town could be next. The film became family viewing for survivalists. *Red Dawn* could be your future!

Oddly enough that by the end of the decade, *Red Dawn* would be a nostalgic trip back at an enemy that was no more. The Soviet Union was in the midst of a bumpy time as their leaders kept dropping dead starting with Leonid Brezhnev in 1982. Yuri Andropov popped off in 1984 while *Red Dawn* was in post-production. What we didn't know was his replacement at the time of the film's release was already on his deathbed. Konstantin Chernenko pretty much spent his entire 13 months in power stuck inside a hospital room. In a work of almost Hollywood magic, the room was a sound stage that would be transformed to make it look like Chernenko was at various places for meetings including his own office. He was in no shape to order an attack on Calumet, Colorado. He was dead before *Red Dawn* came out on VHS. Although he could have seen a "filmed in

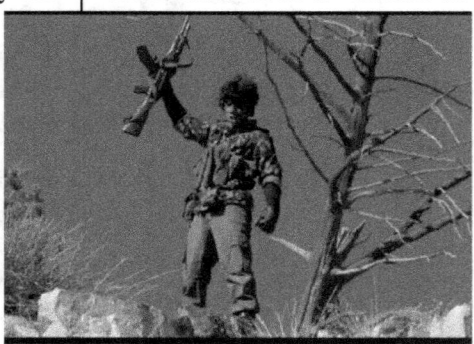

the theater" bootleg copy in his hospital room VCR. By the time *Red Dawn* began running on HBO, Mikhail Gorbachev had taken control of the Soviet Union. He wasn't out to conquer the world. His policies of Glasnost ended up changing things dramatically. By the end of the decade, the Eastern Bloc communist countries broke with the Soviet Union. The Berlin Wall collapsed and David Hasselhoff sang and danced on its ruins. Even the republics within the Soviet Union busted apart so that Russia was by itself. The country that had been the Commie Pinko menace for so long transformed into a democracy and all without having to parachute a bunch of teenagers with guns into Moscow.

After a few decades of peace, we once more fear the Russians thanks to Vladimir Putin making a joke out of his country's democracy and being elected president for life.

Oddly enough when *Red Dawn* was remade in 2012, the Russians were no longer the invading force. Originally the studio had Chinese troops arrive fully armed, but the studio realized this would upset one of the larger markets for Hollywood films. In the middle of post-production, they transformed the Chinese into North Koreans since they're not a box office force. The film was an Olympic level flop as audiences used their ticket money to buy a Big Mac.

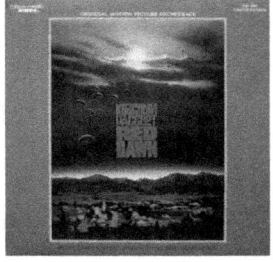

SOUNDTRACK NOTES: You would imagine that a movie about a bunch of teenagers mowing down Soviet soldiers would be rocking with the hottest hits of the early '80s. This was the first film released as PG-13 so people were probably expecting at least a little Loverboy and Billy Squier as music to lock and load by. But there was not a single licensed song between the gunfire. The soundtrack album is all about the patriotic score by Basil Poledouris. He was a good choice since his strong orchestra added strength to *Conan the Barbarian* and *Conan the Destroyer*. He packed the musical muscle onto the Wolverines and their attacks. This a great record to play when you're taking your date into the backyard to target practice on empty vodka bottles.

The Lost Boys

July 31, 1987

Warner Brothers

Directed by Joel Schumacher

Starring **Jason Patric, Corey Haim, Dianne Wiest, Kiefer Sutherland, Jami Gertz, Corey Feldman, Barnard Hughes, Edward Herrman, Alex Winter and Tim Capello**

Rated R - 97 minutes

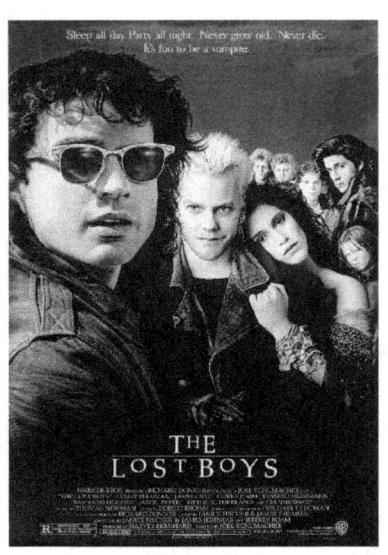

Ever rewatch a film and realize you were rooting for the wrong person to win? This is not a case where the director or the actors later did something criminal or morally disgusting that makes you feel cheated for emotionally wanting them to win. This is all about you. Time has taught you a few lessons between screenings. Such is what happened when after a few decades, I revisited *The Lost Boys* and immediately felt the error in my younger outlook on life.

Have you looked in the mirror lately? If you saw *The Lost Boys* when it was originally released, you're 33 years older. You're middle aged now. If you got into the movie theater with a real ID and no parent or guardian, you're over 50. A few of us might be in prime physical fitness. But most of us are falling apart as we go over the hump of midlife crisis time Why did you cheer for regular kids to kill all the vampires? Why did we think it was a good thing to grow old? It's fine to hit 21 so you can buy liquor. Maybe it's better to be 25 in case you need to rent a car at the airport. But after that, what's the point of getting older? You want a senior citizen discount for your McDonald's coffee?

How could we allow ourselves to turn against all the wonderful things that being a vampire had to offer? What was wrong with eternal youth? Even when the vampires slip into their fangfaces, they're looking a lot better than that Oil of Olay pit that stares back at you every morning. How much time do you spend and money do you waste chasing after the perfect facial rejuvenation cream? Or do you spend time having Botox injected in your face to remove your wrinkles and anything that can be mistaken for a facial expression? Remember when you didn't care to moisturize? And what's the issue with fangs since your gums are probably receding as bad as your hairline...if you still have one. As an adult, you probably worry about having to pay a mortgage, home insurance and property taxes and might think this is going to get worse if you live forever. How many hot water heaters will you have to buy for eternity? The good news is as a vampire, you can live in a cave. There's no need to worry about the monthly rent. You can turn into a bat so there's no more hassles with car issues or dealing with license renewals at the DMV. They won't wonder why your driver's license picture hasn't needed to be changed in 75 years. If they get pesky and ask, just tell them your secret is Oil of Olay.

Somehow, we thought losing our souls was a bad proposition in 1987. Haven't your corporate overlords already claimed that as part of a paragraph in that non-compete contract they forced you to sign as a blood loyalty to them? Or maybe Apple claimed it when you clicked to agree to their terms of service on an iPhone update? When was the last time you ever used your soul? It's like Calculus and the Spanish Subjunctive tense - things that mattered in

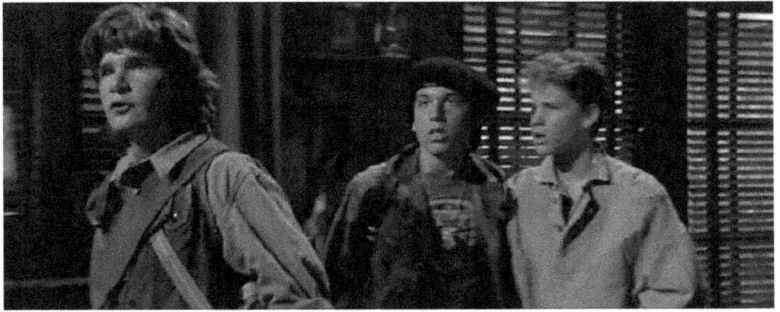

school. But you don't use them in the real world.

The idea of sucking the blood out of another person might seem disturbing. But think how many times you've had the life sucked out of you in a corporate task force meeting? Don't you feel drained on the commute home every night. Wouldn't you rather be on the other side of the suckage? It's a suck or be sucked world that waited for you in the outside world. Just suck it up and embrace the fangs.

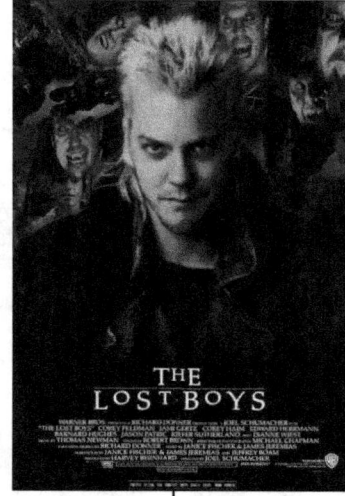

Why did we listen to Corey Feldman or at least his character Edgar Frog? When has listening to a Corey Feldman character been a great idea? He's working at a comic book store, wearing a headband and talking like he anticipated Christian Bale's hoarse voice *Dark Knight* Batman. Why would you trust a guy named Edgar Frog when it comes to the serious decision of embracing the glorious life of a vampire?

Don't you think Jason Patric wishes he was still looking like a lean second coming of The Doors' Jim Morrison or at least the same coming of Michael Hutchenence from INXS? There are probably a few times a year when Patric is half awake trying to remember when is his call time to get his fangs installed. And then he gets crushed remembering that was 33 years ago.

The one person who did stay eternally young as far as you should be concerned is the legendary Saxophone Player who stole the movie during his concert at the amusement park. The muscular musician was bare chested, glistening skin with long hair slicked back as he belted out The Call's "I Still Believe." The crowd was mesmerized by his performance. It was almost a letdown that the Saxophone Player wasn't secretly a vampire. He also wasn't secretly just an actor. You might recognize Tim Cappello from *Miami*

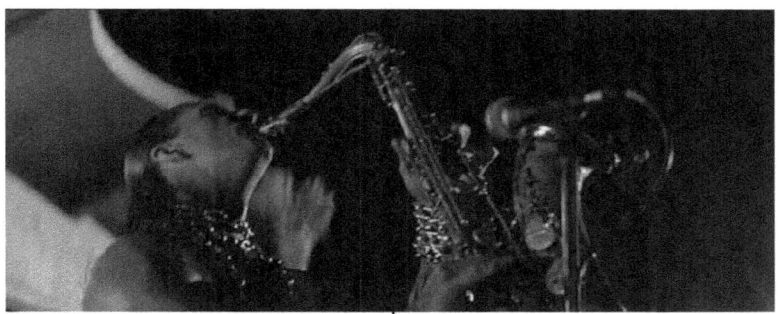

Vice, Equalizer, Bob Dylan's *Hearts of Fire* and the Tina Turner biopic *What's Love Got To Do With It*. You might also remember him as the sax player in Tina's video for "We Don't Need Another Hero" from the soundtrack to *Mad Max Beyond Thunderdome*. But he was not merely a muscular actor flexing and miming his instrument like the ladies in Robert Palmer's "Addicted to Love." Turns out Cappello really was Tina Turner's saxophonist and also keyboardist.

He started playing with Tina in 1984. Before that he hit the road with Peter Gabriel and played on the former Genesis singer's first two albums. He also toured with Carly Simon. The woman who sang "You're So Vain" would walk him around the stage while wearing only a collar, chains and a leather G-string. It was kind of a reverse Spinal Tap "Smell the Glove" moment. He even composed the score for A&E shows about The Rat Pack and Jerry Lewis. He's been part of Ringo Starr's All-Starr Band. He's more than a sweaty and saxy gif that gets retweeted around the internet.

What's completely stunning is that Cappello didn't release his first solo album until 2018 with *Blood on the Reed*. How is this possible? Granted he was busy touring the globe with Tina Turner, but there should have been a side project time for Cappello.

The '80s were still a hot time for selling music on TV. Two-minute-long commercials for albums were the mini-infomercials of the day. They'd take up the entire ad break on a show and let you deep dive on the music that you need on the turntable, but wouldn't think of grabbing at School Kids Records or the Record Bar at the mall. Think back to all those million sellers from Slim

Whitman and Boxcar Willie that insisted you call a 1-800 number and they'd send you a vinyl record, cassette, 8-track or even a compact disc in the mail. Or you could just directly mail them a check to a PO Box in Atlanta or Nashville or Pawtucket, Rhode Island. I know you think that this would be a tough market for Cappello to break since he hadn't already sold more records than the Beatles and the Rolling Stones combined like Slim Whitman. But there were plenty of saxophone records being sold between MTV videos and reruns of *Bewitched*.

Ace Cannon revived his saxophone career with his *Golden Classics* album that wasn't "Sold In Stores." The same is true for Boots Randolph's double album *Boots*. He reminded America that he played "Yakety Sax" as used by Benny Hill for his various chase scenes. Ace and Boots made their ads look like they were at a house party and ready to liven up your own party with their 8-Track in your 4 in 1 compact stereo bought from Sears. Downtown New York avant jazz group The Lounge Lizards were selling albums on late night TV too. Hipster John Lurie was using his cult acting status from *Stranger Than Paradise* and *Down By Law* to entice late night viewers into *Voice of Chunk*. There could have been a place for Cappello on the cable box when *The Lost Boys* arrived on HBO in the summer of 1988.

Imagine being up late at night and seeing a commercial for Cappello's *Music to Neck By*. You would become hypnotized by his soothing notes and savage looks. How could you resist his gleaming chest that outshines his golden saxophone? He would have made a record so smooth and seductive that you could get freaky with your date even if Cappello's blurting out "Yakety Sax." Imagine how many half-awake couples would immediately get into the mood and start making out on their This End Up furniture in the rumpus room? If Cappello produced an entire record of Barry White tunes, the '80s would have ended with everybody in the same bed like last call at Plato's Retreat.

Why didn't this happen? Why can't you find scratchy Cappello records popping up in the used album crates at Flea Markets or second-hand stores? Hard to tell. But I've decided there must have been a conspiracy within the industry. Ace Cannon and Boots Randolph knew their days of selling sax albums during reruns of *Cannon* on UHF channels were numbered if Cappello hit the airwaves. What woman couldn't resist his rocking notes and body? What guy wouldn't think, if I can't have his body at least let me use his music to enhance my chances to score with my date. Cappello could have sold more albums than Slim Whitman and Boxcar Willie combined! He could have been bigger than *Freedom Rock*! Ace and Boots formed the Sax Cartel and shut down any chance of Cappello getting into the business. They informed Cindy Lou's Musical Mail Order and Clyde Records that operators would not be standing by for Cappello. Every hotel room on Tina Turner's tour that Cappello checked into featured HBO on the TV and a chocolate covered horse head on his pillow. This was the Sax Cartel's turn down service. They weren't going to stop until Cappello understood he was not welcome in the not sold in stores universe. That's my conspiracy as to why we had to wait 30 years for Tim Cappello's solo album. If we were vampires, this time passed wouldn't really matter.

SOUNDTRACK NOTES: Right off the bat, Tim Cappello's cover of "I Still Believe" is on the original soundtrack album. You'll have something to play when a bunch of vampires are hanging in your backyard. The record is a mixed bag of hits, not quite the band and who were they? The song that captured MTV was INXS and Jimmy Barnes doing "Good 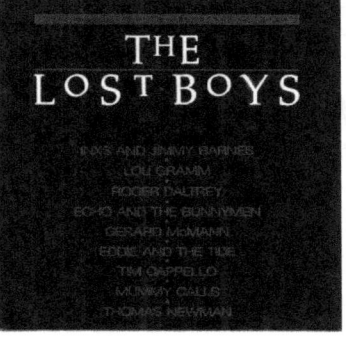 Times." This Down Under party rocker was originally recorded by the Easy Beats. The group and solo artist also teamed up for "Laying Down the Law." Instead of licensing The Doors' version of "People Are Strange," Echo and the Bunnyman did a cover with Doors member Ray Manzarek producing. Echo and the Bunnymen were often described as sounding like The Doors and this collaboration pretty much sealed the deal for that comparison. The Who's Roger Daltrey takes his shot at Elton John's "Don't Let the Sun Go Down On Me" which is an anti-vampire anthem if you think about it. Foreigner's Lou Gramm goes gothy with "Lost In the Shadow." The huh bands include Eddie & The Tide and The Mummy Calls. Eddie & The Tide used to play in Santa Cruz where they shot *The Lost Boys* so it's cool that their crowning achievement was being on the soundtrack. Songs that didn't make it onto vinyl included RUN-DMC & Aerosmith's "Walk This Way," "Groovin'" by the Rascals" and Clarence "Frogman" Henry's "Ain't Got No Home." It's fine cassette to pop in when the sun goes down...even if Roger Daltrey pleads for it to stay shining.

Wednesday - May 20

My Tutor 7:00 p.m.
Private Lessons 9:15 p.m.

After School Special

There was such major relief as the final minutes ticked down to end of the school day. But also, a bit of tension. Students were like runners ready to start their heat and getting down into the starting blocks. You'd begin to slide your handouts into the notebook and sneak extra pencils into your backpack. The final bell was approaching although your finish line varied.

If you lived the great life, you'd already hit your locker before last period class and loaded up all the textbooks that were necessary for homework assignments. You didn't want anything to slow down your route to the cool parking lot so you can get in your car and hit the exit before the bottleneck. Your goal was to get the best space in front of the nearby 7-Eleven. You wanted to show off your Honda Civic with reclining bucket seats for when your date wanted "privacy." There was a joy in hanging with your friends without having the fascist faculty riding your ass for hanging out on school property. You only had to deal with the guy behind the 7-Eleven counter making sure you buy something like the hotdogs that had been rotating all day on the heated rollers. He was last year's stoner cum laude so he's up for cutting you slack. The preferred drink was a blueberry Slurpee so that you can turn your high school sweetheart's tongue blue after a deep bout of French kissing. You'd sit on your car's fender with your pals until you needed to get home for dinner.

If you were denied car keys, you had to scramble to the loser parking lot where the school buses were lined up. You needed to get a window seat in the back of the bus so you can get fresh air and look as cool as you could while being stuck on the bus. When you got to your stop, you didn't walk straight home if you were a badass. You'd wander into the woods and down to the creek to smoke your mom's cigarettes and flip through abandoned Hustlers with the models slightly green from weathering. The goal was to wander back just in time to beat your parents home from their jobs so they had no clue you'd been micropartying on a school day.

If you were an extremely good kid, you'd step off the bus and run to your house because you were eager to see if a new *ABC Afterschool Special* was running that afternoon. From Fall of 1972 until the winter of 1997, these hour-long specials would pop up about once a month during the school year and mess up 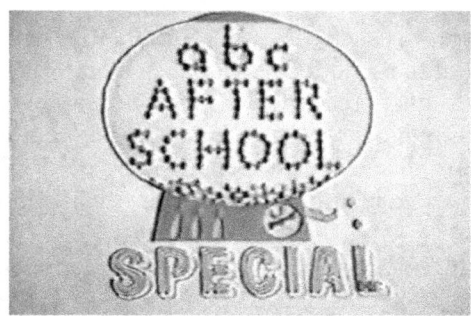 your normal broadcast viewing schedule. You'd sit down waiting for another rerun of *The Flintstones, The Little Rascals, The Addams Family* or *The Brady Bunch* and instead get a semi-educational special. It was a letdown, but you watched since the other option was turn off the TV and read a book. You could have done that at school. You half-assed your homework on the family room floor, ignored your mother asking about your chores and hoped that the subject matter featured tawdry teens.

The *ABC Afterschool Special* featured quite a few of the stars that are part of our film festival. The first season's *Alexander* brought together Jodie Foster (*Foxes*) with Cousin Oliver from *The Brady Bunch* (Robbie Rist) to deal with a retiring clown. The next season brought back Jodie in *Rookie of the Year*. She plays the only girl on a boys baseball team. This is one of the major reasons people swear she was in *The Bad News Bears* when it was really Tatum O'Neal (*Little Darlings*). *The Secret Life of*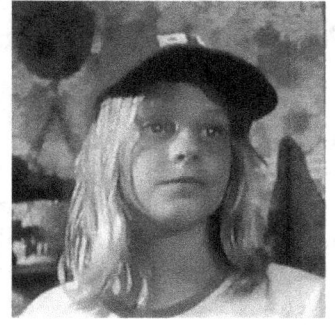

T.K. Dearing returned Jodie for the third season as part of a secret club. *Seven Wishes of a Rich Kid* has Robbie Rist use a genie to impress Cynthia Nixon (*O.C. and Stiggs*).

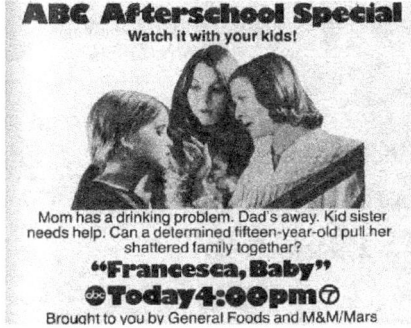

Rob Lowe arrived in *Schoolboy Father* where he wants custody of the baby after he knocks up Dana Plato (*Diff'rent Strokes*) during their summer loving. This was extremely edgy stuff after decades of TV teens being chaste. There never was an episode of *The Brady Bunch* with Greg knocking up Marsha. This was a time where condoms weren't advertised on TV so a generation learned that unprotected sex could lead to Rob Lowe's baby in your belly. *Stoned* has Scott Baio (*Foxes*) become a massive high school drug abuser. The story had him

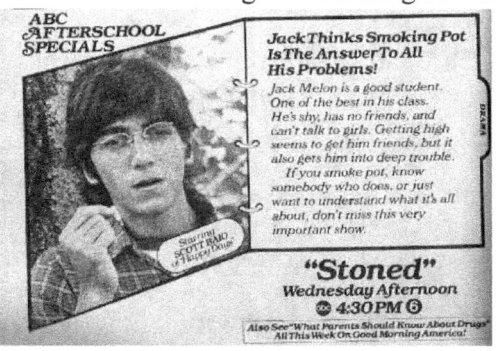

going from pot to the hard stuff in record time. They partied hard in the '80s. Scott returned in a wheelchair for *Run, Don't Walk* where a girl has to understand her life with wheels. *Amy and the Angel* is about suicide and featured Matthew Modine (*Private School*) as neither the angel or Amy. *Have You Ever Been Ashamed of Your Parents* starred Jennifer Jason Leigh after she was in *Fast Times In Ridgemont High*. She keeps her clothes on in this one. *The Great Love Experiment* has Jennifer Grey (*Red Dawn*) enjoy high school without killing Soviet troops. She just has to shoot down nasty boys. *One Too Many* gave us Mare Winningham being friends with Val Kilmer (*Real Genius*) and Michelle Pfeiffer (*Grease 2*) who were better than her pals in *St. Elmo's Fire*. *The Day My Kid*

Went Punk didn't feature a future punk superstar but did have his father be the Doc from *The Love Boat*.

Kids learned about drugs, sex and punk rock from the specials which was a bit more edgy than *Gilligan's Island*. That show only got us hooked on Mary Ann's coconut cream pies.

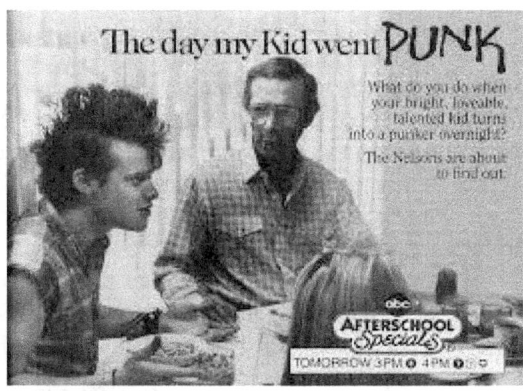

The *ABC Afterschool Special* died out because your local ABC station gave up on kids as a demographic as the '90s started. They were making too much money from running *Oprah* at 4 o'clock to interrupt it once a month. Oprah Winfrey had taken over the specials from ABC and many of the shows were her interviewing kids so it looked like her regular show. Eventually she let the *Afterschool Specials* die and no one noticed. As the decade progressed, local stations expanded their local news coverage. The thirty minute Six O'Clock News started at 3 o'clock. Or they ran judge shows or talkshows aimed at the grown-ups that were hanging around the house in the afternoon. Gone were the days of *Batman* or *Ultraman*. The local stations figured kids would rather watch Nickelodeon on the cable box so why compete?

Tonight's double feature of *Private Lessons* and *My Tutor* are both about kids who get an extra education after the school's final bell has rung. Both were indie films that came off as really exploitive episodes of *ABC Afterschool Special*. Although neither film was going to let you finish your homework or make you feel that educated.

My Tutor

March 4, 1983

Crown International

Directed by George Bowers

Starring **Caren Kaye, Matt Lattanzi, Kevin McCarthy, Bruce Bauer, Clark Brandon, Arlene Golonka, Crispin Glover and Jewel Shepard**

Rated R - 97 minutes

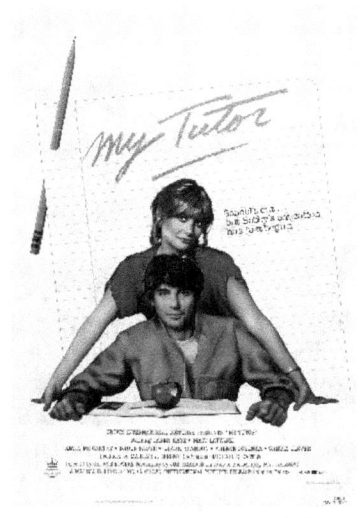

Crown International Pictures doesn't quite get the love and attention lavished on American International Pictures and Roger Corman's New World Films. But the indie studio was a force over the '60s, '70s and '80s with hundreds of releases aimed for movie theaters couldn't book titles from the major studios, but weren't art houses. They made films meant to sell tickets by the carload. During the '70s, over half their bookings were at drive-ins which is the best way to enjoy their films such as *The Van* and *Van Nuys Blvd*. The late "Rock and Roll Bad Boy" Brett Meisner was a major crusader for Crown's releases as part of America's cult cinema culture.

When Crown started, they were into distribution including putting American International's early offering into theaters. But when AIP launched their own distribution, Crown got into the film production game. During the '60s, their focus was on horror, bikers and teen flicks. They were kind of like AIP movies except with even tighter budgets and rougher edges. They rarely featured recognizable actors since they might want money. Several of the films from this era ended up getting a second life in the '90s when they ended up on *Mystery Science*

Theater 3000. *Catalina Caper, Wild Rebels, The Hellcats* and *The Sidehackers* were cut up by Joel Robinson and the Bots.

During the '70s, their output began to focus on more fun time films to keep the teens happy. *The Pom Pom Girls* dealt with the fantasy life of high school cheerleaders. *Malibu High* and *Malibu Beach* made a trip to this affluent coastal community a fun destination. This was a place filled with money and light on fabric for clothes. *The Van* was about the freedom a kid gets when he can finally buy his own van and hit the road while blasting an 8-track of Sammy Johns' iconic "Chevy Van." Ironically the van in *The Van* is a Dodge that was spruced up by George Barris. *Van Nuys Blvd* has a small-town guy get inspired by a news piece on kids cruising Van Nuys Blvd in Los Angeles. He fills up the tank in his van so he can live the dream that weekend. Quite a few of these '70s films starred Bill Alder who would

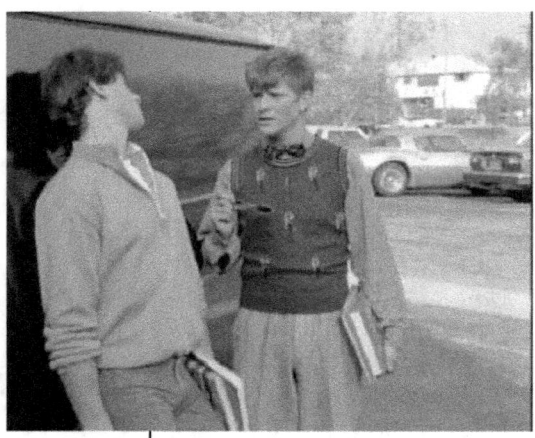

go on to design golf accessories for Tiger Woods.

The '80s saw Crown release two female centered films that weren't complete teensploitation jiggle fests. *Tomboy* has Betsy Russell (*Private School*) as a teenage girl who not only fixes cars, but dreams of racing stock cars. *My Chauffeur* features Deborah Foreman (*Valley Girl*) driving around people for a limo service. She works for Howard Hesseman (*Private Lessons*) who doesn't like having a woman on his male staff. Luckily Hesseman doesn't entice her to sleep with any 15-year-old rich boys.

While *My Tutor* wasn't focused on the female lead, it can be seen as a major step up from *The Beach Girls* in giving its female lead emotional depth deeper than the stretch fabric on her aerobics outfit. Crown

International was doing its best to give gravity to characters without denying an audience the elements they expected when they saw the royal logo on the screen.

My Tutor marked a bit of an attitude change that led to *Tom Boy* and *My Chauffeur* going into production. The film dared to balance the female and male elements of the film, but without alienating the audience. During the opening scene we get a sense that Bobby Chrystal (Matt Lattanzi) is a horrible student as he goes down in flames while taking a test in a classroom. But director George Bowers doesn't want to bum us out. He cuts the academic frightmare with Terry Green (Caren Kaye) and dozens of ladies flexing their goodness during an aerobics workout. There's a lot of thrusting in the workout room. Very quickly we learn two things about Bobby. That he wants to lose his virginity before he graduates high school and if he doesn't pass French, he gets another year to reach that goal.

He gets the ultimate tutor for his first goal when his buddy Jack (Crispin Glover of *The River's Edge*) takes him to a high-class brothel and not a cheap motel on the outskirts of town. Making Bobby's attempt at a first time extra special, the lady chosen for him to pop his cherry is Kitten Natividad. She was the star of Russ Meyer's *Beneath the Valley of the Ultra-Vixens* so Kitten doesn't hold anything back. As you find out, no matter how good of a teacher she is, Bobby screws up like he did on his French final. He has screwed up that test so royally that he might not get into Yale after his dad greased all the rails to the Ivy League. He is given a chance to retake the test. Bobby's father (*The Invasion of the Body Snatchers*' Kevin McCarthy) can't afford a failure so he hires Terry Green to be an intensive tutor. She's set to get a fat bonus if Bobby passes the exam. She moves into the family's mansion to give dawn until dusk assistance. Bobby spots her skinny dipping in the pool after dark, he really wants her to help him pass the first goal more than passing French.

My Tutor gives the sense of a classic Crown International Picture flick with a young guy hoping to hook up with his dream gal. There's plenty of nudity and kinky action that sounds enticing when recounting the movie on the school bus. But Terry is more than an exploitation movie dream date. She has quite a bit going on during her screen time besides shaking her rump in the gym and stripping down at the pool. This isn't a completely mindless softcore romp.

The main actors bring quite a bit to their roles to make the film seem realistic. There's no doubting the on screen pull of Matt Lattanzi. In his first major film, he was a dancer in *Xanadu* who roller discoed his way into star Olivia Newton John's heart. He was the one that she wanted. He married the *Grease* star and appeared in *Grease 2*. How slick is that? Lattanzi is a success story that all bit players dream about when they arrive at the soundstage thinking they'll get lucky with an above the title actor. There's no doubting a guy like Bobby Chrystal would have a chance with Terry Green. He's just inept and needs a little tutoring from someone other than Crispin Glover. While Caren Kaye spent most of the '70s & '80s appearing in various sitcoms including being a regular on *Blansky's Beauties* and *The Betty White Show* along with 10 episodes of *The Love Boat*, she could easily be a tutor. She went to Carnegie Mellon and has a PhD in Psychology. She didn't just play smart for the movie.

My Tutor broke new ground as it went deeper into the genre of student hooking up after the school bell. This went beyond the two things we learned from the cinema du Eric Brown. *They're Playing With Fire* taught us that messing around with your hot teacher can lead to serious consequences. If you paid attention to the plot of *Private Lessons*, you'll remember that it's never good to hook up with any hot ladies that your parents hire full time to take care of you. But what about a tutor? They're not true teachers. They don't hand out grades that are destined to make a mark in your permanent record. They're just there to help. While your parents pay them, it's on a contract basis without any retirement benefits or health insurance. Any fantasies about hooking up with your tutor doesn't appear to get you dragged into the human resources office. This leads to the question: Is getting bonus points with a tutor a true fetish like hooking up with a hot substitute nun at a parochial school?

For most students needing a tutor, the fantasy was that you'd actually want to have a fantasy about the person your parents hired to help you comprehend algebra, physics or jumping jacks. Most tutors were retired teachers or nerds two grades above you that knew the secrets of your teacher's testing ways. They'd either drop by your house for an hour to sit at the kitchen table or your mom would drop you off at the library to meet them. There was rarely talk on the bus about a classmate wanting to write a Penthouse Forum Letter about doing the nasty in the periodical room after they figured out a tangent. They didn't want anything to happen between them and their tutor. During the '80s tutoring started to turn into a lucrative business as students needed to pump up their grades as colleges became increasingly competitive for entry. They would also offer assistance in boosting points on the almighty SAT or ACT test needed to impress university admissions staff. They'd open up study centers at strip malls. Tutoring companies enjoyed hiring young college women that aspired to being teachers. From the stories I've heard,

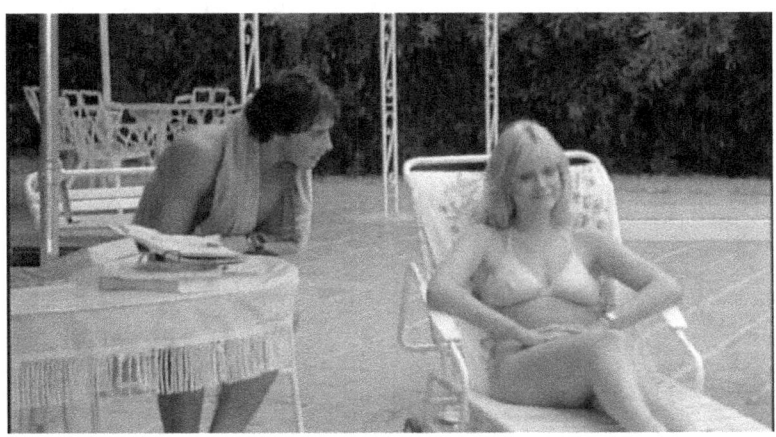

there were a few cases of a college sophomore hooking up with a high school senior to help them celebrate getting into their target college.

My Tutor came out at just the right time as it was a serious hit for Crown. The movie played quite a bit on cable since it had those required frisky elements including skinny dipping and sweaty spandex. It made flunking French look like so much fun.

Crown International Pictures stopped being a thriving indie studio as the '80s came to an end. They were smashed hard by two factors in a cinematic Malachi Crunch. First the demise of the drive-in as a viable business plan. Way too many drive-ins found themselves on valuable property that was targeted by the developers of shopping malls and planned communities. Owners were more than eager to take one fat payday instead of waiting for the next hit to have cars lined up around the highway. The second thing smashing into Crown were major studios releasing their hot titles to thousands of more screens on opening weekend. *Jaws* had only opened on 464 screens in the summer of 1975. *Star Trek III: The Search For Spock* hit nearly 2,000 screens in 1984. The *Avengers: Endgame* opened on 4,662 screens.

The brand new six screen cineplex was eager to book a blockbuster film in more than one of their theaters since they didn't want to turn away money when the first screen sold out. Even though there were more screens, there was less opportunity for Crown International Pictures to put a movie on the marquee. Their kind of movies weren't aimed at the art house. There was no way *Hunks* was going to bump the latest John Sayles film or Merchant Ivory Production out of The Rialto. Crown shut down the production arm and focused on keeping their vault active by running them on cable stations and home video. In the last decade, movie fans have found Crown titles extremely easy to collect since Mill Creek has released box-sets containing 32 or more of the studio's films at rather low budget prices. You don't have to choose to buy *My Tutor, My Chauffeur* or *Tom Boy* since all three can be found with others classics on the various compilations. So even though Crown International doesn't get the critical attention of other American indie studios, their filmography is reasonably priced for those eager to enjoy their glory years.

SOUNDTRACK NOTES: The original soundtrack album for *My Tutor* features the instrumental work of composer Webster Lewis. This is great for when you need some background music while watching your tutor skinny dip in the pool behind your house. The record does not include "The

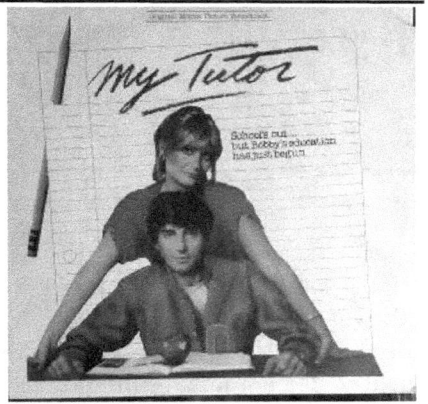

First Time We Make Love" by Kathy Brown, Jimmy Franks "Now You Must Pay" or even the disco-ized "You're My Tutor." The floor should have been pumping at dance clubs across the country with female singers going on about someone being their tutor who would use them like a puppet and they'd obey. How come this wasn't used as background music for tutoring businesses commercials to let the kids know that if they need extra help with French, they'll get intensive tutoring. All songs were written by Lewis with lyrics by Arthur Hamilton. He'd written "Cry Me A River." That might be considered a standard, but "You're My Tutor" is a masterpiece. In a wonderful coincidence, right before he scored *My Tutor*, Webster Lewis provided the music for "The Color of Friendship" episode of the *ABC Afterschool Special*.

Private Lessons

August 28, 1981

Cinema Epoch

Directed by Alan Myseron

Starring Sylvia Kristel, Howard Hesseman, Eric Brown, Patrick Piccininni, Ed Begley Jr., Pamela Bryant and Meridith Baer

Rated R - 87 minutes

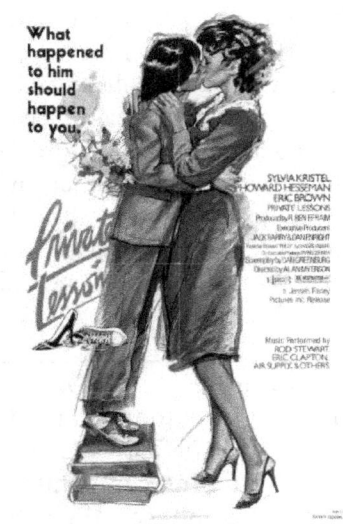

What was the ultimate high school status symbol in the '80s when you're under 16 and can't legally drive a car? A TV set in your bedroom. Nothing made kids on the bus more jealous than letting that little fact drop. Or even better if you invite pals over to the house and they notice in the corner near your Star Wars curtains that you've got a personal boob tube. They were all down for coming over to your house even if you didn't have a pool in the backyard or a used Camaro in the carport. You had the independence of a TV set in your bedroom so your parents couldn't spy on all of your viewing pleasures.

There were different levels of status with having a TV in your bedroom. Where you ranked really mattered on the set and your channel selection. Good was having a black and white set next to your bed. Normally this was the TV that your family had been hanging onto after the upgrade to a color TV in the rumpus room. Odds were high that it was on a rack with wheels so your dad could push it onto the back porch and watch his *Monday Night Football* fix in the early weeks of the season. Your mom preferred this arrangement since she didn't have to hear Howard Cosell all night long. Besides lack of hues, you were stuck with an antenna so your freedom was limited to the local channels.

Nice was having your family's old color TV set brought into the bedroom. Dad had decided to up go wild and buy a new 25-inch screen model. He figured you'd done enough chores to get the older 19-inch model that had once been considered huge. Now you could flip the B&W switch to Color on the Atari 2600 console and see so much more in the games. The only negative was when you had friends over to play Defender; your mother refused to let you take the bag of chips and cans of soda in your bedroom since they'd attract roaches and rats.

Great was getting the color TV and being able to attach the coaxial wire to the back of the set so you get basic cable. This allowed you to change channels without having to get up to tweak the rabbit ears. If you lived in a cool area, MTV was on the basic cable so you'd be watching America's rock station with VJs. You could close the door and tell your folks you were doing homework while checking out Nina Blackwood's latest outfit. Or you could wake up in the middle of the night and catch J.J. Jackson introducing the latest Robert Plant video. On the weekends you could stay up late to watch *Night Flight* on USA Network. The show presented a mix of music videos, indie animation, cult films and concerts from midnight to six a.m. This was as edgy as things got on basic cable.

Godly was not merely getting the color TV, but having the pay movie channels. You want to be the boss on the bus, let word get out that you received HBO, Showtime, Cinemax or even The Movie Channel in your bedroom. You didn't have to sneak watch R-rated

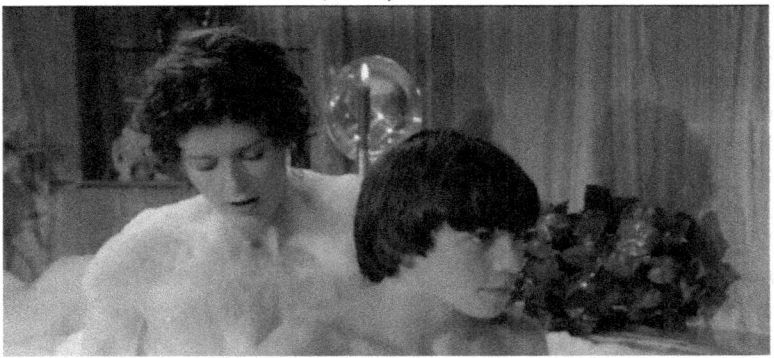

films in the family room. You could turn down the volume, block the light from escaping under the door and watch those naughty films from the privacy of your bed. Every morning, you'd sit down in the seat on the bus and someone would ask, "What did you watch last night?" They wanted to know the films worth risking being caught in the middle of the night. There were plenty of movies and shows to indulge in that you didn't want to watch with your parents. HBO ran quite a few R rated treats after dark. Showtime had a topless skating special called *Spice On Ice* or the T&A comedy of John Byner's *Bizarre*. You could enjoy *Joe Bob's Drive-In Theater* with Joe Bob Briggs on The Movie Channel which showed a lot of freaky stuff that wasn't ever going to show up at your local video store. But the premium channel that really knew how to excite an audience was Cinemax with its Cinemax After Dark time slot. They'd show plenty of English dubbed foreign films about ladies in Europe who had an issue with their clothing vanishing. The ample amounts of nudity earned it the nickname Skin-A-Max. This is where you'd see *Young Lady Chatterley* and anything dealing with a young woman's sexual awakening on a border crossing train. A hazy memory swears the channel showed their share of both *Emmanuelle* and *Emanuelle*. If you had Cinemax, you became the forbidden version of *TV Guide* giving more than the plot summary. You were the kid who could let others know if that film was "arty" or delivered the goods. You were the coolest until someone got a Mustang for their sweet sixteen and then you were a loser who stayed home and watched TV because your parents wouldn't even buy you a Honda Civic.

Even though *Private Lessons* starred Sylvia Kristel, the most famous Emmanuelle, the movie didn't play on *Cinemax After Dark*. It went straight to HBO because it was a massive hit in theaters. Reportedly the film only cost $3 million and scored nearly $30 million at the box office. That's a $100 million score in today's ticket sales.

The success of the film is extremely amazing when you hear the plot. A manipulative chauffeur (*WKRP in Cincinnati*'s Howard Hesseman) gets a foreign maid (Kristel) to sleep with the 15-year-old son

(*Mama Family*'s Eric Brown) of their boss. You know that saying, "They couldn't make this film in Hollywood now." *Private Lessons* is an example of a film that no studio, distributor or movie theater is ever going to allow on the screen. A boy that's under the age of consent getting freaky with Emmanuelle is what we'd refer to in the 21st Century as a felony. Eric Brown was barely older than his character. The story goes that when it came time to shoot the intimate scenes between Davis, Kristel and her body double, the production had to move from Arizona to New Mexico since the age of consent in New Mexico was 16. If they stayed in Arizona, there could have been charges.

Brown does not play the role as if he's an extremely mature 15-year-old. He often sounds like his voice is finally hitting puberty. There's no forgetting that the maid is putting the moves on an awkward teenage boy. As shocking as the movie is now, if you were a 15-year-old boy when it came out or finally arrived on HBO, this was an impressive film. Your hormones are just kicking in. You're naturally going to be intrigued that someone as freakishly inept as the rich kid has a chance to slide into bed with an international sex symbol. Odds are you probably took notes - although mostly what not to do when a European legend asks you to join her in the bathtub. In a sense, *Private Lessons* was as inspirational as *Rudy* would be for a future generation.

What's puzzling is how the moviegoing audience of 1981 flocked to see a film that would normally appeal to a creepier audience. The movie made nearly as much as *The Great Muppet Caper*. What enticed a couple to say, "Hey, let's check out the film about the boy who can't drive that sleeps with the star of that X-rated film about that woman who has a sexual awakening in Bangkok!" There were a couple things that made *Private Lessons* seem a bit more classy than its logline. Dr. Johnny Fever from *WKRP* is in the film so people must have thought it couldn't be that tawdry. The TV series was still being shown on its original network run when ads for *Private Lessons* hit the airwaves. What sitcom star would take this career turn? Although odds are that Hesseman had no idea what the director was shooting when he wasn't on the location. Even Disney veteran Ed Begley Jr (*Superdad*) signed up for the film. The movie did look kind of classy with Jan De Bont behind the camera. The Dutch cinematographer would later shoot Tom Cruise's *All the Right Moves* before becoming a director on Keanu Reeves' *Speed*. Or maybe millions of people flocked to *Private Lessons* because they needed something freaky on the screen since the local adult

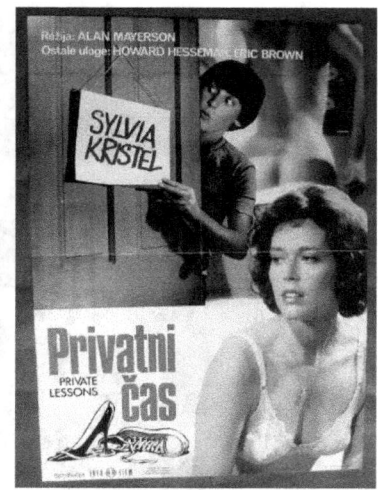

theater was being picketed by their mothers-in-law.

Eric Brown would make what seemed like an unofficial sequel with *They're Playing With Fire* in 1984. This time he's a college student that gets seduced by his hot professor played by Sybil Danning (*Howling II: Your Sister Is A Werewolf*). Except it's not about frisky romance in an academic setting. The teacher is married and she and her husband don't have an arrangement. Brown would also appear on *CBS Schoolbreak Special* which was the network's variation of the *ABC After School Special*. He'd be part of a "Student Court" that put a classmate on trial for shoplifting. He didn't sleep with a teacher or the help during the special. The producers did create a sequel of sorts that you've already seen earlier this week. *Private School* featured producer R. Ben Efraim and screenwriter Dan Greenburg. They even brought back Sylvia Kristel although in a much smaller role that didn't require a body double.

SOUNDTRACK NOTES: If you needed a soundtrack to seduction, *Private Lessons* provided a great piece of vinyl. Right off the bat you get hit with Rod Stewart's "Hot Legs." But then things cool down to a passionate simmer with Earl Klugh's "Spanish Night," Air Supply's "Lost In Love" and Randy Van Warmer's "Just When 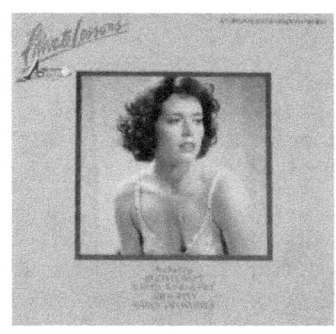 I Needed You Most." That's a good hot streak to hook you up. The first side wraps up with "I Need A Lover" back when John Mellencamp was John Cougar. It's a good way to let your date know what's expected in this relationship. The second side gets funky with Earth Wind and Fire's "Fantasy." Things sizzle with the return of Rod Stewart on "Tonight's the Night" and another Earl Klugh with "Doc." "I Don't Want to Talk About It" is Crazy Horse without Neil Young. The record ends with Willie Nile's "That's the Reason." If you need a little music to smooth out your awkward movies, *Private Lessons* original soundtrack belongs on the turntable.

Thursday - May 21

Class of Nuke 'Em High 7:00 p.m.
Class of 1984 9:15 p.m.

High School Hell

Few things struck horror in the heart of a junior high student more than the fear of being promoted to high school. You think teenage students would be excited, but instead anxieties kicked in. They were about to have their social lives reset to factory settings as they arrived at the next stage in life. The kid who hustled cinnamon sticks in the gym locker room was fearful they'd have to get a connection to upgrade to the hard stuff. But he wasn't alone in the identity crisis.

You'd think this fear would be only true of the loser kids that were picked on since they stepped off the bus from grammar school; the popular kids and the bullies also suffered from the inner terrors. Those students spent three years scrambling to the top of the pecking order. The ninth graders were the faces of the smoking court, laid claim to the best tables in the cafeteria as turf and knew the way to weasel extra credit without making an effort. They were part of the top dog pack that roamed the junior high campus. By the end of summer, they'd be reduced to the fresh meat rookies. Their empires would be smashed like sandcastles by 12th graders eager to prove their dominance. This was a world of pain until graduation or your upperclassman years. High School was like being transferred to Alcatraz except without the great water views.

Some kids had siblings and friends already in high school. They thought they'd be protected, but were they really going to be off limits between periods? Was anyone really safe from those rumors of painful hazing rituals and daily unending nightmares they were used to dishing out to others? Was a big sister really going to protect them if it meant jeopardizing their standing in a clique? Or would they merely advise their younger sibling that they had to put up with the various humiliation techniques and punishments when they were new to high school. Take your lumps, they build character. That would be the true lesson for the newbie. Welcome to Hell, you better give me a cigarette!

A student of the '80s was expected to make so many choices upon arrival at high school. Very few of them were about their academic career. What drug were they going to be taking? Did you want weed? Or sniff "Rush?" Or take speed so they didn't fall asleep during study hall and get sent to detention? Did they learn all the hand signs to flash to your homeroom drug dealer so he'd have your order ready by lunch period for a sneak into the woods behind the cafeteria for a puff and pass refreshment break? Which fingertip would be sacrificed in shop class on the wobbly table top saw? Most importantly was choosing a self-identity crowd to join. This had all the status of joining a prison gang. Were they going to be a Freak or a Jock? What's the difference? Jocks seemed to like to smoke weed as much as the Freaks, but the Freaks didn't like to do any squat thrusts. Freaks just wanted to hang and get high without cheerleaders. Although Jocks did devour speed pills since it allowed them to be full of energy for the school day, all the afterschool practices and hanging with the cheerleaders after dark. What about kids who were considered nerds? They were merely victims for both sides. The Jocks would beat up the nerds to burn off the extra energy from the speed. The Freaks would hit up the nerds to get more weed money when their grandmothers hid their change purses.

About the only thing high schoolers in the '80s didn't have to worry about choosing was their sexuality. Pretty much your "choices" were straight or being straight enough that nobody noticed. The only thing deeper than the closet where the gym coach kept the red utility balls was the one inhabited by any student with the slightest desire to be openly gay, lesbian or the highly unusual for the time bisexual. Smear the Queer was no longer a game restricted to the playground. Anyone that wanted to be a bit different was a threat to the power structure that demanded you wear this year's fashions such as Izod collared polo shirts, khaki Duck pants, dock shoes, jeans, Nike sneakers or cool band concert t-shirts. If you weren't fitting in, you're sticking out and setting yourself up as a target for all.

High school was pretty much the second to last chance to beat conformity into your neighboring peers. The final chance would be the pain inflicted on non-conformists by ghoulish Home Owner Association leadership councils.

Rumors about what was going down in the halls of the nearby high school would get nastier as Junior High days dwindled down. This was like *Scared Straight* except you were going to end up in this future prison unless you flunked. And then you'd have to face the uglier fate of your disappointed parents. You learned to accept your promotion and embrace the fate that was High School Hell. The good news was college would be a massive relief if you survived to graduate 12th grade. But for now, you'd have to choose your gang and that fingertip.

My experience was at a Catholic High School which fostered perhaps the roughest gang of all: Nuns. Instead of priests or monks in charge, it was four Nuns that ruled our academic world. Freaks and Jocks have no chance against a group that wore wedding rings to represent they were married to Jesus. Are you going to mess with Jesus' old lady? If you did something repulsive, there's a chance the Principal Nun wouldn't merely dial up your parents, but make it a three-way conference call with Pope John Paul II. You want trouble? Have your mom answer the phone and hear a voice speaking Latin from Vatican City.

A greater nightmare is that instead of giving out demerits that would lead to after school detention, the nun would use her pull to have you stuck in Purgatory for a few more days. While that doesn't sound that bad, do you really want to spend your initial days in the afterlife stuck with a bunch of crying unbaptized babies and other people whining about how they thought their American Express Black Card would get them in the express lane to Heaven? You'd want to pray for deliverance, but that's talking to the Nun's husband behind her back. She's not going to appreciate that happening and he's not wanting to get an earful from her.

Rarely did Hollywood want to reflect the true nightmare of high school on the silver screen. They wanted to show all the fun like a propaganda film. Tonight's double feature reflects the raw brutality that existed in secondary education. *Class of Nuke 'Em High* and *Class of 1984* will make any junior high student consider just transferring straight to a juvenile youth prison to avoid the brutality of 12th Graders. This double feature is going into your permanent record.

Class of Nuke 'Em High

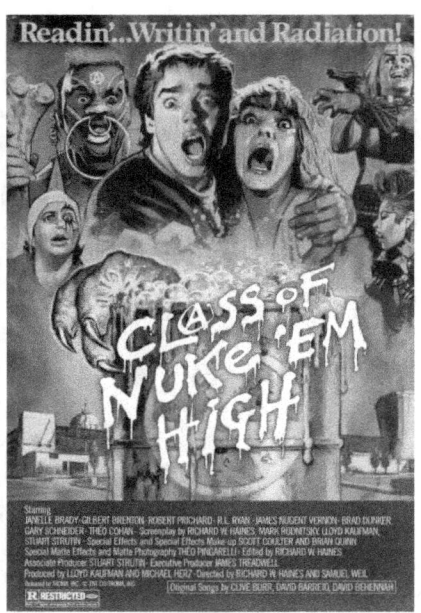

December 12, 1986

Troma Entertainment

Directed by Richard W. Haines & Lloyd Kaufman

Starring Janelle Brady, Gil Brenton, Robert Prichard, James Nugent Vernon, Gary Schneider, Gary Rosenblatt, Mary Taylor and Lauren Heather McMahon.

Rated R - 94 minutes

You can't find Tromaville, New Jersey on a map which is probably a good thing. Doubtful too many families are eager to pack up the Chevrolet Caprice Estate station wagon and hit the road for a weeklong vacation in the "Toxic Chemical Capital of the World." But millions have enjoyed the town's largest non-chemical export: Troma Entertainment.

This plucky indie company has been making and distributing movies since 1974 with the brain trust of Michael Herz and Lloyd Kaufman. Besides distributing films during their early years, they helped out on big Hollywood productions which is how Lloyd's name ends up associated with *Rocky, Saturday Night Fever* and *My Dinner With Andre*. These are three films that never played in Tromaville. There's no arthouse or cineplex inside the corrosive city borders.

Tromaville established itself in 1984 when health club janitor Melvin Ferd leaped out a second story window and planted himself inside a drum of industrial waste. Instead of melting away, Melvin transformed into the horribly disfigured yet powerful *Toxic Avenger*. People couldn't get enough of Tromaville as a city that didn't care about the EPA standards. It was a land that thought Love Canal was the right way to run a city. America wanted another visit to Tromaville and Lloyd Kaufman and Micheal Herz zipped up their yellow toxic waste safe suits to step deep into the city's public education system with *Class of Nuke 'Em High*.

President Richard Nixon signed off on the establishment of the Environmental Protection Authority, the Clean Water Act and Clean Air Act in the early 1970s. America had figured out the dirty secrets of the industrial revolution. Companies would randomly dump dangerous chemicals in rivers or property. Exhaust from factories was rather toxic and caused acid rain. People feared that pollution was going to snuff out the country by making the land inhabitable. How bad was it? The Cuyahoga River in Cleveland caught fire in 1969. How do you put out a fire on burning water? The smog from auto exhaust in Los Angeles was thicker than a studio's special effect smoke machine used to create London Fog in a Jack the Ripper flick. The new rules to reduce pollution were helping clean things up. Less rivers were burning.

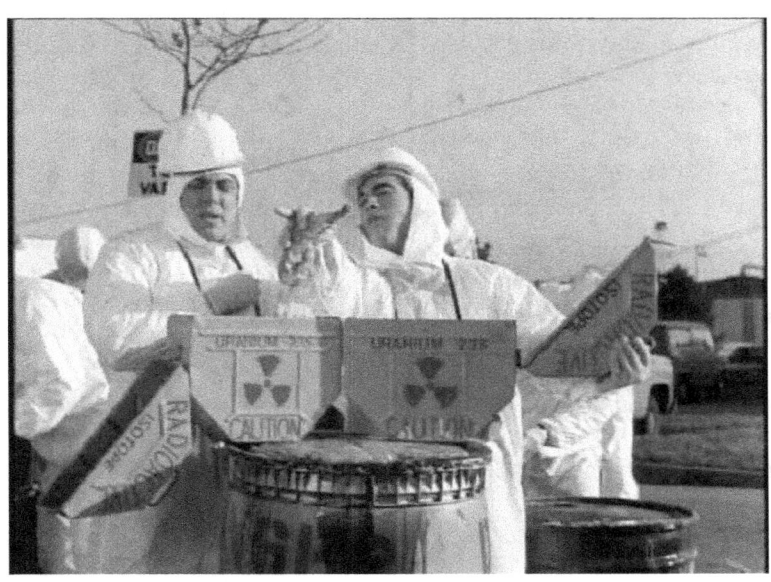

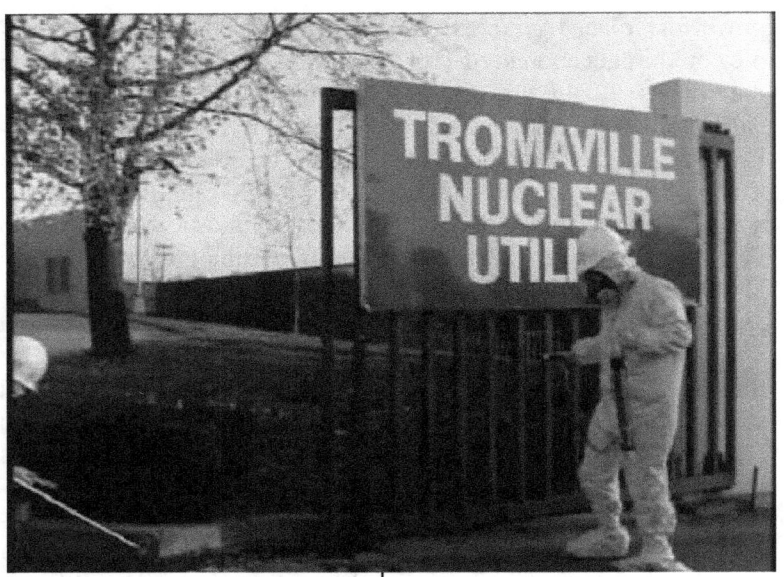

Naturally as things were getting better, industrialists kept protesting all the outrageous regulations. They missed the good old days when they could just dump their various toxic wastes in nearby creeks or a nasty patch of land outside the factory. They kept claiming they couldn't afford to scrub the air leaving their chimneys. People whined about various pollution devices installed in cars as reducing their fun behind the wheel. They missed leaded gas. And they found a savior in Ronald Reagan. The former star of *Death Valley Days* was depicted as a great outdoorsman riding horses and chopping wood. But he wasn't exactly all about preserving the beauty of nature. He ran for office complaining about government over regulation. When he was elected president, he immediately began to give his corporate backers a little relief. He slashed the budget of the Environmental Protection Agency. He made it harder for the agency to enforce the rules and penalize the culprits. His head of the EPA Anne Gorsuch constantly attempted to destroy the Clean Water and Air Acts. Reagan had no problem allowing private companies to set up oil, gas and mining operations on tens of millions of acres on Federal lands. He also tried his

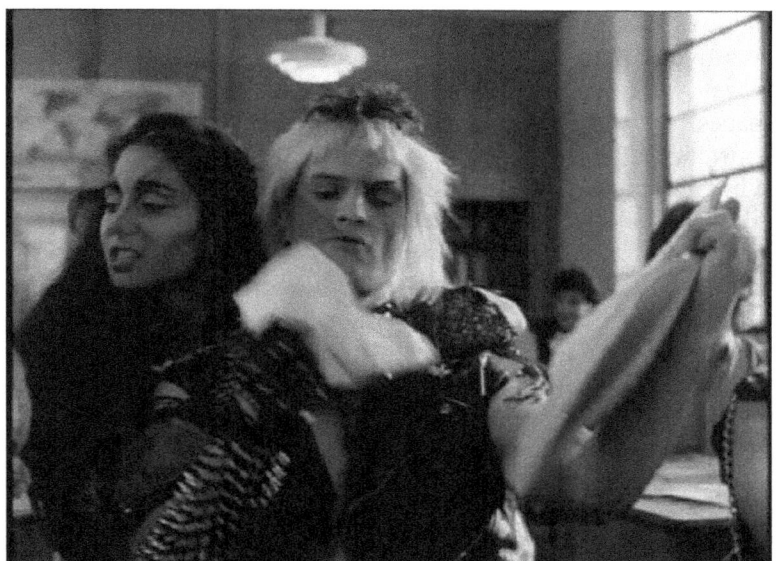

best to cut back on government oversight with the belief that private industry can watch itself. America was sold on the idea that corporations are extremely truthful about any disasters on their property or involving their toxic waste. Money came before quality of life in the '80s.

While the concept of a high school being next to a nuclear plant seems comical, there are quite a few cases of schools in danger zones. A study back in 2002 concluded that 1,200 public schools were located less than a mile from toxic waste dumps listed by the federal Superfund or state agencies. This study only included New York, California, New Jersey, Michigan and Massachusetts. There are still 45 states to go on that list. There are high schools in California that have working oil wells on their campus that might have been exposing students to harmful elements. Why would anyone build a school near these poisonous places? Because the land was cheap?

During the '80s, my college had to admit that they had been dumping toxic waste from the chemistry department and textile school on a patch of land near the football stadium where people tailgated. The excuse was there was no law against it at the time. The school didn't seem concerned about any of the alumni who had spent years grilling wieners over the toxic soil since those weren't the parking spaces reserved for the fat cat boosters.

While the concept of a Tromaville's shoddily maintained nuclear power plant being next door to a high school might seem like an absurdist joke; there had to be a few people in the audience pondering why they can't do this in their neighborhood. Tromaville at its core is a Libertarian dream where if you build it and let it fall into disrepair, who cares? You know the guy on the block who says, "Why does the government have any say about what I want to do on my property?" Why does the government need to have regulators and inspectors at a nuclear power plant? A little radioactive waste leaking into a nearby high school adds character to the students.

And what characters it adds to *Class of Nuke 'Em High*. Being a Troma film, nothing is underplayed on the screen. When it comes to having the radioactive waste ooze next door, it's nasty. Troma has it flow from the water fountain. In the fallout shelter basement, the nastiness drips onto a pair of teens getting freaky next to the boxes of ancient Civil Defense crackers. The effects of radioactivity are not quite scientifically accurate. One of the ways that Troma keeps production costs down is to not hire any technical advisors to keep things authentic. That money saved by not providing lunch to an educated know-it-all is spent on numerous gross effects. The toxic waste has turned Tromaville High's Honor Society into a group of barbarian punks that are selling weed to the kids. But it's not just any weed. They're scoring this fast-growing marijuana off workers at the nuclear power plant. Turns out it's extremely potent and will alter the students who didn't drink the water. This is *Cheech & Chong Smoke The China Syndrome*.

Like *The Toxic Avenger*, *Class of Nuke 'Em High* became a hit for Troma. The movie became a big favorite at mom and pop videostores. When they had that 2 Rentals for the Price of 1 Tuesdays at Videorama, there was a chance someone wanted to rent both VHS tapes to have an evening in Tromaville. The movie also played quite a bit in the '90s as part of USA's *Up All Night* with Rhonda Shear. She ran quite a bit of Troma films and even visited Lloyd Kaufman at Troma studios which turns out wasn't really in Tromaville, New Jersey. How successful was *Class of Nuke 'Em High*? They have so far made 4 sequels including *Class of Nuke 'Em High 2: Subhumanoid Meltdown* (1991), *Class of Nuke 'Em High 3: The Good, the Bad and the Subhumanoid* (1994), *Return to Nuke 'Em High Volume 1* (2014) and *Return to Return to Nuke 'Em High AKA Volume 2* (2017). The half-life of radioactive waste guarantees there will be *Nuke 'Em High* movies for thousands of years.

SOUNDTRACK NOTES: There is a soundtrack album, but fans had to wait a long time for the disc to hit the rack. Turns out the record wasn't released until 2014, but it was worth the wait since the vinyl had the same coloration as the radioactive toxic goo. Right off you get the "Troma Leader" aka the 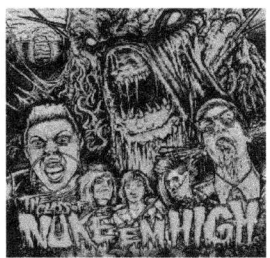 company's iconic credit song. Not only do you get Ethan & the Coup "Nuke 'Em High" theme song, but their "We Are One" which was supposed to be in the film. The band didn't get the song to Lloyd Kaufman in time. "Angel" is by GMT, a band of guys who split Motorhead. Swiss metalheads Stormbringer swing down with "Rock 'N' Roll Paradise." "Run For Your Life" was recorded by Stratus, a metal band made by ex-members of Uriah Heep, Praying Mantis and Iron Maiden. I haven't a clue who Praying Mantis were. David Behennah's "Emotional Refugee" really sums up so much of the movie. The big "get" for the soundtrack was "Much Too Much" by New Jersey's own The Smithereens. After working on *Class of Nuke 'Em High*, The Smithereens had a string of indie rock hits including "Only A Memory," "Behind the Wall of Sleep" and "A Girl Like You." In an odd twist, the producers also included Glen Acker & Michael Brody's "Class Of Nuke 'Em High Part 2 Theme." That'll get you eager for the sequel though. This is the perfect album for when you think the water at school tastes extra chunky and makes your teeth glow

.

Class of 1984

December 12, 1986

United Film Distribution Co.

Directed by Mark L. Lester

Starring Perry King, Merrie Lynn Ross, Lisa Langlois, Timothy Van Patten, Stefan Arngrim, Michael J. Fox and Roddy McDowall

Rated R - 94 minutes

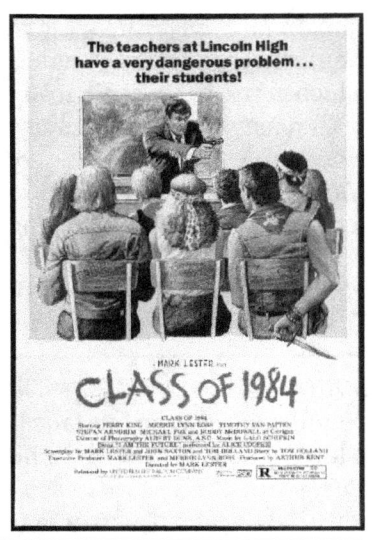

As an actual member of the Class of 1984, it's pretty badass to be able to say that in a crowd. There hadn't been too many Class of (insert numbers here) that struck fear into people. Class of 1969 got plenty of snickers whenever an elderly principal said '69 during an assembly. Class of '76 sounds like a great Bicentennial souvenir. But thanks to George Orwell and his book about a dystopian world, 1984 was seriously ominous. Big Brother was coming and we were going to greet him during our ring ceremony. The only other class that could make people fear them is Class of 1999 since that's the year the Moon flew away from the Earth in *Space: 1999*. Although by the time 1999 rolled around, not many people were talking about the science fiction TV show that starred Martin Landau and Barbara Bain. All people cared about in 1999 was seeing *Star Wars Episode 1 - The Phantom Menace*...that was until they saw it.

Likewise, being a part of the Class of 1984 sounded impressive until you sat down and read George Orwell's novel. It was a rather downbeat story that features a guy having a cage with rats strapped to his face. This was a tough and depressing read even in the Cliff's Notes version. Making

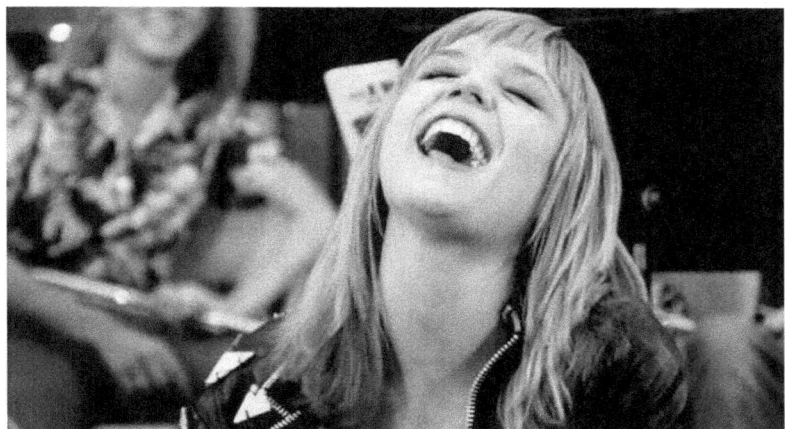

matters worse for those of us who'd rather digest the film in under two hours was the lack of a movie before our graduation. Michael Radford's movie of *1984* didn't come out in America until March 22, 1985 although it played New York and Los Angeles at the end of 1984 to qualify for the Oscars. It received ZERO nominations because who wanted to watch *1984* in 1985?

The makers of *Class of 1984* didn't make that foolish mistake. They released the film right at the end of the summer of 1982 just in time for the back-to-school crowd. The real Class of 1984 were assuming their role as upperclassmen so we were ready to flex our new muscles as a new batch of lowly freshmen arrived. Also, by putting the movie out long before 1984, *Class of 1984* would be readily available on home video including Beta. By senior year, the tale of destructive honor students would be on cable. By the time it played through the release windows, you'd swear Peter Stegman (*The White Shadow*'s Timothy Van Patten) was your prom date and Andrew Norris (*Riptide*'s Perry King) conducted the band during graduation. When your children ask you about your biggest memory of 12th grade, you'll talk about the time those punk rockers went on a murder spree.

Punks always meant trouble in movies and TV. They quickly became the new savages when it became less hip in Hollywood to have Apaches attack settlements and burn down the forts. While punk took root in New York City during the mid-70s, it wasn't perceived as violent and angry with bands like the Ramones, Television and Blondie being more into their music than causing chaos. This all changed when English teens embraced this new attitude and shed off the conventions of Pub Rock for the colorful wildlife. America got its first big scare of punk rock when the Sex Pistols went on their infamous tour of the South in 1978. Stories of the ugliness inside the shows spread like a forest fire across the country. Lock up your children, Johnny Rotten was going to destroy humanity. The audiences weren't there to enjoy the music, but to inflict damage on each other with their early slam pits. There were reports of people with mohawks spitting all over the place and on each other. The punks were mean and ready to bust crap up. These troubled teens wore ripped clothes, leather, chains, outrageous facial piercings and multi-color hair. They were worse than beatniks! And Hollywood quickly used them as their new band guys because there was no way they could complain about their depiction in film and TV. Marlon Brando wasn't going to send Sid Vicious onto the stage to accept his Oscar as a protest. If punks complained, they were just whiny punks. Nobody's cultural traditions and rituals were being mocked and exploited. Nobody that mattered to filmmakers. Plus because of the outlandish outfits and makeup worn by punks, directors could stick feathers in their hair and wipe war paint on their cheeks to get their new Apaches.

Parents around the country cringed when *Quincy M.E.*'s "Next Stop, Nowhere" episode aired. The big murder is at a Mayhem show when during violent slam dancing, a kid gets stabbed in the neck with an ice pick. Quincy wants to know what's wrong with the kids? Why are they so nihilistic and have to wear so much product in their hair? Why wasn't the music happier like the stuff Mitch Miller made in the days of black and white radio? At the end of the episode Quincy and Sam don't sharpen up their elbows and jump in the pit at a Fear show. Mostly your parents get to question why you have a Germs logo painted on your old jeans jacket. The punks also showed up on *CHiPs* in "Battle of the Bands." Jon and Ponch investigate a punk band that's stealing stuff. The positive part of the episode is having a fake band called Pain perform "I Dig Pain" as the slam dancing overtakes the club. The crowd tears up the bar in a violent frenzy. This episode got a lot of parents to fear their children wanting to go to an "All Ages Show."

A real view of the Los Angeles punk scene was found in Penelope Spheris' *The Decline and Fall of Western Civilization*. A documentary about the various bands and kids in the underground of Tinseltown. The film grabbed legendary performances from Black Flag, Circle Jerks, Fear, Germs, X and Catholic Discipline in their native habitats. The film upset LAPD chief Darryl Gates so much that he demanded the movie never be shown in his precious city again. Punk rock was meant to be feared. *Saturday Night Live* was nearly destroyed when Fear was booked as the musical guest on an episode with Donald Pleasence (*Halloween*). They let punkers on the stage to skank around and smash into each other. It was not the passive response usually given during the musical segment. Even John Belushi returned to the show to stage dive into the mayhem. This made Halloween night in 1981 truly fearful to parents across America.

Although having hung out in my small city's punk rock scene during the '80s, there was little to be feared by most punkers besides tripping over their personalized skateboards. The weekends were spent drinking cheap Olympia beer and Boone's Farm Strawberry Hill while hanging out on rooftops. There was a low budget peaceful nature to most events. Things could get nasty when a hardcore band hit the town. You never wanted to be at a show full of jarheads from Camp Lejeune. The young Marines were eager to show off their fighting skills in the pit. They were all elbows and knees as they circulated in front of the stage. Even worse were the kids who identified as Skinheads. Their shaved heads, matching "working class" outfits and testosterone heavy attitude was rather scary. They came off as a really angry cult. If you ever want to see a nightmarish film check out Russell Crowe in *Romper Stomper*. The simple rule was if you were at a party and spotted two or more skinheads in the living room, you'd back out the kitchen door and head home. Nothing good was going to happen that night.

Even the most "compassionate" of punk rock movies had the punkers depicted as dangerous characters even when they're supposed to be comical. *Rock 'n' Roll High School* ended with the Ramones and PJ Soles destroying Vince Lombardi High School. She even lured the preppy Vince Van Patten (*The Bionic Boy*) into being a crazed anarchist. He's not nearly as violent and vile as Timothy Van Patten in tonight's film. And for clarification purposes, Vince and Timothy are about the same age, but they are not brothers. Vince is the son of Dick Van Patten (*Eight Is Enough*). What's the deal with Timothy? He's really Dick's half-brother which makes him Vince's half Uncle. Is your mind blown like a mouse at listening to the Ramones? Timothy is now an Emmy Award winning director working on HBO's finest shows including *The Sopranos, The Wire, Deadwood, Boardwalk Empire, Game of Thrones* and *Sex and the City*. Pretty good for a punk.

Were the punk rockers so fearsome in their leather and asymmetrical haircuts or just Hollywood hype? The people society really had to fear in the '80s turned out to be the Preppies. They're the ones that coldly calculated how to destroy America with their various schemes like junk bonds, subprime mortgages, Roth IRAs and avocado toast. Preppies are the reason why our lives are being constantly monitored. Everything we do has been transformed into a way to track us and sell us out to Wall Street companies.

Their social media companies do their best to manipulate users into doing stupid things in order to make them think they're being creative. Did you "plank" or Harlem Shake? Have you done your cover of a Tik-Tok video? Or joined in on a foolish challenge like eating ghost peppers or laundry detergent gel packs? Why did you do it? Did you crave the likes and the hits? Was it worth it to be one of the millions who made that video? Do you feel pretty stupid that you got caught up in the trendiness of online assimilation? Preppies will soon have kids going on various websites to post their selfie shot viral #RatCageOnFaceChallenge videos. Preppies are the reason why this country feels like *1984* in 2020. Don't blame the punks.

SOUNDTRACK NOTES: For some unknown reason, *Class of 1984* doesn't appear to have an official soundtrack release or even an EP. "I Am the Future" gives us an amazing collaboration of Alice Cooper singing to the music of composer Lalo Schifrin. Some countries did get a 45 single release of the song But doesn't appear to be true in the USA. Fear gets to strut its stuff with "Let's Have a War" and "Fresh Flesh." Teenage Head also doubles up with "Ain't Got No Sense" and "Little Boxes." Even Timothy Van Patten could have had his version of Stegman's Concerto on the vinyl. This would have been the record to play when you want to scare the substitute teacher in homeroom.

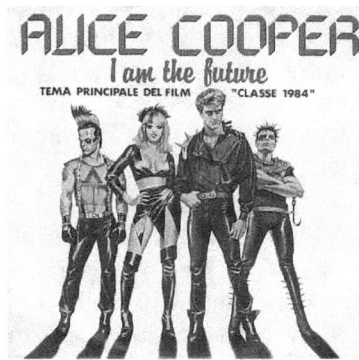

Friday - May 22

No Small Affair 7:00 p.m.
One Crazy Summer 9:15 p.m.

One Night Only! Demi Moore Sings!

The US Army admitted they had found the remains of UFO near the desert town of Roswell, New Mexico on July 8th, 1947. The military put out a press release describing the crashed flying disc. Newspapers across the country ran with news of government confirmation of aliens. Immediately afterward officers at the Roswell Army Air Field denied it was an alien invasion and the wreckage was merely a weather balloon. Similarly, there are reports that on November 11, 1962, Demi Moore was born in Roswell, New Mexico. The military has yet to deny this event ever took place. Demi Moore can't be explained away as a weather balloon.

Once I hung out with Oscar winning screenwriter Ted Tally. He spoke of working on the script for *The Juror* with Demi Moore. She kept wanting to make her character more vulnerable. But Tally was having an issue with that since Demi was the fiercest person he'd ever met. This is a writer who found the lovable side to Hannibal Lecter in his screen adaptation of *The Silence of the Lambs*. Demi Moore was like that girl you knew in college who was sexy, fun to hang around and would get her revenge on you for wronging her.

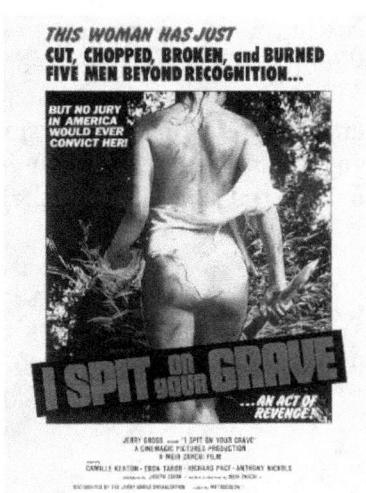

Her first impact in the movie business was having her sweaty and barely clothed backside being on the VHS box for *I Spit*

- Page 1 -

On Your Grave. She wasn't in the film and received no credit as the model. But plenty of teenage boys rented that tape in hopes that the girl on the cover was doing the spitting. She did appear and fought strange creatures in *Parasite*. Later she played the daughter that didn't sleep with Michael Caine in *Blame It On Rio*. She truly entered the universe of '80s teenagers with *No Small Affair* that featured Jon Cryer, E.G. Daily, Tim Robbins and Jennifer Tilly. Then she graduated to *St. Elmo's Fire* with the core of the Brat Pack.

While many of her peers had career that had them doing indie films and TV series, Demi Moore kept pushing her stardom. She was not part of those "Where Are They Now" features in the '90s about the Brat Pack actors. Demi was everywhere for quite some time. She was showing off her baby bump or posing in a latex paint suit on the cover of major magazines. She came out of *St. Elmo's Fire* with a lead in *About Last Night...* The film was supposed to be called David Mamet's *Sexual Perversity in Chicago*, but that wouldn't look good on a suburban marquee. The title was toned down for fear of the cops raiding the theater as if they were running a Christy Canyon film. Demi started the '90s right with *Ghost* as she mourned for the spectral Patrick Swayze. She handled a lot of military truth with Tom Cruise in *A Few Good Men*. Robert Redford was willing to pay a million bucks to sleep with her for *Indecent Proposal*. She stripped down for *Striptease* and packed on the muscle for *G.I. Jane*. She made bank as a producer of the *Austin Powers* trilogy. She even proved a worthy enemy for the second *Charlie's Angels* film. She did so much and yet we pretty much forget that in her early screen years, directors wanted us to view her as a singer. Which made sense since she had a bit of stage presence and a rasp in her voice that made it seem like she could lead a bluesy rock band a lot better than her one-time husband Bruce Willis. Did you survive Willis' *The Return of Bruno*? Tonight, we bring you both of her films where she's the headline attraction at clubs. Was she ready to rock a movie audience?

Having an actor sing in a movie was why sound was wired into the motion picture houses. *The Jazz Singer* was all about getting people hot for Al Jolson busting out "My Mammy." They studios didn't stick speakers in theaters just so you could hear Shakespearean dialogue. A hot song from a movie was a great way to publicize the release. People could hear the tune on the radio and be eager to drop cash at the box office when the film arrived at the local Bijou. This was the game plan for decades. Musical numbers proved to be an extra revenue stream during a time when there was no home video to sell six months after opening weekend. You couldn't own the movie, but the soundtrack album would look so nice next to your record player. The movie industry went crazy putting the teenagers' favorite singers into movies so they could tap into that sweet soundtrack cash. Early on they gave us Bing Crosby, Doris Day, Dean Martin, Frank Sinatra and Elvis Presley. During the '60s, the *Beach Party* films made sure when the fun in the sun was getting exciting that Frankie Avalon and Annette Funicello broke out in song instead of doing what teenagers really want to do at the beach. The Beatles made the musical film so mod with *Hard Days Night* and *Help!* The '70s gave us the full disco explosion with Donna Summer winning an Oscar for the classic "Last Dance" in *Thank God It's Friday*. Olivia Newton John and John Travolta gave us "Summer Nights" in *Grease*. The trend of singing on the screen wouldn't stop in the '80s although it was a bit more motivated and less fantastical.

The era started out right with *Fame* as Irene Cara scored major hits with the theme song "Fame" and "Out Here On My Own." She played a singing student at the performing arts high school so it wasn't unnatural for her to break out in song. Cara would score another movie hit with "Flashdance... What A Feeling" that also won her an Oscar. But she wasn't in *Flashdance*. Diane Lane became a punk sensation in *Ladies and Gentlemen, the Fabulous Stains* before returning to clutch the microphone in *Streets of Fire*. Justin Bateman (*Family Ties*) became a rocker girl playing beach gigs with her band in *Satisfaction*. E.G. Daily was singing at the dance in *Better Off Dead* after starring in *Valley Girl* and *No Small Affair*. Madonna was merely the singer at a club in *Vision Quest*, but became the third biggest name in the cast.

The relationship between a soundtrack and movie changed a few years into the decade with the arrival of MTV. No longer did a film need musical moments involving the cast in order to promote the songs on the soundtrack with the arrival of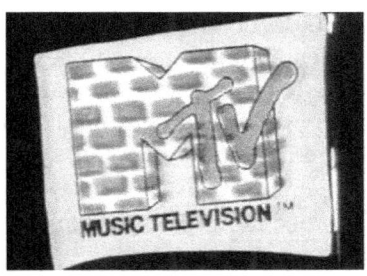
the music video. Directors and producers didn't have to come up with awkward excuse scenes to get the movie to a concert or have a notable band play a small club. They could make a music video featuring the singer, a few cast members and tons of clips from the movie. The video was a great way to sell the movie and the soundtrack without messing with the plot. And when it went into heavy rotation on MTV, it was an infomercial to lure the kids into the theater and the record store. If Martha Quinn thought the movie looked cool, '80s teens were eager to buy a ticket. Berlin could take your breath away without appearing on the deck of the aircraft carrier in *Top Gun*. Orchestral Manoeuvres in the Dark didn't have to play the prom in *Pretty in Pink* to win your hearts with "If You Leave." Simple Minds didn't have to accidentally show up in the Shermer High Library to make sure "Don't You Forget About Me" was remembered from *The Breakfast Club*. This also meant that producers and directors no longer had to make a movie with a character in a band to be able to tap into the MTV gravy train of promotion. But luckily for us the directors and producers of *No Small Affair* and *One Crazy Summer* wanted Demi Moore to be a singer and not merely a model who likes to listen to pop songs on the radio.

Casting Demi as a singer wasn't farfetched since she had a history with music. Her last name came from a short marriage to singer Freddy Moore. She was born Demi Guynes back in mysterious Roswell, New Mexico. She co-wrote "It's Not A Rumour" for Freddy's band The Nu-Kats. The song isn't exactly a Big '80s megahit. The video did get played a bit when MTV didn't mind running videos that weren't from major labels. Demi Moore prominently appears in the video with a side ponytail like an audition tape for *Napoleon Dynamite*. She struts, teases and pouts around the band. We'll be showing the video before each screening tonight so you have "It's Not A Rumor" stuck in your head for the entire weekend. Jan De Bont (director of photography for *Private Lessons*) shot the video and captured the young Demi in her early '80s glory.

The one thing Demi doesn't do around the Nu-Kats is sing. And not to burst your dream, but you don't need to go digging around used record stores in search of rare Japanese imports of Demi Moore albums. This isn't like Phoebe Cates, Mare Winningham or Molly Ringwald. During her marriage to Freddy Moore, Demi did record a five-track demo in the hopes of landing a contract with RCA records (the same label as Elvis). They even brought in Stan Lynch, the drummer from Tom Petty and the Heartbreakers to keep the beat. But no dice on getting signed.

You would think with dreams of a recording career, she'd use these two roles to finally get on vinyl. This didn't work out completely. Her voice in *No Small Affair* belongs to Chrissy Faith. And the movie didn't try to cover up the truth since Chrissy Faith's performance on the soundtrack led to Faith getting a Grammy nomination for Best Female Rock Vocalist. So that's not Demi, but an artist rendering of what Demi would sound like. At least in *One Crazy Summer*, we get to hear Demi's true voice when she sings "Don't Look Back." But when she returns for "Take A Bow," you're hearing Jaime Segel's voice. Segel would later be heard singing in *Betsy's Wedding* starring Molly Ringwald and Ally Sheedy. Demi would get a chance to sing once more in Emilio Estevez's *Bobby* (2006) when she busted out an unconventional version of "Louie Louie."

There's no *Demi Moore Sings* cassette for sale in the concession stand. Tonight, we will imagine that Demi Moore was a singing sensation and the world wanted her on stage.

No Small Affair

November 9, 1984

Columbia Pictures

Directed by Jerry Schatzberg

Starring **Jon Cryer,** *Demi Moore, George Wendt, E. G. Daily, Jeffrey Tambor, Tim Robbins, Kene Holliday & Jennifer Tilly*

Rated R - 102 minutes

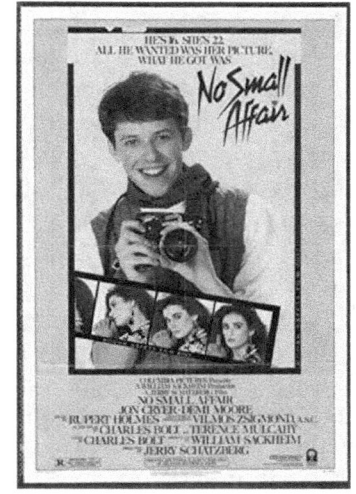

Now that we're deep in the digital age, you probably don't think about the price of photography anymore. When you get in the mood to take photos, you pull out your smartphone and snap away without a care in the world. It feels limitless when you want to capture the perfect shot. But this wasn't the case in the '80s. Charles Cumming (*Pretty In Pink*'s Jon Cryer) lines up the perfect shot and gets upset when Laura Victor (Demi Moore of *St. Elmo's Fire*) and her friend get into the frame on the wharf in San Francisco. Today we ask, why does that matter so much? "Just keep snapping away" is our 21st mindset. But in 1984, Charles had 24 frames in the camera. His vision for the shot was screwed up. He doesn't have the cash for screw ups. He's stuck with a photo that he didn't seek to capture. Luckily his frustrations melt away when he sees the photo of Laura. Otherwise, we don't have a movie.

Photography in the '80s was rather costly even on the simplest terms. You had to buy the film that went inside the camera. After you took all the pictures, you paid to develop the negative and then you paid to have the prints made. Not to mention the price of a flashbulb that only worked once. Every time you pressed the red button and heard a click, you were also hearing a cash register go "cha-ching." And you weren't guaranteed a brilliant photo when you opened up the envelope at the K Mart photo center. This was the era when you lived with a sense of impending doom when your father would flip through the new photos and get angry because someone made a stupid face or had their eyes closed. There are probably quite a few people who break out in a cold sweat when a nostalgia website runs pictures of the little yellow roof Fotomat kiosks that sat in parking lots and promised next day photo processing. You had one day to sweat it out that dad missed your rabbit ears flashed over your little sister's head. The ominous parking lot promised a "safe space" for the back of dad's hand to come over the seat if you ruined a picture. Every snapshot was precious to dad and mom had his back on this one. As far as they were concerned; they were Ansel Adams and Diane Arbus and you were the idiot who ruined their upcoming show at MOMA because you stuck your tongue out.

Even if you had your own Kodak Instamatic, the act of taking a photograph was serious business. You didn't just take hundreds of pictures of you and your buddies hanging out behind the Tastee-Freez. First off was the fact that processing the film could easily take a dent out of your birthday money. It was easy to understand dad's anger when you discovered a photo was ruined because someone turned their head away when you said, "Say Cheese!" You wanted them to pose as if they were stuck inside a Rembrandt painting. You had a secondary

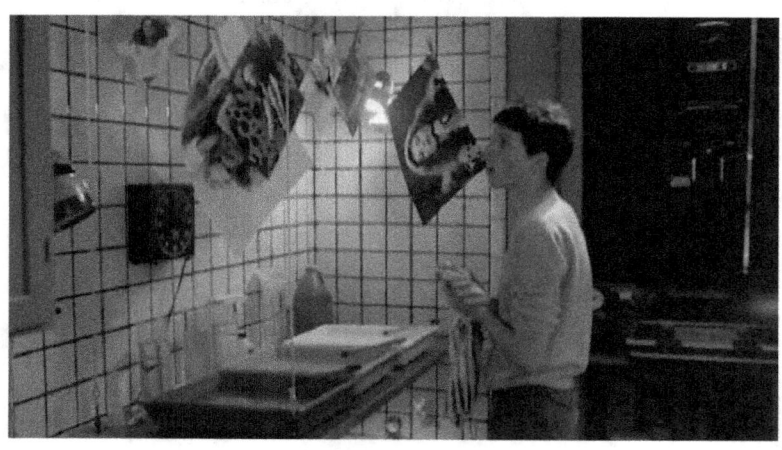

fear that your thumb blocked the lens since the viewfinder on an Instamatic did not go through the lens. If you ordered double prints, you had to pay for the mistake twice. The biggest nightmare was that the technician that processed the film spotted something illegal amongst your friends in the printed photograph. If the tech was the guy at your family's drugstore, they might tip off your mother that your friends are up to bad things. Worse was the tech calling the cops to report that you and your friends are underaged drinking, smoking the reefer or exposing their private parts. There was a reason why your local weekly entertainment rag ran classified ads for places that offered "discreet film processing." Sure, it cost a little more than the Fotomat, but you weren't going to get grilled by Officer Friendly in front of your parents as to which of your friends owned the bong. This doesn't happen in the digital age until you decide to post such a photo on your social media site and forget that Aunt Edna is part of your circle of friends. And then you have to worry about Aunt Edna wanting to get hooked up since her dealer is unloading stems and seeds in her package.

If a kid was lucky and had a bit of money, they could build their own darkroom in the basement bathroom and learn the secrets of photography. If you couldn't pull it off at home, there was a chance to explore it at high school with the photography club that was usually attached to the Yearbook. This was a great way to learn how to take pictures and get someone else to pay for the film. If you were lucky, the school would have a tiny darkroom squeezed in a broom closet instead of sending the film off to get processed. Most of the time, you still had to burn a pile of birthday money to buy a camera and a few lenses. The school didn't trust you to be responsible enough to keep track of a Nikon. These kids had the advantage when it came to working on the photography staff of the college newspaper. This is where they stepped up into a truly dedicated darkroom space with photo paper and chemicals paid for with your student activities fees. It was tough to break into my college newspaper's photography department because it was dominated by kids who had been snapping

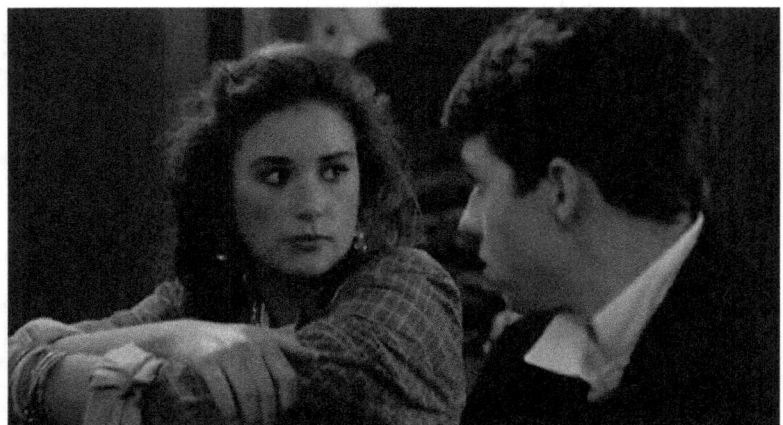

away for years. They had parents that didn't freak out if they touched the F Stop.

There were ways to sneak onto the photography staff. For me it was being an entertainment writer who covered the more obscure bands that were playing nightclubs. Photographers fought to cover The Rolling Stones at the football stadium. But They Might Be Giants at the Brewery when the band didn't hit the stage until 11 p.m. didn't get any takers. I borrowed a newspaper camera, grabbed a few rolls of black and white film, received a few tips on settings and away I went to shoot the show. Later one of the photographers took pity on me and gave lessons on how to not merely process my negatives, but make prints. In the dark and under the red light, it was like an alchemist sharing his secret on how to turn chemicals into images. Every step was a series of surprises as shapes showed up on the negative roll. Eventually a white sheet of paper would soak in the chemicals and become that moment from the show. This was magic at my fingertips. I also learned to never eat fried chicken after using the fixer. Your fingertips needed to be thoroughly cleaned and not merely rinsed. There was also a massive amount of heartbreak when I unwound the negative from spindle and saw nothing in the frames. What went wrong was hard to tell. There were so many things that could have gone wrong from camera settings to accidentally exposed film to my fault. All I had were memories as I accepted the blankness on a strip of 35mm.

There isn't the same anxious thrill in digital photography as all pictures can be immediately checked to see what the camera or smartphone captured. There's not so much magic as reliability in the digital process.

The only thing as magical as developing film is making a movie. There's always a sense that at any moment a film's production is going to go up in flames. From pre-production jitters that the money is going to fall through to production jitters that the money is going to fall through to the post-production jitters that the money is going to fall through, a film's future is always in jeopardy. *No Small Affair* suffered through a bumpy ride getting onto the screen although it wasn't because the money fell through.

Originally the movie was being made in 1981 with Martin Ritt as the director. He was best known for making *Hud* with Paul Newman. After directing *Norma Rae* and *Back Roads* with Sally Fields, the duo started on *No Small Affair* as their third collaboration. Sally was going to be the nightclub singer. To play the role of the 16-year-old high school photographer, they had cast the completely unknown at the time Matthew Broderick (*Ferris Bueller's Day Off*). While it's hard to imagine, Broderick hadn't even started his run Off-Broadway in Harvey Feinstein's *Torch Song Trilogy* and was a few years away from the Tony for Neil Simon's *Brighton Beach Memoirs*. This was going to be Broderick's big break in movies. What went wrong? Director Ritt had a heart attack that shutdown the production. While there was talk of bringing in a replacement director, the movie was abandoned and Broderick returned to Manhattan to find success on the Great White Way before breaking out on the silver screen with *WarGames* in 1983. Producer William Sackheim wasn't willing to walk away from the project and take a complete

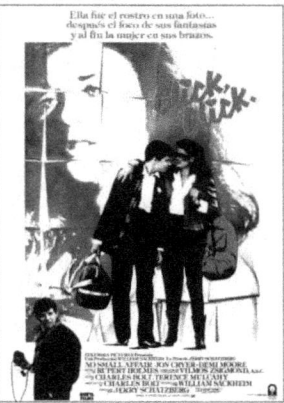

loss. He eventually got the production back on the rails with Jerry Schatzberg in the director's chair. Schatzberg started his career strong with *Puzzle of a Downfall Child* and *The Panic in Needle Park* and after *No Small Affair*, he'd make the sensational *Street Smart* with Morgan Freeman as a pimp out to pull the cape on Superman Christopher Reeve. The cast changed since it'd been a while since the red light flashed. Broderick was rather busy at this point in his career. They cast Jon Cryer who had replaced Broderick in *Torch Song Trilogy*. Broderick still has a slight presence in the film since Charles and his family live on Broderick Street which is a real street in San Francisco. It's athe same street where the family on *Full House* supposedly lived. *No Small Affair* is considered Cryer's first film, but that's only because Robert Altman's *O.C. and Stiggs* was still stuck in post-production after being shot in 1983. We'll have more about that movie on Saturday night. This was Cryer's first film to make it to the cineplex. Sally Field was no longer the singer. She was off making *Places In the Heart* that won her the Oscar because we can't deny the fact that we like her—right now, we like her! The replacement was Ellen Barkin (*The Big Easy*). But late into pre-production, a change was made and Demi Moore was brought to play Laura. Barkin ironically had just made a film called *Enormous Changes at the Last Minute*. Luckily for Barkin, she would end up in the theaters around this time in *The Adventures of Buckaroo Banzai Across the 8th Dimension*.

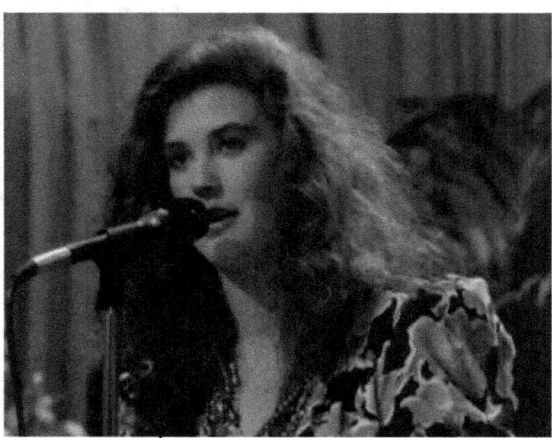

After all the perseverance to get the movie into theater, *No Small Affair* didn't make a lot at the box office. Even with the promise of an R Rated love scene between Demi and Jon Cryer in a bed that looks like it starred on *Love American Style*, the teens didn't flock. The film did well on VHS after Demi Moore hit her stride in *St. Elmo's Fire*. Just like in photography, it all matters when you press the button and you don't know what you really have until you drive away from the Fotomat.

SOUNDTRACK NOTES: Most of the music for *No Small Affair* was written by Rupert Holmes. You might remember him best for the Yacht Rock classic "Escape (The Piña Colada Song)" that ruled the marinas and single bars in 1979. He also did "Him." This music is perfect for seducing an old bluesy 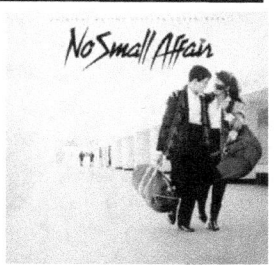 singer. Demi Moore doesn't actually sing on the soundtrack. Her voice belongs to Chrissy Faith. The album features Faith singing "My Funny Valentine," "Itchin' For a Fight" and "Hot Headed." While the record didn't sell blockbuster numbers, Faith was Grammy nominated for Best Rock Female Vocal. The fact that Demi came on so late to the production might also explain why she didn't sing on the soundtrack since Faith's tracks must have been recorded early in pre-production for Ellen Barkin (or even Sally Field) to lipsync. There's a bit of hard rock with MTV staples Twisted Sister giving us "I'll Never Grow Up" and "Shoot 'Em Down." Plus, you get a touch of Zebra with "Hard Livin' Without You." In a punky move we get "Eiffel Tower" from Malcolm McLaren and the McLarenettes. Malcolm was the manager for the Sex Pistols before he decided he could do this music thing too. The love theme "Love Makes You Blind" is sung by Fiona who would go on to play Bob Dylan's love interest in *Hearts of Fire* and Don Johnson's fling on *Miami Vice*. The record sounds mixed for a marathon dark room session when you're waiting for the hands of the giant countdown clock to let you know the negatives have developed.

One Crazy Summer

August 8, 1986

Warner Brothers

Directed by Savage Steve Holland

Starring **John Cusack, Demi Moore, Curtis Armstrong, Bobcat Goldthwait, Joel Murray, William Hickey, John Matuszak, Rich Little, Jeremy Piven & Taylor Negron**

Rated PG - 89 minutes

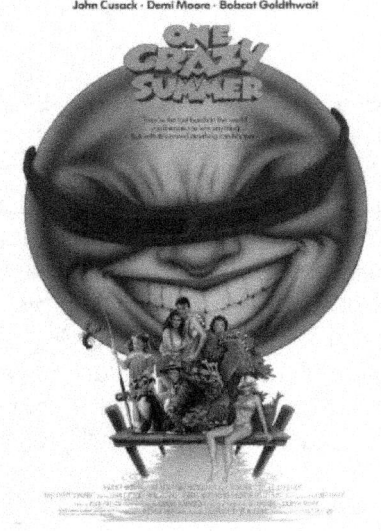

Are you ready for the beach? During the late '70s when you were coming to the end of elementary school, odds were good that your local UHF station would bust out a week's worth of the *Beach Party* movies in the afternoon before reruns of *Gilligan's Island*. For two hours from Monday to Friday, you received an amazing fantasy of the fun and sun that awaited you at the coast. As soon as you'd turn into a teenager, you could load up a modified jalopy, surf all day, hang by the fire on the beach all night and rock out to Dick Dale for days. That's what Frankie Avalon and Annette Funicello did. And if the waves broke right, you could hook up with Jody McCrea, John Ashley, Candy Johnson or Deborah Walley. Everybody knew Frankie and Annette belonged together so don't even fantasize about that. This seemed like the dream life that awaited you until that horrifying day when you realized that you were still going to stay at the beach with your parents until further notice. They weren't ready to let you run free as the high tide rolled in. Even though you were old enough to order from the adult menu, you were still a kid in their eyes.

You weren't going to be able to enjoy the beach until you could arrive with a bunch of high school or college pals and pretend to be your own parental supervision. The party could get out of hand without your parents' watchful eyes. Excess was expected. There was a reason why bars had Dwarf Tossing nights. I remember one trip to Myrtle Beach when I drank a cup of orange juice and felt it tasted funny. And indeed, it did, but not because the citrus drink had passed its Best Used By date. The sunshine in a glass was lacking vodka. You didn't mind pushing your boundaries at the beach because for the most part everything seemed temporary. Everybody was just down for the week and most of the people working at the beach seemed to only be there for the season. This was why Spring Break in Daytona was pure hedonism. You hunted for hookups during the wet t-shirt and beer bong contests. You didn't have too much of a worry about seeing those people in October.

What are the chances during a college beach trip with pals that you'll meet someone, fall in love, get married after graduating from college, live around the world, have three kids and be together for over 50 years? They're pretty good if you're my parents. But for other people? Teens were just looking for a beach bang that they can brag about when they get back home. You wanted a "What I Did on My Summer Vacation Story" that could be

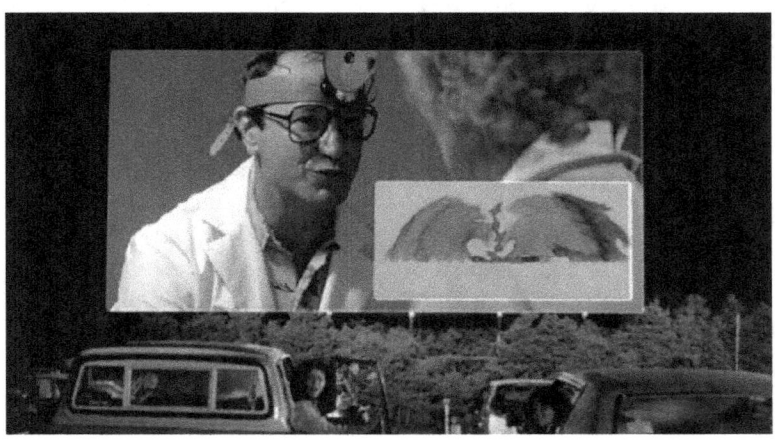

printed in the *Penthouse Forum* and not presented to a third-grade class.

The '80s had quite a few films that updated the teens going to the beach theme that didn't stick with the morality of the *Beach Party* films. These jiggle by the sea flicks went all out for that sweet R-rating. The plots let the kids in Iowa know that there was a reason to buy a ticket for Florida and not merely hang out in the swimming hole by the hog lagoon. The films were rather inexpensive to make since most of the wardrobe was bottles of Hawaiian Tropic Suntan Oil. Oh yes, it was during that time when we wanted to be extra crispy from staying out in the sun. People didn't talk about Sunblock in the '80s. Suntan lotion was designed to turn your skin various shades of leather. Nobody wanted to be a great white whale on the beach. The plots might have varied between the films, but for the most part, the teen viewers didn't care as long as there was plenty of bikini action and an occasional top that comes loose and is abducted by a seagull. You may ponder why teens went to a movie about people lathered up in suntan lotion and tiny swimsuits when they could have just gone to the beach and seen it in the flesh or even hit the local pool for such a carnal view? Turns out that most people in swimsuits get uncomfortable and sometimes extremely angry if you keep staring at them for a long time. They might kick sand in the face of the person who keeps staring where their eyes aren't. In a movie theater, nobody gets angry if a teen fixates on how a bikini top defies gravity.

Spring Break was a massive success as it raked in $24 million on a budget that might have been $4 million. What was the plot? Two nerds go down to Fort Lauderdale, Florida for Spring Break and get lucky. It had an R rating. Do you need any more storyline or did you already order a copy of this gem? *Hardbodies* had a twist with a young guy helping a few middle-aged men learn how to get laid by tanned ladies at the beach. *Hardbodies* had always been a special film to me since back in college, actress Monique Gabrielle dropped by our student radio station during a promotional tour. I have fond memories of her entering the control room with her perfectly coiffed blond hair and a smile that made me melt. She wore a bright red tanktop and silver parachute pants. She was prime 1984 and the image of her still dazzles in my mind. When she laughed at my joke, she snatched my heart. I wanted her to take me away to Hollywood or at least proposition me to guide her back to the hotel for a little room service. She wrapped up talking on the radio and left without me. Although I'd see more of her after tracking down her *Penthouse* magazine Pet of the Month issue (December 1982) and later renting *Emmanuelle V*. I nearly cried when she appeared as the major temptation to Tom Hanks in *Bachelor Party*. Her silver parachute pants left their mark on my soul. Over a decade later, I shared this memory with Mark Griffiths, the director of *Hardbodies* when he visited the Moving Image Archive and hung out at my office. He smiled and only had kind words about Monique Gabrielle. Oddly enough I had a startling revelation a few years ago while looking up the movie on IMDB.com. Turns out Monique Gabrielle wasn't in *Hardbodies*. She was at NC State promoting *Hot Moves*. That film was about four guys at the beach wanting to get laid so you can understand my confusion. Although I'm not sure why Griffiths thought she was promoting *Hardbodies* when I told him the story. He probably was being kind. Ultimately this experience proves my theory that most '80s beach films have the same plot: People Wanting to Get Laid at the Beach. And who am I to com-

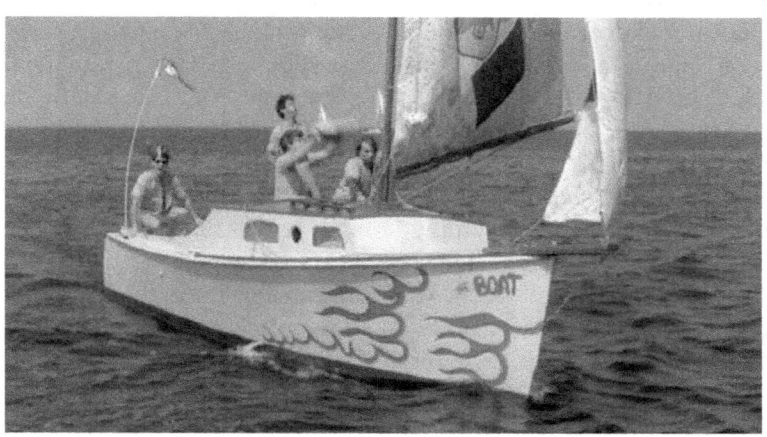

plain about this box office winning formula? Although one film that dared to go against the formula was *One Crazy Summer* which was extremely crazy since the movie had a PG Rating. After taking us to the ski slopes in *Better Off Dead*, Writer-director Savage Steve Holland headed to the beach. John Cusack (*The Sure Thing*) and Curtis Armstrong (*Risky Business*) rejoined him, but it's not a sequel. This time Curtis Armstrong isn't the wing man friend. That role belongs to Joel Murray (*Mad Men*) as George Calamari. He's the one who has to take Hoops McCann (Cusack) to the beach so his pal can finish the project that gets him into art school. Instead of getting laid, Hoops big quest turns into helping Cassandra Eldridge (Demi Moore) save her grandfather's estate that's being targeted by an evil real estate developer for prime beach property. You won't be seeing Curtis Armstrong, Bobcat Goldthwait, William Hickey, John Matuszak, Rich Little, Jeremy Piven or Taylor Negron dripping in gallons of Hawaiian Tropic. This lack of glistening in the sun also includes Demi Moore since she over dresses for Cape Cod action. She's more beach appropriate in *Blame It On Rio*. She does take the nightclub stage in order to save her beach inheritance, but there's no serious R Rated hooking up in the dunes goodness.

There turned out to be one major artistic hook up from the shooting of *One Crazy Summer*. But it wasn't romantic. Sometimes we make pals at the beach that remain in touch for a long long time. Such was the case for Bobcat Goldthwait and Joel Murray. Nearly 25 years later, the duo met up to make the masterpiece *Good Bless America*. The film was written and directed by Bobcat. Joel played a guy sick of reality show stars and other parasites of culture. He does more than click the remote control to get them off his TV screen. He's not going to save Demi Moore's grandfather's estate. He's going to save us all. *God Bless America* is a lot more potent than *Beach Blanket Bingo*. We'll be showing it as part of Bobcat Goldthwait Cinematic Icon weekend in November.

Ultimately American society was so much better in the '80s when we could just lay back and watch teens jiggling on a cinematic beach. Coat yourself in Hawaiian Tropic Professional Tanning Oil and prepare to catch the rays glowing off the big screen.

SOUNDTRACK NOTES: There appears to have been no real soundtrack release from *One Crazy Summer* on vinyl, cassette, 8-Track or the brand-new compact disc format. Although in the 21st Century, quite a few people have put together playlists of the songs from the major motion picture. The music does 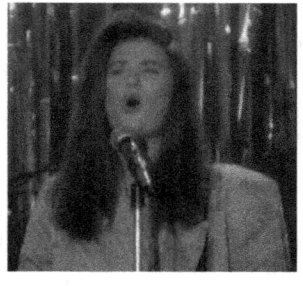 make a fine '80s mixtape. First, we get "Don't Look Back" sung by Demi Moore. There doesn't even appear to be a Radio Stations only 45 single to make us hear Demi's big musical moment. "Take A Bow" was her other big song in the movie, but it was sung by Jaime Segel. By 1986, David Lee Roth had left Van Halen, but he hadn't split for Savage Steve Holland's heart. Diamond Dave gives us a rousing "Easy Street." Twisted Sister gets nasty with "Be Chrool to Your Scuel." Canada's Honeymoon Suite contributes "What Does It Take." The Little Ol' Band from Texas, ZZ Top gets nasty with "Dirty Dog." Peter Allen's epic "I Go To Rio" goes to my heart. Classic rock strikes with Steppenwolf's "Born To Be Wild" and Creedence Clearwater Revival's "Down On the Corner." This wouldn't be a beach film without the Beach Boys and the soundtrack is loaded up with "In My Room," "Do It Again," "Wouldn't It Be Nice" and "Fun, Fun, Fun." You can sit under the rays and listen to hits from *One Crazy Summer* on your smartphone.

Saturday May 23

Losin' It 2:00 p.m.
The Sure Thing 4:00 p.m.
Valley Girl 7:00 p.m.
Ferris Bueller's Day Off 9:30 p.m.
O.C. and Stiggs Midnight

Road Trip!

"Mom, Can I have the keys to the car?" Very few sentences in the English language can strike as much elation in the speaker and abject horror in the listener than a teenager asking for the keys to the family car.

This is when a teenager feels like an adult and the adult feels like their parents. Their child passed driver's education and fooled the DMV agent during the road test. But can they be trusted to drive safely without adult supervision? Or will they use the station wagon for an audition to join Joie Chitwood's Helldrivers? Were they going to remember any of the safety rules? Were they going to keep both hands on the steering wheel and their eyes on the road? Are they use the car as their sex hook up machine and mess up the perfect headrest position? Are they really going to the library or will they just be cruising the 7-Eleven parking lot? Will they wreck the car?

The fear of wrecking the car wasn't a false anxiety in my family. Both of my younger brothers totaled my mother's cars. Neither brother was injured during their wrecks. Mom wasn't happy. She had discovered the perfect headrest position. Two times she had to start adjusting again. Why didn't I wreck the car? Because every time I took the wheel, her voice haunted me to watch my speed, use my blinkers and slow down at yellow lights. Her scariest warning was a promise that if I got a single ticket, I'd be paying for my own car insurance. That's a price I couldn't afford. I'm willing to admit that I drive like my mother. But I survived my teens and twenties without visiting to traffic court.

There had to be an incredible level of trust between a kid and their parents in the '80s. Nowadays a parent can constantly call their kid's cellphone to check when they are driving back from their friend's house. A parent can turn a kid's smartphone into a tracking device to monitor where the kid took the car. But in the '80s, there was none of that. If you had to check in with your parents after getting to the mall, you better have a few quarters for the payphone. In order to spy on their kid, a parent could check the mileage against the alleged distances but that required math. Who wanted to revisit that after high school? Sometimes they would call the friend's house to talk to your friend's parent to make sure you were both really at the library. That could get ugly if you both went to the mall instead of studying. A teenager always had to check the oil and their alibis when borrowing the family car. The last thing you wanted to do was lose access to the car. This was even worse than having your parents disconnect the cable TV as punishment.

We were a generation that grew up with tales of hitting the road. Whether it be Jack Kerouac's *On The Road* novel, *Easy Rider* at the Drive-in or the Beach Boys songs about the glory of a hotrod that dad blasted on the car stereo, we were raised to take the wheel to achieve true freedom on the asphalt.

True freedom didn't really kick into gear until you left for college with a car. Now you had the ability to go anywhere without having to constantly cover your tracks. You wanted to go to Richmond to see Sonic Youth in concert, there was nothing stopping you. You could drive to Chapel Hill to see if your old high school buddy knew of a better party on a Saturday night. If you were really adventurous, you could head up to New York City to finally see those clubs raved about in *Trouser Press*. The only thing limiting your journey was imagination, desire and gas money. Gas money being the most important element.

In 1983, the price of a gallon of gas was $1.16 which doesn't sound too bad until you remember that the minimum wage was $3.35 an hour. If your car was a gas guzzling hand me down from the '70s, you weren't going too far on a fill up. That badass Chevy Camaro only got 13 miles per gallon. The gas tank did take 21 gallons. You were going 273 miles after working 7 hours at Harris Teeter bagging groceries. Oh wait, your paycheck deducted taxes and social security. This means you worked at least an entire 8 hour day to pump that sweet gasoline into your car. You really needed friends to join you on the journey that could chip in for gas money. Especially if you were going to Manhattan to see West German industrial legends Einsturzende Neubauten.

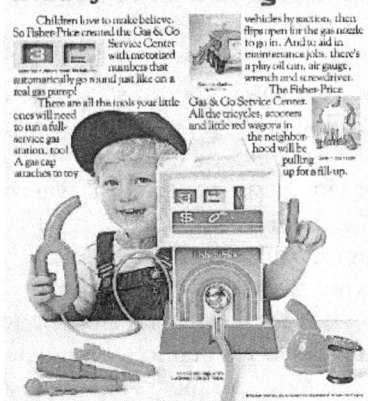

John Swain, the departed owner of the Record Hole, swore he never met a teenager with money that had a car or a girlfriend. "And what happens if they have both?" I asked him. "You're flipping through his collection right now." The second biggest reason a guy dumped his albums was joining a religious cult. They needed to banish all the demon music from their dorm room and pocket a few bucks in return for the collection plate.

Movie producers knew that teens and cars were still a hot topic in the '80s. They cranked out quite a few road trip movies. *Licensed to Drive* had Corey Feldman and Corey Haim reunite after killing off the teen vampires in *The Lost Boys*. Now the Coreys want to drive a 1972 Cadillac to impress Heather Graham (*Boogie Nights*). *The Wraith* had supernatural Charlie Sheen zip around in a futuristic car to impress Sherilyn Fenn (*Twin Peaks*). In *Back to the Future*, Michael J. Fox takes an extreme road trip in time using a modified DeLorean and accidentally impresses his mother (*Some Kind of Wonderful*'s Lea Thompson).

Tonight's movies are all about people hitting the road in various ways to various destinations. *Losin' It* takes Tom Cruise and Jackie Earle Haley over the border to Tijuana, Mexico in search of adult kicks. *The Sure Thing* is a journey across America as John Cusack shares a ride with show tune singers and a grumpy Daphne Zuniga so he can hook up with the ultimate California beach girl. *Valley Girl* might be the shortest of trips, but culturally is a massive distance going from the dangerous streets of Hollywood across the mountains into the quaint suburban San Fernando Valley. *Ferris Bueller's Day Off* borrows the ultimate dad car to commit hooky in Chicago. Our final film *O.C. and Stiggs* allows two teen troublemakers to cruise around in the Gila Monster to commit an "Utterly monstrous, Mind-Roasting Summer" all over Arizona and Mexico.

Perhaps there's a teenager in the audience that had to ask mom for the keys. We're grateful that you decided to take a road trip to our theater tonight. Remember to turn off your cellphone in case your mom calls in the middle of the film to confirm you're getting her Pontiac Fiero back in the driveway by 2 a.m.

Losin' It

April 8, 1983

Embassy Pictures

Directed by Curtis Hanson

Starring **Tom Cruise, Shelley Long, Hector Elias, John Stockwell, John P. Navin, Jr., Henry Darrow and Jackie Earle Haley**

Rated R - 100 minutes

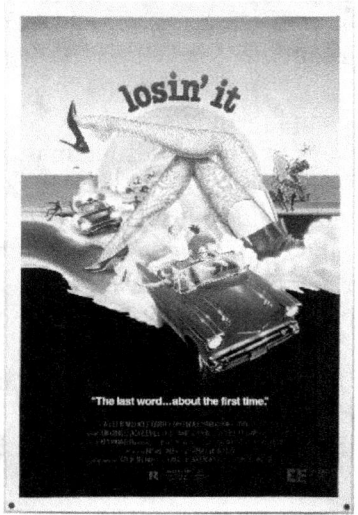

Jackie Earle Haley is the greatest trouble teen actor of all time.

That's not to say he was a troubled teen who spent more time on the cover of supermarket tabloids than on the screen like certain actors that are part of this film festival. There are no torrid rumors about his early years in Hollywood when he appeared on *The Partridge Family*, *Marcus Welby M.D.* and *The Waltons*. He became a fixture at Hanna-Barbera studio's sound booth as a voice on *Wait Till Your Father Gets Home*, *Those Are the Days* and *Valley of the Dinosaurs*. Where's the trouble?

Trouble came in 1976 when Jackie Earle Haley stole the spotlight in *The Bad News Bears*. This wasn't the sweet story about little kids discovering the joy of baseball. The misfits and discards that proudly wore jerseys supplied by Chico's Bail Bonds were given bad life lessons from a coach played by Walter Matthau. The only thing going for them was the pitching of Tatum O'Neal. Even as they found a bit of talent in their castoff crew, they needed a second star. This arrived one day in the ballpark when Kelly Leak was lurking behind the outfield fence. He's smoking a cigarette while on his motorcycle. Kelly grabs a ball and fires it back to third base. A park security guard tries to act tough and get him off the property. Kelly flings his cigarette in her

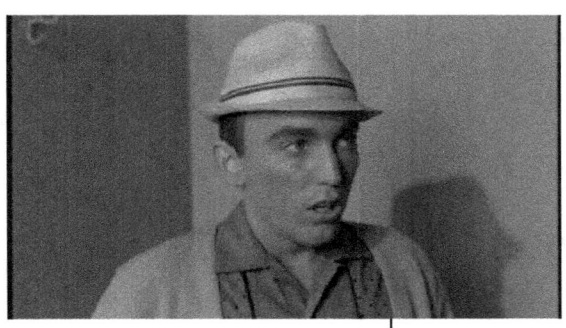

face and drives off. In a few seconds, Kelly Leak has become the attitude idol of millions of teenagers. He cements this reputation at the arcade where he burns an adult in air hockey while smoking away. He beats Tatum O'Neal in a game and gets her to be his date for a Rolling Stones concert. His skills would impress Damone.

After years of seeing people who you'd aspire to be when you grow up, Kelly Leak was the person you wanted to be now. There was no someday when you watched him on the screen. There was only now. Are you ready to be Kelly Leak or you going to putz around? Jackie Earle Haley was not the kind of cute handsome that made nauseous pin ups that filled *Tiger Beat* magazine. Who could be as pretty as Scott Baio? Kelly Leak's magnetism was all about attitude and confidence. When you looked in the mirror, a teenage boy didn't think, I'm not as big of a Hollywood hunk as Kelly Leak. Focus on your stare and not your entire face. And if your stare wasn't quite there; get some kickass tinted sunglasses like Kelly would wear on his motorcycle. The motorcycle said so much about the glory of Kelly Leak. He didn't ride a Huffy bicycle with baseball cards clothespinned to the spokes so he could imagine he was riding a motorcycle. He didn't scoot around on a moped. He didn't tinker in the garage to make a dirt bike using an old lawnmower engine. Kelly Leak rode a Harley Davidson Z90. Let that sink in. He rode a Harley Davidson. He was the son of Billy and Captain America from *Easy Rider*. He wasn't going to settle for second best when it came to his ride. He didn't aspire. He owned. He smoked cigarettes and drank beer like he was already in high school. Kelly Leak was the American dream and he didn't need a driver's license.

Kelly Leak was the badass of baseball with his only peer being Dave "The Cobra" Parker of the Pittsburgh Pirates. Both players had cannons for arms, could crush a baseball and knew how to party in the '70s. The Cobra and Kelly Leak made baseball the cool sport in the '70s. Both didn't have a problem lighting up a cigarette while resting in the dugout and waiting for their turn at the plate. Both Kelly Leak and Dave Parker are not in the baseball Hall of Fame. Dave should be enshrined with all the hall of famers he gunned down or chased off the mound into the showers with his towering homers. Kelly Leak ought to get in the same part of the Hall of Fame that gave a plaque to Abbott and Costello. Little league kids knew if they did just a little bit more, they could be an all-around stud like Kelly Leak.

After *The Bad News Bears* became a massive hit, the studio was ready for sequels. While most of the major talent on the original split including Matthau, O'Neal and director Michael Richie, Jackie Earle Haley stuck around as Kelly Leak. Neither *The Bad News Bears In Breaking Training* (where they go to the Astrodome) and *The Bad News Bears Go to Japan* (where they go to Japan with Tony Curtis) are worthy of the original. The films didn't allow Kelly Leak to even glimpse his original Trouble Teen glory. But he wouldn't be stuck at home plate for the rest of his career.

Luckily in 1977 Jackie was cast as a teenage hero in a massive science fiction movie that Fox Studios swore was going to be their blockbuster of the summer. It had strange mutants, a cool vehicle and a sense that humanity would be lost if the teen's mission failed. Do you think I'm talking about *Star Wars*? Nope. That was the other science fiction film Fox was putting out that summer. Jackie was in *Damnation Alley* with George Peppard and Jan-Michael Vincent. Thanks to the success of *Stars Wars*, *Damnation Alley* was damned to not last long in theaters. The kids wanted to see spaceships firing laser beams and saving the galaxy. They wanted nothing to do with a giant armored van cruising across a post-nuclear apocalyptic America that's covered with giant radioactive mutant roaches.

Jackie would be part of another sports themed hit as a member of the Cutters in the bicycle classic *Breaking Away* with Dennis Christopher, Dennis Quaid and Daniel Stern. The film also featured Paul Dooley as the father character before also doing the same role in *Pretty In Pink* and playing the evil father in *O.C. and Stiggs* (tonight's midnight movie). *Breaking Away* was popular enough to be turned into a TV series on ABC with Shaun Cassidy replacing Christopher. Haley returned as the Moocher. The show was dropped after eight episodes. This brings us to *Losin' It* in Jackie's filmography.

Jackie still brings a bit of trouble to the screen when he drives a car with Tom Cruise and Shelley Long across the border to Tijuana. His mission is to get laid by willing senoritas. By the end of the film, Jackie comes off as more of the chauffeur than the car owner as dorky innocent Tom dominates the movie.

I'm not accusing Tom Cruise of being a heat vampire who used this film to absorb the buzz of Jackie Earle Haley. Tom did play the lead in *Interview with a Vampire* so he's got it in him. But this was not a classic case of pickpocketing a co-star's career since Tom didn't snag the roles that Jackie was ever going to get. We didn't miss out on Jackie buzzing the tower in *Top Gun* or getting shown the money in *Jerry McGuire* or even intensely staring in Stanley Kubrick's *Eyes Wide Shut*. For a while the roles dried up for Jackie after doing guest gigs on *McGuyver* and *Murder She Wrote*. The same wasn't true

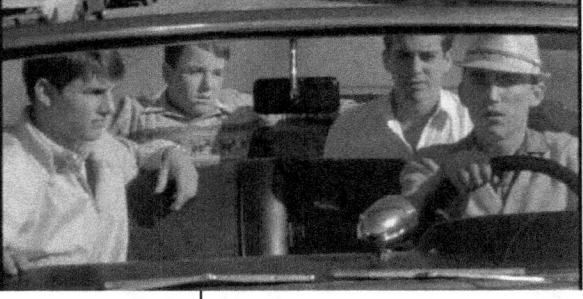

for Tom Cruise in the wake of his drive to Mexico.

Tom Cruise had a banner year in 1983 with four films that saw him go from a supporting greaser in *The Outsiders* (March 25) to co-star in *Losin' It* (April 8) to underwear dancing teen pimp in *Risky Business* (August 5) and finally a high school football phenom in

All the Right Moves (Oct. 21). This was a huge career leap for an actor who only two years before had smaller roles in *Endless Love* and *Taps*. After 1983, Tom was no longer auditioning for parts as directors were pitching their projects to Tom. Oddly enough *Losin' It* was not a hit when it was released. Because the VHS came out after *Risky Business* was still forming lines outside cineplexes, mom and pop rental stores were eager to stock the videotapes. It's doubtful anyone came into the

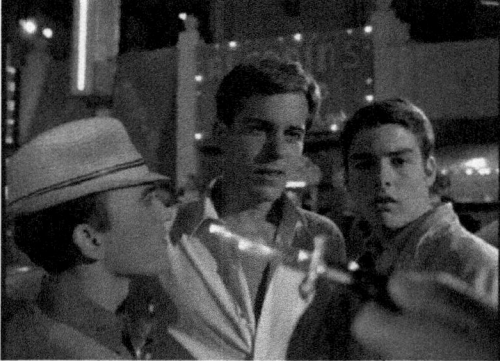

Videorama looking for that new Jackie Earle Haley film. Jackie had lost his heat in pursuit of Spanish Fly. Jackie must have taken this downtown in acting career in stride since he didn't end up on the cover of Supermarket tabloids like so many other child actors from his heyday. He didn't write an autobiography such as co-star Tatum O'Neal's *Paper Life* that gave a horrifying insight into her life, troubles and demons including heroin addiction. People might ponder whatever happened to the guy who played Kelly Leak, but they didn't see his mugshot in *People* magazine.

F. Scott Fitzgerald once wrote "There are no second acts in American Lives" in *The Last Tycoon*. Well F. Scott Fitzgerald didn't know about Jackie Earle Haley. In 2006, Jackie not merely landed a meaty role in the remake of *All The King's Men*, but his follow up part in *Little Children* earned him numerous critic group's honors and an Academy Award nomination for Best Supporting Actor. He followed it up with Rorschach in *Watchmen*. He dominated his scenes as the vigilante that came off as Batman without the Wayne Foundation's wallet. He ended up in Martin Scorsese's *Shutter Island* and Tim Burton's *Dark Shadows*. He assumed the scars and blades of Freddy Krueger in the reboot of *A Nightmare on Elm Street*. He's probably had a more successful career in his comeback than his child actor years. Oddly enough the one film that didn't cast him was Richard Linklater's updating of *The Bad News Bears*. Why didn't he make a cameo as the owner of the strip club that sponsors the team? Don't you think that's what Kelly Leak would have been doing in thirty years after he returned from Japan? The one time I ended up meeting Linklater, our conversation was too brief to ask him about the lack of Jackie Earle Haley in his movie. Perhaps he feared that having the original Kelly Leak on the set would inspire too much trouble in the kids who weren't allowed to be as badass as him in the original? Jackie Earle Haley might have grown up, but with a flick of a cigarette; he'd still be the greatest trouble teen actor in history.

SOUNDTRACK NOTES: Because *Losin' It* was a period piece about those Happy Days of the late '50s, the original soundtrack album is like a supplement to the hits found on *American Graffiti*. We get Dee Clark's "Hey Little Girl," The Shirelles' "Will You Still Love Me Tomorrow," The Miracles' "You've Really Got A Hold On Me," 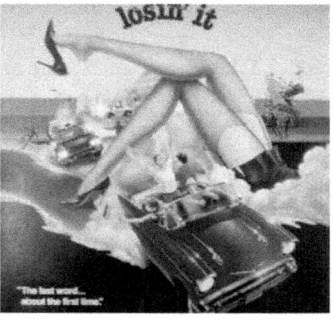 Del Shannon's Runaway and Rockin' Rebels' "Wild Weekend." It's a fine mix of classic hits that are bound to please your pals that want something the Fonz would elbow out of the jukebox at Arnold's. There is a new track with an early '80s movie vibe. The Jeff Alan Band does the original theme song "Losin' It." It's the classic pop synth cheese with Jeff Alan constantly repeating the words "Losin' It" in case you can't remember the title of the film. This appears to be the only song that the Jeff Alan Band released on vinyl. The score was composed by Kenneth Wannberg who had previously edited John Williams' compositions for *Star Wars*.

The Sure Thing

March 1, 1985

Embassy Pictures

Directed by Rob Reiner

Starring **John Cusack, Daphne Zuniga, Nicollette Sheridan, Viveca Lindfors, Anthony Edwards, Tim Robbins, Boyd Gaines, Lisa Jane Persky, Fran Ryan, Larry Hankin and Sarah Buxton**

Rated PG-13 - 95 minutes

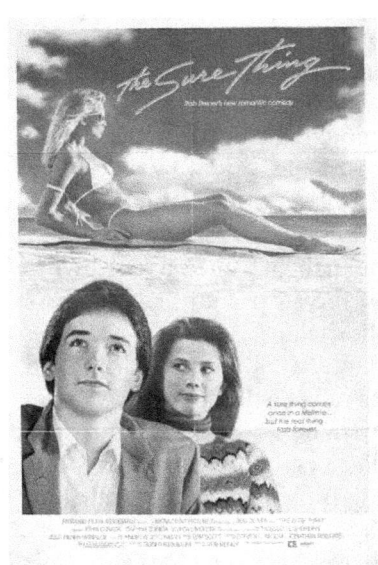

How far would you travel for a "Sure Thing?"

Remember that during the '80s people didn't have things like smartphones with "dating" applications so that you could easily find other who were DTF with NSA when you're feeling horny. You couldn't sit there in the safe confines of your dorm room swiping over a series of photos and clicking on that special someone that you want to hit up for a one-night stand. The closest thing we had was the personal ads at the back of the classifieds in your local alternative weekly entertainment newspaper whether it be the Village Voice, The Boston Phoenix or The Spectator. You read the tiny print description by a person that described themselves as a SWF, DBM or GAM who were into pina coladas, long walks on the beach and the music of Rupert Holmes. Instead of contacting them directly, you'd have to address the envelope to a PO Box or the periodical's special personnel's department. Between writing your letter, mailing the letter, waiting for the post office to deliver your letter, hoping the classified ad writer responds with a letter, getting a letter back in the mail, writing your response to them, mailing your response, waiting for the postman to deliver it and maybe getting another response, you're sitting by the mailbox for 2 months before you meet at P.D. McSwingers for fuzzy navels in a corner booth. Your initial libido desires had pretty much petered out before you could say, "You don't look like your Polaroid." Of course, they didn't look like the Polaroid since they had originally snapped the instant photo three years back when you originally wrote them.

Let's face it, today you can go on your cell phone, hit up an app, find someone looking for lust, give them directions to your place, be naked and humping faster than Dominos delivered a pizza in 1985. Although that doesn't guarantee your partner in pleasure won't look like the Noid. People today enjoy using all those wonderful digital filters to shave away the wrinkles and pounds as if they're a cover photo editor for Cosmopolitan magazine.

There was a faster option to get freaky action in the '80s. Just show up at P.D. McSwingers and look for that special someone on the dance floor who says, "I'm not here for a spouse" between New Order 12" remixes. But that could be a lie. A one-night stand can get ruined with the horrifying phrase, "What are you doing tomorrow night?" It's the old bait and switch. You want to find the person who was just living in the moment and not using sex as way to sink their hooks into you with the deceptive act of cuddling. You

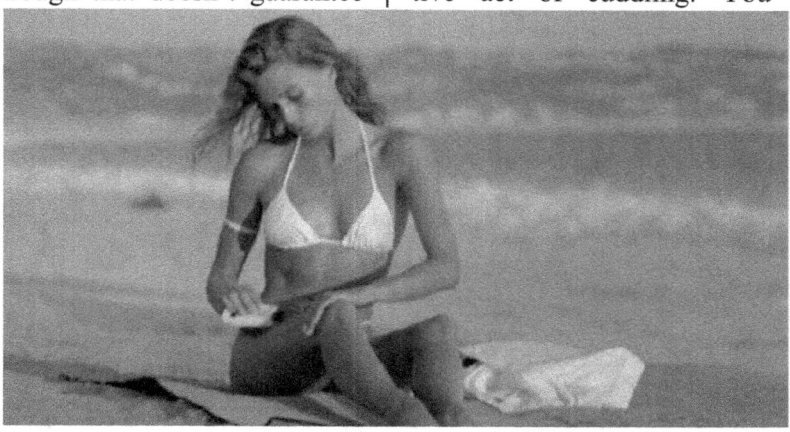

wanted someone that truly appreciated the sexual revolution and didn't mind if you were out the door before they were done showering.

The Sexual Revolution exploded in the late '60s and '70s with the introduction of the birth control pill and the discovery of doctors that weren't going to guilt a female patient from getting a prescription. This was a serious improvement over the previous decades (or centuries) with the condom being the main birth control employed if you were looking for carnal pleasures with no consequences. Of course, that meant a woman had to trust a guy was buying a reliable rubber and not a cheap rejected clown balloon from the vending machine at a greasy truck stop bathroom. She also worried that the rubber had been in his wallet for five years waiting for that special night like a barrel of Scotch. Age and heat made condoms disintegrate upon impact. The lack of rubber in a rubber can lead to an unexpected pregnancy. This holey rubber creates a string that ruins the appeal of No Strings Attached sexual encounters. After the pill became legal and available, women who wanted to enjoy the pleasures of sex weren't fully relying on the guy and his Trojan. Things were pretty good for the '70s if you wanted to be an independent libertine. Even if you caught a venereal disease such as syphilis, chlamydia and gonorrhea; a trip to the Free Clinic for a little penicillin was all you needed to be ready to swing into action at P.D. McSwingers in a few weeks. There might be a touch of shame if the local health inspector had to track down your temporary lovers to make sure the VD didn't spread too far around town. What was a little VD for all the fun you were having with numerous partners at P.D. McSwingers?

The notion of free love was immediately attacked by religious figures and politicians. The Holy Roller Religious leaders didn't even want you having sex after you were married if you weren't aiming to pop out kids. Now they were going nuts that people could enjoy the pleasure and not merely do their "fruitful and multiple" duties. The Pope was not a fan. Uptight politicians got into the act as they attacked the concept of a birth control pill. Quite a few proposed that someone enjoying

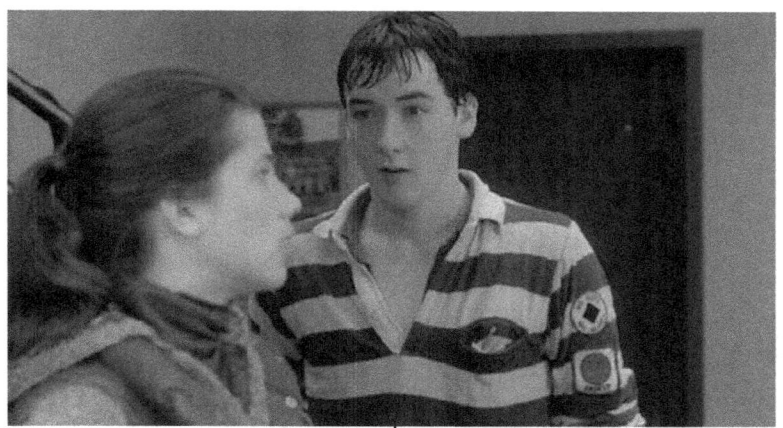

sex would be led to communism. Perhaps after a big orgy, people were ready to read a few chapters from Mao's *Little Red Book*. Karl Marx's "From each according to their ability, to each according to their needs" sounds exactly like a great mindset for 12 strangers in the watery Grotto at the Playboy Mansion. Attending orgy parties with multiple Sure Things pretty much guaranteed you weren't looking for a relationship. The mathematical implications of group sex seemed infinite in this brave new copulating world.

Everything came crashing down in the '80s when Herpes and HIV/AIDS became the headlines after the shock of the star of *Bedtime For Bonzo* being elected president. While Herpes wasn't life threatening, it wasn't curable. It quickly became a bumpy stigma. HIV/AIDS was fatal. While most people viewed it as something that affected the male gay community, it could spread to heterosexual folks. The fun and frivolity of the '70s came to a bit of a halt or at least a pause. Oddly enough the item that became the primary line of defense in not catching HIV was the condom. And we're back to questioning if the guy cared enough to buy the very best at the Kerr Drugstore and wasn't holding onto his dad's vintage prophylactics from his time in Vietnam.

Because of these new VDs, the Sure Thing of the '80s was a bit iffy. Hooking up became more complicated. Did you trust this other person to not be a disease carrying angel of death? Very quickly the urban legend spread of the girl who wakes up, finds her one-night stand has split and written on the bathroom mirror in lipstick is "Welcome to the World of AIDS." Sex became an infectious David Cronenberg horror flick such as his version of *The Fly*. Likewise, guys weren't so sure if they wanted to get freaky with a woman who enjoyed multiple partners. Health agencies would guilt people with PSAs that pointed out that you're not merely having sex with a person, but with all the people that person had slept with and the people that slept with those people and those people. There could be hundreds of people in that bed with the two of you. It was like the Faberge Organics Shampoo commercial for your pubes. Do you want to have the same germs as the people who came before you? Swingers in the '80s got a bit cautious although there were a few daredevils who didn't care. But it was still tough to find a partner who wanted to enjoy death defying pleasures.

I had a school pal who was openly bisexual which was rather rare in the '80s. During a party I asked him what was the difference between hooking up with men versus women - in a non-physical way. I wasn't looking for a Penthouse Forum letter. He declared that within a minute of talking with a guy, he knew if they were going to be getting sexual. When it came to a woman, he could be naked in bed with her for hours and have zero clue if she was up for sex. Even if he'd been tipped off that she was a Sure Thing, it wasn't a guarantee that she was always up for it. Plus, you had no idea if your friend was lying and just wanted to hear

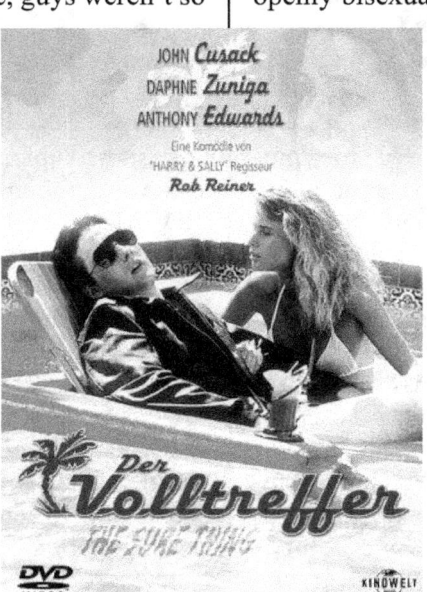

about you getting slapped or maced for coming on too hard with your date.

The worst thing you could do if you were tipped off that your date was a Sure Thing was take them out to a movie. Why? Because Hollywood studio films hated casual sex in the '80s. The '70s had quite a few movies about women going on erotic journeys to enjoy themselves. Granted most of them featured a character named Emanuelle or Emmanuelle. Or they were fun party people at the beach jiggle fests made by Crown International. But in the '80s, the movie theaters became as puritanical as a snake handling church. *Fatal Attraction* has Michael Douglas enjoy a fling with a woman and she boils his kid's bunny. Even in *Fast Times At Ridgemont High*, Stacy Hamilton wants to enjoy sex and gets knocked up on her second try. At the end of the film, we're told that Stacy and The Rat are a couple, but haven't gone all the way. While it's a sad fate for Stacy, it could have been worse if she'd gone to Camp Crystal Lake.

Hollywood studios got deep into the Teen Slasher genre in the '80s. *Friday 13th*, *Halloween*, *Nightmare on Elm Street* and their sequels and impersonators flooded the cineplexes. Those films had one thing in common: the people who enjoyed sex were marked for death. Those that got laid, paid with their lives. The monsters with the machetes, razor gloves and chainsaws were eager to slice up any teenager that had an orgasm outside of marriage. Very rarely did the Final Girl have a post coital glow as she escaped the serial killer. The Hollywood films were as bad as those little religious comics that promised eternal damnation for having a libido and carnal thoughts. By the end of the film, your Sure Thing would decide they don't want to be hacked to pieces and will skip your proposition. They didn't want to hear how you'd hang a sock on the doorknob to alert your roomies to not knock or complain about the moans. They wanted to go home and not worry about anyone peeking out of the closet.

We come back to the original question: How far would you travel for a Sure Thing? The Hollywood studios' answer was the graveyard. Your answer could be Newark. Either way, pack fresh certified condoms.

SOUNDTRACK NOTES: There was not a soundtrack album for *The Sure Thing* although bootleg CDs are available. How could this happen? Don't people want a mixtape for when they're driving cross country to get laid? The producer secured a bunch of major songs for Gib's journey. The tunes kick off with Rod Stewart's "Infatuation." 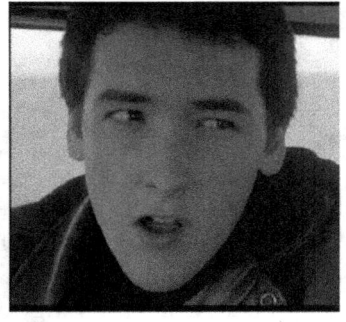 You might remember the video featured Rod stalking a woman in his apartment complex. This is the perfect song if you're stalking Nicollette Sheridan in her bikini at the beach. The Eagles' "Heartache Tonight" was always on the radio in the '80s so it seemed natural to hear on a car trip. We get a dose of Wang Chung with "Dance Hall Days." The Cars are at their pop tops with "You Might Think." There are even cute older numbers including The Fifth Dimension's "Aquarius - Let the Sunshine In" and Mel Torme's "The Christmas Song." The uncomfortable part of the soundtrack represents the divorce of America's premiere house party band. After the massive success of *Freeze Frame*, The J. Geils Band had creative differences. We get both halves of the split. Lead singer Peter Wolf's "Lights Out!" blasts away with the soulful power and energy expected from the Woofa Goofa. The remaining members that stayed in the J. Geils Band can only muster up "Concealed Weapons." This a musical number that you'd expect from the *Benny Hill Show*. If you played "Concealed Weapons" for your Sure Thing; they would immediately get up, get dressed, get out and get a new phone number.

Valley Girl

April 29, 1983

Atlantic Releasing

Directed by Martha Coolidge

Starring **Nicolas Cage, Deborah Foreman, Elizabeth Daily, Cameron Dye, Michelle Meyrink, Lee Purcell, Colleen Camp and Frederic Forrest**

Rated R - 99 minutes

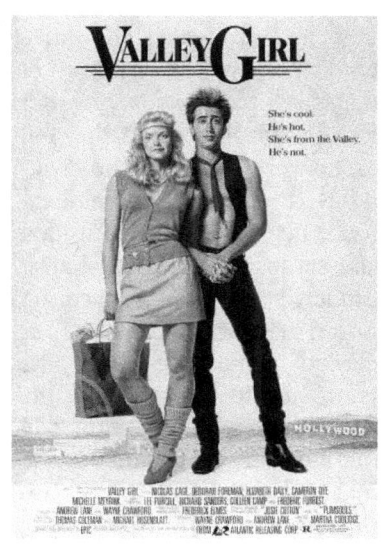

Gag me with a spoon! In the middle of the night, Frank Zappa woke up his teenage daughter Moon Unit. He wanted her to come downstairs to the Utility Muffin Research Kitchen recording studio in the house. Earlier in the day, her and her friends were doing goofy accents and mocking the girls from San Fernando Valley. He needed her to repeat the routines on the microphone. She was happy to get to spend time in the studio with her dad and collaborate on what seemed like a goofy song. Little did Frank know that they would create the biggest hit in his career and produce a pop culture sensation with "Valley Girl."

Moon Unit Zappa did not invent the Valley Girl or Valspeak. She lived in Laurel Canyon on the other side of the mountain. But her impersonation of a girl from a really good side of Encino captured and conveyed the mindlessness. In less than five minutes of a vinyl groove, Frank and Moon conveyed how the Valley Girls were very materialistic and not quite so smart. They lived to shop at the mall and get their nails done by others. They weren't aiming to do anything deep or intellectual. Moon sounds like she's on the phone all night with a friend giving a rundown of her day in Valspeak. She talks about her love of fashion, her distaste for kinky sex, how her English teacher creeps her out as he flirts with the boy students, a bad trip to the nail saloon, her mom's insisting that she scraps off the plates after dinner, her issue with wearing a retainer and her game of choice being Pac-Man. She loads up her lines with the proper lingo of fer sure, gag me with a spoon, grody to the max, omigod, bitchin', I'm like so sure, No way!, beastie, bag your face, bag those toenails, barf out, space cadet, tubular and totally!

Moon's voice reflected a girl waiting for frozen yogurt with massive amounts of Uptalk. She ends her sentences with "ya' know?" It feels like she throws exclamation marks into the middle of words. And there's always an extra "like" that can get tossed into her word stew. She delivers her lines in a way that united the classical pop speech song of Lorne Green's "Ringo" with hip hop raps found on the Sugar Hill Gang's "Rapper's Delight."

"Valley Girl" wasn't an individual effort, but a duet between Moon and her father. Although it's not a normal duet since while Moon gives the rundown of her day, Frank comments on this new breed of airhead floating up in the '80s. He mocks them the same way he had fun with the vapid dance club crowd on "Disco Boy" or "Dancin' Fool" back in the 1970s. He had also poked fun at Punky Meadows of the band Angel with "Punky's Whips." If you were here Friday, you remember Angel being the musical act featured in *Foxes*. Who knew

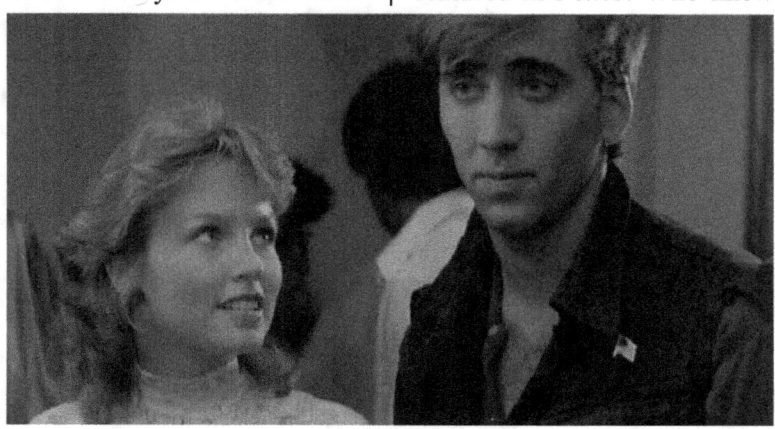

Frank Zappa would have such an influence on this festival? He used their own lingo to ridicule the Valley Girl including fer sure as part of the chorus. This was quite strange to hear a dad demeaning his daughter, but Moon was playing a character named Ondrya Wolfson. This wasn't nearly as creepy as another Frank's duet with his daughter. Do you not remember Frank Sinatra and his daughter Nancy singing "Something Stupid" where they sound like a couple having a fling that gets ruined when one of them admits they're in love? That is cringeworthy. In "Valley Girl," the other Frank just wanted his daughter to grow up to not be an airhead. I'm not sure what Sinatra wanted from his daughter. But it wasn't for her to avoid being vapid.

In a sense "Valley Girl" tied back to Zappa's "Plastic People" on The Mothers of Invention's *Absolutely Free* album that came out in 1967. He was having an issue with materialistic people that were extremely superficial. Fifteen years later, the children of the Plastic People's children were even more synthetic. Zappa wanted to warn the world of what was festering in the San Fernando Valley before it infected America with a bit of comedy and a funky beat.

Strangely enough the song became the biggest hit in Zappa's career. Casey Kasem got to count it up to 32 on the Billboard's Top 40 song chart. Moon Unit found herself a celebrity for more than her dad naming her Moon Unit. She performed on *Solid Gold* with the Solid Gold Dancers as her army of Valley Girls. (We'll be showing this clip before today's screening.) Frank was nowhere near the stage. But he seemed sort of pleased that his warning about this new scourge was being heard around the globe.

Instead of the world being shocked or laughing along with Zappa, quite a few people embraced the Valley Girl as their new persona. America in the early '80s was a land of indoor shopping malls where teenagers would retreat after school and drift aimlessly from the Food Court to the Merry-Go-Round for fashions to The Record Bar for cassettes. Very rarely would they venture into Waldenbooks because who has time to read when your life is inside a shopping bag? They needed an identity that really spoke to them. Somehow

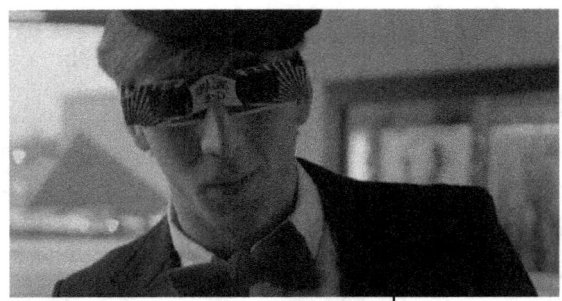

Ondrya represented their life of shopping and avoiding cleaning up after dinner. And thus, way too many impressionable teenagers sought salvation in the Valley Girl spirit and slang. The summer of 1982 saw kids and even adults dropping "for sure" and "omigod" into conversations. Think about how annoying people got after the release of Austin Powers or Borat movies with repeatedly saying, "I'll shag you rotten" and "Can we have sexy time?" "Gag me with a spoon" and "Grody to the max" became legitimate responses in a conversation especially if you're hanging out at the mall's food court. People constantly said "like" since this is all they had before the invention of the word "literally."

In the end, Frank's warning became the infection that spread this attitude from one mall record store to the next. Record Bar, Strawberries, Peaches, Sam Goody, Turtles and more played "Valley Girl" to the kids browsing the overpriced racks as they took a break from the dressing room at The Gap. They said, "Omigod! She's like speaking to me! I hate saliva on my retainer! Gag me with a spoon, too, like!"

The mall was the center of a Valley Girl's existence and Ondrya Wolfson name checks the Galleria mall that's in Sherman Oaks. She calls it Encino since that border is nearby and frankly if you're in the Valley, there's no real break between the towns. Does that location sound familiar? Sherman Oaks is mostly known to hip kids as where Garry Shandling lived on *It's Garry Shandling's Show*. But what about the mall that was the sacred shrine to the Valley Girls? Turns out that if you were there opening night. Sherman Oaks Galleria was the mall where all the action happened in *Fast Times At Ridgemont High*. That's right. The establishing shot for the exterior was the Santa Monica Place mall in Santa Monica. They put up a sign declaring it as Ridgemont Mall. But the movie theater, the arcade and Perry's Pizza were inside the Sherman Oaks Galleria. The mall itself was a child of the '80s since its grand opening was in 1980. The place was a modern sensation and quickly became a major location for teen flicks. Besides popping up in *Valley Girl*, the shopping center appeared in two other classic '80s teen flicks that were also science fiction nightmares. A deserted version of the Galleria appeared in *Night of the Comet*. This is where Catherine Mary Stewart and Kelli Maroney went after most of humanity was wiped out overnight. Where else would Valley Girls go in the midst of a crisis? Shopping is a great way to forget about the mutant zombies that want to eat what passes for a Valley Girl's brain. Kelli Maroney would be back in the Galleria for *Chopping Mall* with Barbara Crampton. This time she and Crampton (*Fraternity Vacation* & *Re-Animator*) are being chased around the food court by a trio of security robots that have gone out of control. The Galleria was getting rather sketchy. Seeing how Kelli Maroney was in *Fast Times, Night of the Comet* and *Chopping Mall*, she could probably challenge Ondrya Wolfson for the title of Queen of the Galleria. Although she did not win the title when *Real People* hosted the Ultimate Valley Girl competition in 1983. Moon Unit was one of the judges.

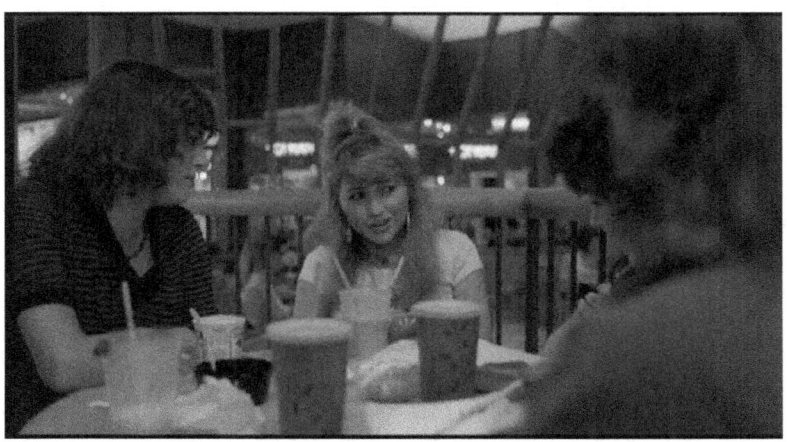

If you consider an '80s Flashback Mall-cation, be warned that you won't be visiting the cinematic Sherman Oaks Galleria. During the early '90s, Mall Decay struck the massive indoor structures. Even though the Galleria was the Temple of the Valley Girl, it found itself dealing with an economic downturn. The mall closed its doors in 1999 for a major renovation. When the building reopened in 2002, things had changed. A majority of the space was dedicated to offices. They still showed movies on the third floor. But instead of the Pacific 4 where the Rat ripped your tickets, there's now an ArcLight Cinema with 16 screens. You can't catch Linda and Stacy slicing salami since Perry's Pizza is gone.

Although there is a Cheesecake Factory. The arcade is gone which isn't that bad since Damone is probably scalping concert tickets online. The new Galleria isn't a place for teens or people who want to remember their teenage years.

If you do find yourself in Los Angeles, you'll be happy to know that the mall from the opening of *Valley Girl* is still there. Del Amo Fashion Center still stands although it's really located in Torrance which is by the coast and not in the Valley. While the Mall has undergone renovation over the decades, according to our research, the Hot Dog On A Stick is still open at the mall's food court. There's one last place you can live the Valley Girl dream. Omigod!

SOUNDTRACK NOTES: You'll notice one song is missing from Valley Girl. Where's "Valley Girl" from Frank and Moon Unit Zappa? Turns out he had nothing to do with this movie. The producers were trying to cash in on the Valley Girl craze and didn't care. Frank had been talking to other producers about 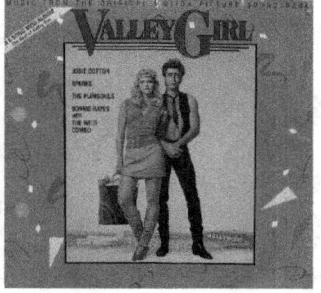 making an "official" Valley Girl movie. There was a lawsuit that didn't quite work Frank's way. The soundtrack for *Valley Girl* is a bit of a mess since the movie's end credits claimed there was a soundtrack album. The original soundtrack from Epic Records was scrapped because of clearance issues with a few songs. The studio tried to put out a mini-album with six tracks. The EP never made it to the bin at Tower Records. Ultimately in 1994, Rhino Records was able to release a CD of the soundtrack with the new wave tunes from Plimsouls ("Million Miles Away"), Men At Work ("Who Can It Be Now"), Payola ("Eyes of A Stranger"), Psychedelic Furs ("Love My Way") and Modern English ("Love My Way"). They even included Josie Cotton's "Johnny Are Your Queer." The soundtrack caught the first wave of '80s nostalgia and sold well enough to get a second volume released. The second volume had more from the soundtrack and even a few songs that were intended for the film, but the producers couldn't afford. The tacks included Toni Basil's "Mickey," Sparks and Jane Wiedlin's "Cool Places", Bananarama's "He Was Really Saying Something," Culture Club's "Do You Really Want to Hurt Me," The Jam's "A Town Called Malice" and even Toto Coelo's "I Eat Cannibals." It was like the lost *Living In Oblivion: The '80s Greatest Hits, Volume Six* that was supposed to come out at this point in the '90s. To give you an idea of how much music can cost a production, the production budget to make Valley Girl was $350,000. The cost of licensing the music was around $250,000. But the gamble paid off because it grossed nearly $17 million in theaters and sold bitchin' units on home video.

Ferris Bueller's Day Off

June 11, 1986

Paramount Pictures

Directed by John Hughes

Starring **Matthew Broderick, Alan Ruck, Mia Sara, Jennifer Grey, Jeffrey Jones, Edie McClurg, Charlie Sheen, Ben Stein, Louie Anderson & Richard Edson**

Rated PG-13 - 103 minutes

Ferris Bueller, you're not my hero.

The popular view of *Ferris Bueller's Day Off* is that a super slacker high schooler inspires empowerment within his best friend Cameron when they skip classes. Cameron goes from being weak to assertive during an amazing fun time in Chicago. Ferris Bueller comes off as the ultimate friend you'd ever want.

Many critics and fans consider this the masterpiece of not only John Hughes' teen movies, but his entire directorial career. This ultimately is Hughes' masterpiece of misdirecting an audience. Superficially it all feels good at the end. But was it? John Hughes' ad campaigns for Virginia Slims cigarettes made high schoolers feel good about embracing cancer in their lives. Now he was selling teenagers a cancer called Ferris Bueller.

Over the course of the film, we're being lured into caring for a guy who is a massive narcissist that manipulates everyone around him. This isn't a "Day Off" for Ferris since this is his regular routine. The school year has barely started and he's already skipped over a week. Of course, he can do this because he has the skills to hack the school computer and fix his absentee days. Ferris brags about his techniques to fake illness by talking straight to the camera. He wants us in on his games. By breaking the fourth wall, Hughes immediately creates a bond between the folks in the theater and Ferris. The audience becomes less judgmental if they think the people on the screen are paying attention to them. He's their pal and not someone they're just watching go along with his daily activities. He's taking everyone along for the ride. And Ferris ends up taking everyone for a massive ride including a few people who consider themselves so smart.

George Will called the movie, "Most true to the general spirit of the movies, the spirit of effortless escapism." Even co-star Ben Stein was dazzled by the film that featured him as the dry and boring teacher. Stein has described *Day Off* as "the most life-affirming movie possibly of the entire post-war period.... There's nothing mean-spirited about it. There's nothing sneering or sniggering about it. It's just wholesome. We want to be free. We want to have a good time. We know we're going to have to eventually become family men and women, and have responsibilities and pay our bills. But just give us a couple of good days that we can look back on."

But there's nothing escapist or good for Ferris' victims. Think of all his classmates that wasted their school day thinking about poor Ferris dying at home. How many tears were shed and prayers sent to God for Ferris to live? How risky was it from people to paint "Save Ferris" on the water tower? Who spent all that money for flowers and the telegram stripper nurse? Where did all the money collected for

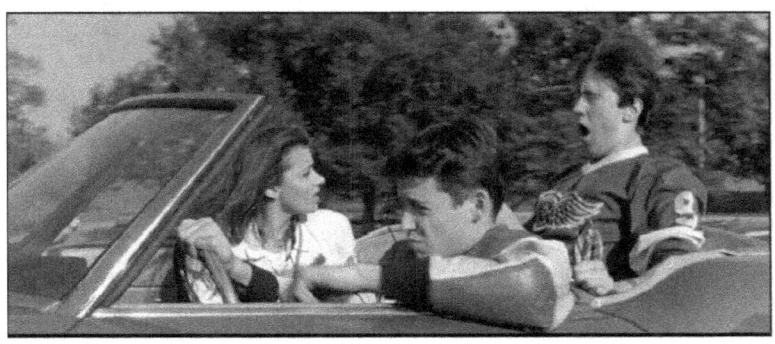

Ferris end up? He was "sick" the next day so did that charity money get dumped on his doorstep? The students of Shermer High School were just a faceless pack of suckers that could be easily duped by Ferris. He had a bigger fish to hook for his big *Day Off*.

Cameron Frye (Alan Ruck of *Class*) was the perfect mark for Ferris. Audiences didn't see Cameron as a target because of the way Hughes framed the neglected rich kid with no spine. You are led to believe that he needed therapy that only Ferris can deliver. How do we know this? Because Ferris keeps telling us this fact. We don't look at Cameron and ask, "Why do you put up with such an asshole as a friend?" Hughes had already made us friends with Ferris. Ferris was there only to help. Or was he?

Why do we not question what's happening to Cameron? The same way Hughes made us not question why a woman needed to light up a cigarette to be liberated. He used a simple narrative identity misdirection to make us view this story all wrong. He played on a preconceived notion of who the story is about.

Writers and filmmakers end up creating works about that person that turned around their life. That one outrageous character that somehow made them either go the straight and narrow or aim higher. The film or book is a payback to someone they idolized that fixed them. Jack Kerouac's *On the Road* was a fictionalized tribute to his driving pal Neal Cassidy. The audience tolerates the outrageous friend's bad behavior because we know they elevated the schlub that at one point was the director or writer.

We imagine that John Hughes' alter ego in the movie is Cameron. Anything Ferris does to Cameron is balanced out by that feeling that Cameron is the writer-director's character so it's all good. Hughes was from Detroit and moved to Chicago which is why Cameron roams around Chicago in Gordie Howe's Detroit Redwings hockey sweater. Gordie Howe was Hughes' favorite player. Cameron is the observer which naturally we assume is the position of the future writer/director as he lionizes his cool friend. Alan Ruck and Hughes share that same doughy look. Ruck was only six years younger than Hughes when they made the film. That's right, Ruck was 29 playing a high schooler which is normally a nightmare people have at 29.

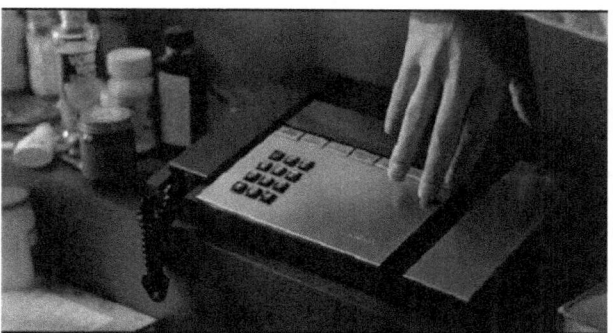

It's easy to imagine that Hughes saw himself in Cameron. Hughes even used his own hand to get the shot of Cameron pushing buttons on the answering machine. We get a sense that the real life "Ferris" is what Hughes needed to emerge from his ineffectual cocoon into a massive success.

But turns out that Hughes wasn't Cameron. He was Ferris. You doubt?

John Hughes knew how to skip work. Supposedly when John Hughes was working at Leo Burnett Worldwide in Chicago, he would fly to New York City for meetings with the folks at Virginia Slims cigarettes. But he kept the meetings short so he could skip over to the National Lampoon magazine offices. Later he would get cocky enough that he'd show up early at his office in Chicago, move stuff around his desk, tell the secretary he was heading out to get something, grab the first commuter jet to New York City, hang with the Lampoon folks for lunch, fly back to the Second City and sneak back into the office before the evening whistle blew. That's something you can easily imagine Ferris Bueller doing as an adult.

You want hard evidence of this connection?

In the director's commentary on the DVD, Hughes admitted that he decorated Ferris' bedroom himself. This was a personal touch to make Ferris's bedroom resemble John Hughes' high school bedroom. The director had every inch of the walls covered in record sleeves and photos he cut out of English magazines back in the '60s. Although the space above his bed was probably covered with the Beatles instead of a poster for Bryan Ferry's "Slave to Love" single on 7" and 12" vinyl.

Later on, he explained that the address of Ferris' family house is the same the Hughes family had in his childhood. On the Bueller's refrigerator was a portrait of John Hughes done by his son. However, this isn't John Hughes' family home since the Bueller's residence is located in Long Beach, California. In case your curious, Cameron's father's garage is outside of Chicago in Highland Park, Illinois.

Hughes completely exposed all his cards in the commentary when he reflected on Cameron, Ferris and Sloane Peterson (*Legend*'s Mia Sara) roaming the city. He pointed out that this was taken from his life. "My wife, who used to be my high school girlfriend. We were always three. Me, my wife and one of my friends...troubled buddies," he uttered on the track. John Hughes was Ferris Bueller. He's the character that never changed from his day off.

Hughes confessed that "Cameron was based in large part on a friend of mine in high school. He was sort of a lost person. His family sort of neglected him. He took that as license to really pamper himself. When he was sick, he actually felt good. He was relaxed." So, we get the sick Cameron stuck in bed with a legit excuse to not show up for school. But Ferris isn't going to let his friend's cold medication take hold. He badgered Cameron because he wanted something and it's something more than Cameron's companionship. He wanted the key to Mr. Frye's 1961 Ferrari 250 GT California Spyder. The classic car at the time was worth $200,000 which is now close to half a million bucks. But don't worry about the inflation difference. Recently this model sold at auction for $17 million.

Before Ferris could borrow the car, he had to put Cameron in a position where he can't say no. This came when he had Cameron pretend to be Sloane's father to spring her from school with the old "her grandmother died" excuse. Cameron overplayed things with Dean of Students Edward R. Rooney (Jeffrey Jones) to the point where they might get busted when they picked her up. This leads to a bit of a fight between the duo. On the commentary track, Hughes broke down how Ferris operates on his "friend" Cameron. "Ferris has hit him, embarrassed him and now he's drawing him back in," described Hughes.

"He's making him pay for his mistake which is very important for the plan. He's got to make Cameron make a mistake so he can get the car. Cameron has to pay for getting too confident with Rooney and this is the price he has to pay." How dark does this friendship get? How much can Ferris manipulate Cameron. Just remember that as they drove off from school, Ferris steered the wheel, Sloan rode shotgun and Cameron squeezed into the back space that isn't really a seat. He gets talked into taking out his father's precious car and can't touch the gas pedal. He's really being taken for a ride by Ferris. Although why does the car's license plate read "NRVOUS" since we're supposed to believe Mr. Frye is more in control of his emotions than his son? Perhaps the father got the personalized plate in honor of his nervous son? Maybe dad knew someday he'd leave the precious car for the kid. This car was an investment that would even take care of Cameron's kid. The car has increased in value by $16.8 million in 34 years. But it all doesn't matter as Ferris turned the key and hit the gas. He's a teenager that's not on the car's insurance policy having the ride of his life.

In the ritzy restaurant's bathroom, Ferris gave a monologue about how he took the Ferrari out of the garage to get Cameron to overcome his fears. He even got Cameron to "dig" riding in the car. Ferris justified his actions by claiming it's all for Cameron's benefit. But then Ferris threw in how he loved driving it. This was the car he deserved to drive. Cameron was only allowed to think that Mr. Frye loves the car more than him. He didn't get to think that Ferris wants the car more than their friendship.

Even Hughes on the commentary track pushed that Ferris was justified in his coveting the car. "I think Cameron really wanted him to take it," he declared. Who didn't want their friend to drive their parents' expensive sports car? It's strange that Hughes didn't really know what Cameron wanted. He didn't know how Cameron feels about Sloane. "Cameron was probably secretly, desperately in love with her," Hughes guessed. He wrote the character and doesn't seem to have a clue about the guy. But he knew Ferris. It's almost like Cameron didn't exist emotionally outside of being a troubled rich friend that needed soaking. When Cameron got upset about their day in Chicago being a waste, Ferris pushed back with "You haven't seen anything good today?" That's the problem because Cameron was basically a spectator to their adventures in the city. Ferris stole the Sausage King's reservation at the restaurant. Ferris caught the foul ball at the Cubs game. Ferris drove the 1961 Ferrari 250 GT California Spyder around the city. Ferris got to take his girlfriend to share the views of great art at the museum. Ferris hijacked the parade float and became the sensation singing "Danke Schoen" and the Beatles "Twist and Shout" while Cameron stood on the sidewalk. Ferris had all the fun and Cameron was there to just watch his "friend." And Ferris felt Cameron was ungrateful for not enjoying the privilege of basking in his glory.

The second crisis with the car happened when they drove back to Shermer and Cameron realized there's a few extra hundred miles on the odometer. Cameron went into catatonic shock. Instead of dealing with the issue at hand, Ferris went off on how Cameron will be doomed for a miserable marriage like his parents if Ferris doesn't help him overcome all this. "He'll marry the first girl he lays," Ferris directly warned the audience. This is confusing since Ferris just said he wants to marry his high school sweetheart. Even weirder that John Hughes married his high school sweetheart. These two appear to have married the first girl they laid. Making matters more frustrating was that Ferris did nothing to help Cameron get laid in the film. He didn't even introduce his buddy to the "Danke Schoen" girls on the float. He merely let

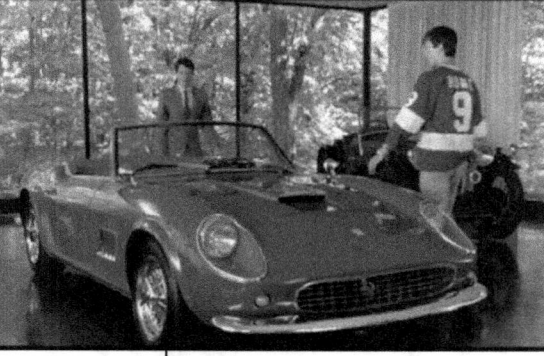

Cameron stare at his naked girlfriend and gave a goofy grin when this fact came out.

At some point, he will use this incident to manipulate Cameron. Perhaps Mr. Frye owned a private jet?

Ferris can't focus on his pal's nightmarish problem. Is it really his problem since it's not his dad's car? Ferris and Sloane take the traumatized Cameron to an unknown backyard pool and for an equally unknown reason left Cameron in a folding chair on the diving board. Naturally Cameron fell into the water wanting to drown instead facing his dad over the extra miles. Ferris came off as a hero diving into the deep end to save the suicidal drowning Cameron. But he wouldn't have been at the bottom of the pool if Ferris hadn't driven the Ferrari to Chicago and just used Cameron's car. Why did Ferris not have a car, but his sister (Jennifer Grey) drove a Fiero?

The final car crisis hit when Cameron discovered Ferris' brilliant plan to fix the odometer was worthless. There was no way they'd fool Mr. Frye. Finally, Ferris' manipulative ways have come up short. Cameron lost control and we get the shocking moment of what happened to the expensive Ferrari. Ferris claimed that he'll take the blame and talk to Cameron's dad. But Cameron refused letting Ferris rightfully take the blame. "I got to take a stand. Right or wrong, I'm going to defend it," Cameron declared. Ferris must have known that he'd hooked Cameron to be the fall guy when his plan fell through so he could offer up to take the blame, but knew the offer wouldn't be taken.

John Hughes on the commentary track made Ferris look noble after screwing over the rich kid. "He's accomplished the day," Hughes claimed. "If he didn't know exactly what the day was going to mean. He put in motion circumstances that have led to this. He had something to fix in Cameron. He didn't know the specifics, but set up the circumstances where he did deal with what he needed to deal with." There are better ways to fix a friend than make them confront their father over what happened to the $17 million car.

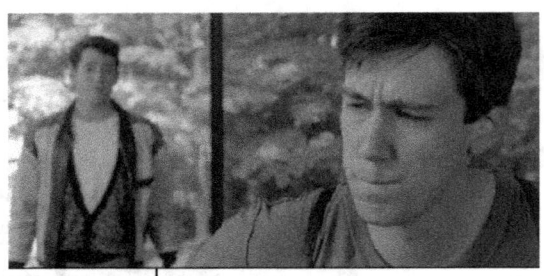

When Sloane got worried about Cameron's fate, her boyfriend blew it off. "For the first time in his life, he'll be OK," Ferris claimed. And with that the movie completely forgot that Cameron existed. The film races to the end of the reel with an invigorating slapstick chase. Ferris bolts across yards to beat his parents and sister back to the house so he could be safe in his sickbed. Ferris didn't become an honest son. His sister protected him from Rooney. Once more Ferris duped his parents into thinking he's sick enough to miss another day of school. The only difference between this day and tomorrow was he won't have a Ferrari to drive. Cameron's fate was ignored. He's not even mentioned during the post end credits stinger when Ferris told the audience to go home. Ferris suffered no consequences for his actions. And we don't need to care about Cameron because he wasn't Ferris.

Ferris successfully manipulated everyone in the greater Chicago area. Likewise, John Hughes manipulated everyone in the theater into believing Ferris was the greatest friend you can ever have. He made you completely forget that Cameron was sitting in the garage waiting for his dad to come home. All that mattered was Ferris talking directly to viewers about how you need to enjoy the day. This is a masterwork from John Hughes like his cigarette ads that made high schoolers dismiss those pesky Surgeon General warnings about cancer. We embraced the fantasy of Ferris and dismissed the harsh realities facing Cameron. Hey

George Will, where's Cameron's "effortless escapism?". John Hughes made a film that celebrates self-centered brats who have to get their way and don't have to change. He paved the way for millions of people that call themselves influencers. Think of all the Youtubers who keep talking directly to the camera as they drag us along on their off days. He made it possible for the stardom of Paris Hilton, the Kardashians and all those men and women that are on the *Real Housewives* shows. He made us think somehow having that asshole friend was essential because they'd eventually be as cool as Ferris. He allowed too many people to accept an egotistical gameshow host as the perfect president. He made a narcissistic manipulator be the cinematic hero without having to change his wicked ways in the third act. And people loved it. John Hughes was a dark genius.

Back in 2012 during the Superbowl, Matthew Broderick returned to the Ferris Bueller character in order to sell the Honda CR-V compact sports utility van. He lies to his agent that he's sick and can't make a film shoot. He hits the city in the SUV. But who is missing from the commercial? A visit with Cameron. You want to know why he isn't there? Let's remember the stories that John Hughes wrote for *The National Lampoon*. You can't believe the man who wrote "My Penis" and "My Vagina" would originally end Cameron's fate with him just waiting for his dad?

"This will define his relationship with his father for the rest of his life," Hughes said on the commentary track. But Hughes's imagination couldn't have let this "lost" person's final scene end without one final "lost" moment. What could have happened to Cameron if this was a story in the *Lampoon* instead of a Hollywood studio production?

Mr Frye comes home and sees his precious car destroyed. Cameron takes a stand against his father only to take a tire iron in the head and go tumbling out the already shattered window. His body hits the remains of the Ferrari. The father calls the cops and reports his son has died in a freak auto accident. The police believe the dad because he's rich and white. The mom dies from heartbreak. Dad collects the insurance money from his wife, son and car. He's a free and single guy now with a new classic Ferrari. Mr. Frye gets a happy ending. The next day at Shermer High, nobody notices that Cameron is dead because all the classmates are worried about Ferris missing school again.

I would have been laughing in the darkness at such a dark ending. John Hughes could have used his wicked sense of humor in his movies and become Chicago's version of John Waters. But Hughes wasn't going to take the risk of being a true indie filmmaker with edgy material. He wasn't going to spend his time having to raise miniscule budgets, spend a year doing the personal touch to publicize the release, eke out a minor profit and do it again for the next film. John Hughes might not have liked Hollywood studios and making movies in Southern California, but he enjoyed the paydays and the power. He dialed the darkness back and created his masterpiece that celebrated himself as the heroic Ferris Bueller and made us ignore the fate of a lost person.

SOUNDTRACK NOTES: Have you been scouring used record stores looking for the original soundtrack on vinyl? You can't stop your fruitless search. John Hughes decided that there didn't need to be a soundtrack album. He couldn't figure out how to make it happen thanks 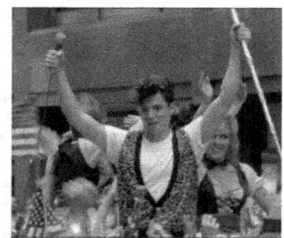 to "Danke Schoen." How could you put that cheesy Wayne Newton song in a mix with Yello's "Oh Yeah" or Sigue Sigue Sputnik's "Love Missile F1-11"? How many people would be ticked off that "Danke Schoen" was left off the album? A&M records was eager to put out the soundtrack, Hughes declined. He put out a 7" single to members of his fan club. Yes, John Hughes at this time had a fan club. He pressed 100,000 copies of the 45 featuring The Flowerpot Men's "Beat City" and Blue Room's "I'm Afraid." Neither band struck it big in the '80s although Hughes used two other Blue Room songs on the soundtracks of *Some Kind of Wonderful* and *Trains, Planes and Automobiles*. A limited-edition soundtrack CD was released in 2016. It featured "Danke Schoen" and Ira Newborn's orchestral score.

O.C. and Stiggs

July 10, 1987

MGM/UA

Directed by Robert Altman

Starring **Daniel H. Jenkins, Neill Barry, Jane Curtin, Paul Dooley, Jon Cryer, Ray Walston, Tina Louise, Cynthia Nixon, Louis Nye, Dennis Hopper, Martin Mull, Melvin van Peebles & Bob Uecker**

Rated R - 109 minutes

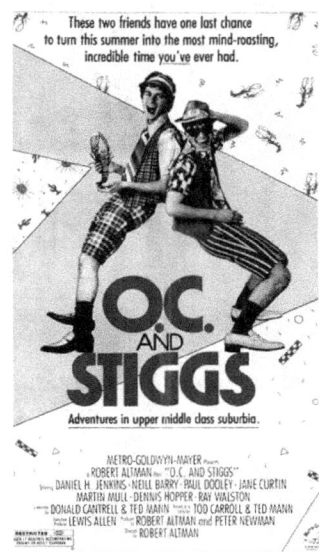

Did you know that Robert Altman made an '80s Teen Flick? Shocked?
Did you know that Robert Altman made an '80s Teen Flick based on characters from The National Lampoon?
Quit saying I'm a liar. Even the most hardcore people who constantly reference Robert Altman in film school classes will draw a blank if you mention *O.C. and Stiggs*. You might have well been mentioning an episode of *Bonanza* that Altman directed. But *O.C. and Stiggs* really happened. Although it barely happened.
Why would anyone hire Robert Altman to direct a teen flick with a script that came from characters in the *National Lampoon*? Why would Robert Altman want to make a movie based on outrageous teens summer adventures that hijacked an issue of The National Lampoon? This is the man who directed *M*A*S*H, McCabe and Mrs. Miller, The Long Goodbye* and *Nashville*. What could motivate him to pursue this project?
There are quite a few reasons why the auteur director landed the gig.
Altman launched his Hollywood studio career with films aimed at teenagers. *The Delinquents* was an indie feature he

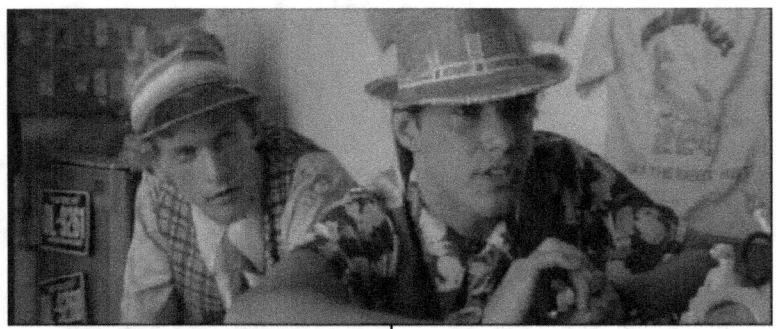

made back in Kansas City to break out of making industrial films. This was quickly followed up by *The James Dean Story*. The documentary was a rush job made shortly after Dean died in the car wreck to give teenagers a reason to flock to the cinema one more time to find out more about the gone to soon star of *Rebel Without A Cause* and *East of Eden*. The two teen films got Altman plenty of gigs directing television shows including *Bonanza, Combat!, The Millionaire, Hawaiian Eye* and others. He was hanging with Alfred Hitchcock who had him do a couple episodes of *Alfred Hitchcock Presents*. There was a history of him in the teen genre.

But what made him want to make a teen flick at this point of his life? Altman had recently made the musical *Popeye* that was one of the biggest box office successes of his career. He wasn't able to really get any clout out of it at the major studios because of his issues during the production. Robin Williams wanted Altman fired. Indeed, the former *Mork and Mindy* star referred to the Popeye village in Malta as "Stalag Altman." The director had a falling out with Harry Nilsson which led to Van Dyke Parks taking over the music element of the film. The production went over budget on money and time. While the film sold plenty of tickets, *Popeye* didn't come close to the predictions the studio bean counters had made when the greenlight was lit. His success was viewed as failure in Hollywood which is never good. He seemed doomed to helming episodes of *The Love Boat*. Things were looking bleak for Altman until he discovered the *O.C. and Stiggs* script which was viewed as a fast-track project at MGM after they outbid Paramount. He sold himself as perfect for the project since O.C. and Stiggs were teenage versions of *M*A*S*H*'s Hawkeye Pierce and Trapper John except they didn't waste their time in med school learning to be surgeons. He was sold on the characters even though it doesn't appear he subscribed to the *National Lampoon*.

O.C. and Stiggs were the saviors of *National Lampoon*. The magazine was having another changing of the guard. The first batch of writers left and struck showbiz gold with *Saturday Night Live*, *Caddyshack* and *National Lampoon's Animal House*. The next generation of writers including John Hughes were now splitting for movie gigs at the start of the '80s. After a decade in publication, the magazine was sagging in subscribers with a circulation around half of its peak of a million readers in the mid-70s. Even worse than the drop in sales was the average reader's age going higher. Those that still read it were no longer the hip and young at colleges and high schools which wasn't good for advertisers. The magazine needed to connect with those teenagers hanging out and being up to no good. Writers Ted Mann and Tod Carroll created Mark Stiggs and Oliver "O.C." Oglevey. The O.C. was for "Out of Control." The two high schoolers were rude, crude and lewd to the extreme. They didn't take no for an answer. The delivered revenge to anyone that opposed their will. They acted without caring about the consequences. Since O.C. and Stiggs "wrote" their dispatches in the magazine, they were always the winners. Their "Annual Gash Report" was a disturbing breakdown of how much the duo had gotten laid over the last year in the

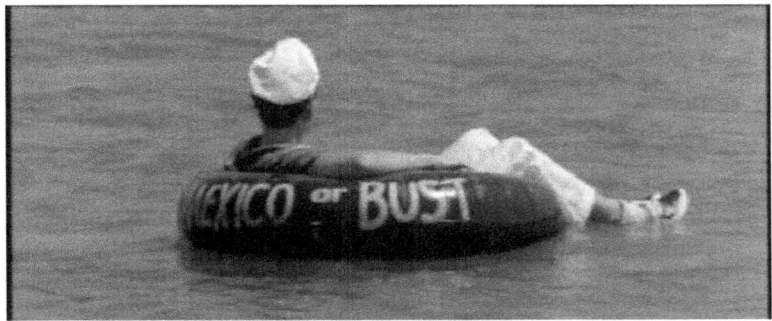

form of a business report you'd get from a Fortune 500 company. Except those companies didn't include questionable photos of their executives wearing pig masks in the shower or sound like a Penthouse Forum Letter. This was the level of tasteless comedy that your mother wouldn't get a laugh out of. Because of that revulsion "Annual Gash Report" was an instant hit with teenagers looking for comedy of a questionable taste.

After being a feature, the duo took over the magazine in October of 1982 with "The Utterly Monstrous Mind-Roasting Summer of O.C. and Stiggs." The magazine featured story after story of their Arizona based antics from when school let out for the summer. Most of it involved attacks on insurance company owner Randall Schwab and his dysfunctional family. Their pranks get completely out of control including giving a loaded weapon as a wedding gift to Schwab's daughter that ends up in the trigger finger of Schwab's son. There's Stiggs' birthday party which involves a hotel, a hooker and their friends dressed as train engineers. They make a twisted trip to Mexico. Finally, there's more destruction with a helicopter involved. This is not the essay about your summer vacation you'd submit on an application to Princeton. But it was a great way to get Hollywood studios to notice the characters.

Paramount and MGM wanted a piece of the O.C. and Stiggs action. The success of *National Lampoon's Animal House* and *Porky's* made the duo look like a sure bet for stardom in the same way that Beavis and Butthead exploded a decade later. Paramount was looking to develop the film as a project for Sylvester Stallone as documented in Hunter Stephenson's "The Utterly Monstrous Mind-Roasting Sage of O.C. And Stiggs" that ran in *Apology* Magazine. MGM was more desperate for a teen hit and countered with an immediate green light and didn't care that Robert Altman was in the director's chair. They were just eager to have a low budget teen flick hit like *Porky's* to make up for the damage left by *Heaven's Gate*. What they got was a teenage version of *Heaven's Gate* although at a fraction of the price.

Altman wanted to get the show on the road immediately for fear that someone at the studio

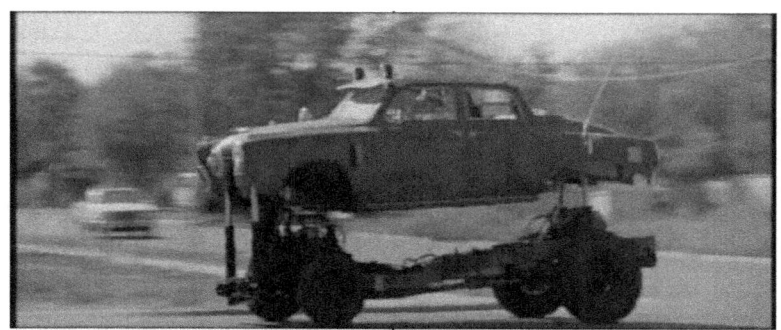

would pull the plug if they let it linger too long in pre-production.

Production started during the summer of 1983 in Phoenix, Arizona. It had barely been six months since the first draft of the script had been written. Altman wanted to strike while the iron was hot and other things were burning. The temperatures were in the 100s on the cooler days, but Altman wasn't going to wait for Fall. He had cast Daniel H. Jenkins as O.C. and Neill Barry as Stiggs. Neither had any real credits at this point in their careers. They were fresh faces to the teen flick genre. By the time *O.C. and Stiggs* arrived in a theater or two, Jenkins was a Tony nominated actor for playing Huckleberry Finn in *Big River* on Broadway. Barry was already in *Amityville 3-D* and the version of *Heat* with Burt Reynolds during this delay. Altman cast another semi-unknown in Jon Cryer to play Randall Schwab Jr. He did cast two familiar faces to fans of Teen Flicks with Paul Dooley (*Sixteen Candles*) as Randall Schwab and Ray Walston (*Fast Times at Ridgemont High*) as Gramps. This was not going to look like any other teen flick of its time. He did his usual audio tricks so audiences automatically knew Robert Altman was in control and not a fresh out of film school newbie.

The production was noted for Altman and the crew's partying ways back at the hotel they'd taken over as a production compound. He probably smoked as much weed as the fictional O.C. and Stiggs. Bob didn't stick to the script and had the cast improvise quite a bit. When Martin Mull was given a part, Altman told him to not waste his time memorizing the lines. He was going to ignore the script. This is probably where the troubled history of *O.C. and Stiggs* begins.

Even though Altman turned in a cut of the film in early 1984, the MGM was not happy. This was not the edgy teen romp they'd imagined. Why? Because Robert Altman didn't merely make the cinematic version of "The Utterly Monstrous Mind-Roasting Summer of O.C. and Stiggs." Altman had ulterior motives when he trashed the script and went with the improv. "It was a satire of teen sex comedies, gosh darn it, not an example of that dubious breed!" Altman declared during an interview featured on the DVD. Teens weren't ready for a satire of their genre since the John Hughes teen flick era hadn't even begun.

MGM had zero desire to release the film. Unlike directors who get angry when a studio dumps their movie on a vault shelf, Altman couldn't muster a protest. He didn't go on a press tour screaming about the evil and controlling studio like Terry Gilliam did when things got messy on releasing *Brazil*. The rumor is that Altman checked himself into rehab after seeing his final cut of *O.C. and Stiggs*. This was cinematic rock bottom for the partying director.

O.C. and Stiggs remained trapped in the vault at MGM for years and only one person seemed eager for its release. That was Nigerian singer King Sunny Ade. Why wouldn't he want the film to come out since King Sunny Ade and His African Beats contribute a fine musical performance at the center of the film. This exposure could have elevated his career as he was trying to break out in the America market. Being in a Robert Altman film was a big deal for a musician. Keith Carradine won an Oscar for Best Song in *Nashville* and the theme to *M*A*S*H* became iconic. King Sunny Ade was stuck waiting and talking up the film that so many people had forgotten went into production. He did stay busy by releasing at least 7 albums before he could buy a ticket and see himself on the silver screen.

MGM wasn't sure what to do with the movie. The studio did copyright the film in 1985, but there was no release. It didn't help that the studio went through a few ownership changes including that time Ted Turner bought and sold it in less than 3 months in 1986.

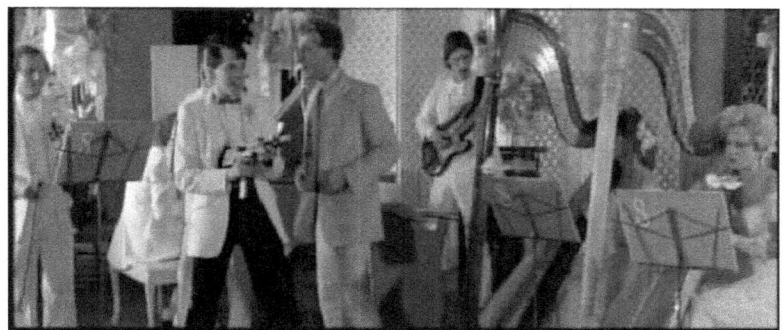

The film finally saw the light of a projector in 1987 in Los Angeles for an extremely short test release. The movie didn't play Manhattan until almost a year later when it opened on March 18, 1988 and closed the following Thursday. The total box office was under $30,000. There would be no great comeback story for the troublesome teenagers. These minor releases were probably done as a way to sell the VHS rental cassette as a theatrical release and not straight to video. A film that went into production in six months took nearly five years to see the darkness of an empty commercial theater.

The film had no buzz by 1988. *O.C. and Stiggs* hadn't appeared in *National Lampoon* for five years. *National Lampoon* wasn't a hot buzzword so the magazine wasn't part of the title. Robert Altman's career had gone completely to the art house with *Secret Honor, Fool for Love* and *Beyond Therapy* doing middling business. When *O.C. and Stiggs* finally showed up, Altman was directing *The Caine Mutiny Court-Martial* as a TV movie for CBS. He was a few years away from *The Player* revitalizing his bankability. Jon Cryer had become a leading man star with *Pretty in Pink, Dudes* and *Hiding Out*. People showing up had no clue that Cryer was neither O.C. or Stiggs. He played a rather quiet character on the screen which seemed wrong. Even Dennis Hopper looked like he'd taken a step back in roles by playing the crazy army guy after dominating *Blue Velvet* and earning an Oscar nomination for *Hoosiers*. But King Sunny Ade got his wish.

Even after the anemic theatrical release, MGM has never been sure what to do with *O.C. and Stiggs*. When the studio put together a collection of 10 teen movies from the '80s in 2011, they left out *O.C. and Stiggs* and gave us *Secret Admirer* and *Last American Virgin*. The movie did come out on DVD from MGM in 2005 in a non-anamorphic form with a transfer that looked like it was an EP speed recording off a second-hand VHS videocassette. As so many of Robert Altman's films get upgraded to Blu-ray, there seems to be no great push for the Criterion Collection to give us *O.C. and Stiggs* in 1080p. Tonight, you'll get to see that time Robert Altman made a teen movie based on National Lampoon characters. *O.C. and Stiggs* is getting the midnight movie love those boys deserve. Please don't leave your lobster shells on the floor.

SOUNDTRACK NOTES: This shouldn't be a surprise, but there was no original soundtrack album released for *O.C. and Stiggs*. The opening song is a jingle for Schwab's Insurance company about "Misery Loves Our Company." King Sunny Ade and his African Beats perform "Mo Ti Mo" in their club scene. They also contribute the 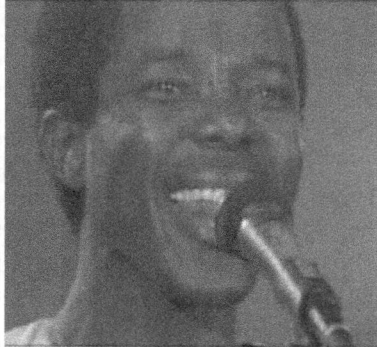 music for the closing credits. But most of the film is sparse music since Altman has dialogue coming from characters all over a scene. This "silence" might also be from MGM giving up on the film and not wanting to waste money securing the rights to pop songs for a film that wasn't going anywhere. Anything they bought in 1983 would be pure nostalgia by 1988. Or maybe this was part of Altman's satire of teen films by not giving music for montage moments. Was he playing against expectations? Either way, you just need to buy King Sunny Ade and his African Beats' *Aura* album that came out when *O.C. and Stiggs* should have been originally released.

Sunday - May 24

The Pick-up Artist 2:00 p.m.
Fresh Horses 4:00 p.m.
St. Elmo's Fire 7:00 p.m.
Less Than Zero 9:15 p.m.

Growing Up In Public

Growing old sucks. When you're a kid you think getting older and becoming an adult will be amazingly great. You imagine all the wonderful things you'll be able to do when you're not a slave to a school schedule. You create a never-ending list of things you'll be able to accomplish in your life without the burden of your parents saying, "No!" You'll drive your dream car. You'll have weekend long parties in your own swinging apartment. You'll get hooked up with a lover or a spouse or even a lover and a spouse that are cool with your arrangement. You'll transform into a vampire. Staying up until the sunrises and sleeping during the boring parts of the day is your new life. Good times were just around the corner as soon as you got that diploma.

And then the day comes when you retire from college and enter the real working world. The first thing you have to contemplate is not how many martinis can you down during your first lunch hour with fellow employees or which co-worker wants to get freaky in the VIP bathroom. You're forced to ponder "What is the difference between an IRA and a Roth IRA?" Being a grown up isn't nearly as fun as you imagined. You have to remember all the bills to pay every month. You get the cold hard reality of not only how much you have to pay monthly for your dream car, but how much your insurance company wants to charge you. Every time you go to the doctor, you're given another new pill to supplement your aging body. Have you already figured out what body parts are getting surgically replaced first? And when it comes to your dating life, it gets bleak fast. Remember that if you get married and decide to break up, you're setting your bank account on fire. You end up going to bed early because you're just tired after a long day at the office. Plus, you have to go back the next morning. All this glorious entropy grows exponentially if you have kids. One morning you use the toilet and realize your bathroom smells exactly like your grandmother's bathroom. Welcome to the sad truth of transforming into an adult.

You can cling to your youth and keep doing childhood games. You can join a kickball league, keep drinking at the same bars that took your fake ID when you needed one and dress up for various comic conventions. But at some point, you will be called out by the kids who are the age you imagine yourself still being. They'll ask you what it was like 10 years ago. Or check to see if you went to school with their parents. You'll go back to your apartment, cry and reflect on how *Logan's Run* really wasn't that bad of a concept. Maybe you needed to visit the Carousel to be renewed?

But don't be too distraught. There's nothing wrong with being an adult outside of losing hair, gaining weight and sagging all over. It's just different from the life of a high schooler. You can ease into adulthood by performing simple things like framing posters that you had thumbtacked on your bedroom walls. That looks more adult-like. Also buy a vacuum cleaner. This amazing device makes your rugs less crunchy when you use it properly. Even more important is to wash, dry and fold your own laundry instead of dumping it off with your mother every other week. You can still cheat by hiring a laundry service. But maybe you can do it all by yourself? Maybe you can be an adult.

Can you be accepted in the adult world? That's a toughie. This was a massive fear for so many of the young actors that were in the teen flicks of the '80s. Would people want to see them as an actor outside of being a high school classroom? And by people, we're not just talking audiences, but producers, directors and casting directors. Would the actors be allowed to grow up before the camera? Or would they find the offer of roles drying up as suffer the same sad fate of Rodney Allen Rippy and Mason Reese? Adding to this nervousness was the simple fact that there were so many young actors who had been doing well in the high school films. How many adult roles would there be waiting for them? Could they compete with Harrison Ford, Robert Redford and Meryl Streep for the juicy adult roles? Could they continue to be a movie star? Would they have to consider TV roles? Or maybe it was time to go back to school and get a degree.

There were a few names from this group that became immediate adult superstars. These are people who aren't so much a "Whatever happened to…" so much as a "When is their next movie coming out?" Tom Cruise grabbed stardom with *Risky Business*. He was not having to beg for roles. And he quickly was accepted as an adult on the screen with *Top Gun, Cocktail, Rain Man* and *Born on the Fourth of July*. Sean Penn shed his stoner surfer boy image as a prisoner in a juvenile detention center in *Bad Boys* with Clancy Brown, Alan Ruck and Ally Sheedy. This also allowed him to skip continuing doing comedy and get edgy material such as *The Falcon and the Snowman, At Close Range, Shanghai Surprise* and *Colors*. He didn't get stuck in *The Wild Life*; Cameron Crowe's follow up to *Fast Times At Ridgemont High*. They cast his brother Chris Penn in the lead role instead. Jennifer Jason Leigh also took on edgy characters in both *The Men's Club* and *Last Exit To Brooklyn* that led to her long career. She didn't have to get a job at the mall. Matthew Modine enlisted into Stanley Kubrick's *Full Metal Jacket* and was killing Viet Cong fighters. Jodie Foster went on to Oscar glory after taking a little time off to get a degree at Yale.

As the Brat Packers aged out of the teen flicks, people were astonished that none of them died early. There would be no James Dean, Freddie Prinze or John Belushi from this group of kids that were notorious for their outrageous partying ways. The biggest of the messed-up kids was Robert Downey Jr. He could be found in the tabloids quite often as he didn't seem to ever get cleaned up. One morning he woke up in a child's bed. Trouble was, the bed did not belong to his child. He was like Goldilocks except this time the Three Bears called the police. He became an amazing recovery story. Downey not only cleaned himself up, but transformed into a box office monster. He made the GNP of most countries as he played Tony Stark in *Iron Man* and all the other Marvel superhero films. Judd Nelson also seemed bent for obscurity. I had pals down in Wilmington who ran into him one night at a donut shop. He was in town starring in the legal drama *From The Hip*. As they said hi, Judd reached into their box and took a donut without asking first. They let it slide, but the story of his bad manners spread fast. His donut thievery didn't ruin his film work. He's had a rather busy career over the years and did make waves in *Billionaire Boys Club*. Rob Lowe looked like his career was going to take a severe detour when a sex tape came to the attention of the authorities that featured him and a 16-year-old girl. Lowe was around 24 at the time. He didn't go to jail because of various legal maneuvers and the fact that 14 was the age of consent in Georgia at the time. Lowe now sells diet candy bars on TV and hunts for ghosts with his kids. Molly Ringwald launched a singing career and was on *The Secret Life of American Teenager* without being the teenager. She's currently on *Riverdale* which is an update of *Archie*. She is neither Betty or Veronica. Ally Sheedy emerged from Shermer High and graduated to *Short Circuit* and *Maid to Order*. She reconnected with Molly on *Betsy's Wedding*. Emilio Estevez did well for a while with Stephen King's *Maximum Overdrive*, *Stakeout*, *Mighty Ducks* and *Young Guns*. He even got into directing with *Wisdom* and *Men At Work*. His focus lately has been in directing movies and TV episodes. Anthony Michael Hall was in the Oscar nominated *Foxcatcher*, the box office champ *The Dark Knight* and the upcoming *Halloween Kills*. He also ended up in *Freddy Got Fingered*. Andrew McCarthy will be in plenty of the films you see today. We'll talk about him later. James Spader and John Cusack went on to massive successes over the years. Spader has made a career playing sophisticated douchebags of various degrees from *Sex, Lies and Videotape* to the series *The Blacklist*. Cusack revisited the '80s in *Hot Tub Time Machine*.

The only major star from our festival that has passed away is Patrick Swayze. He became a massive leading man with *Dirty Dancing, Ghost, Road House* and *To Wong Foo, Thanks for Everything! Julie Newmar*. Swayze passed away in 2009 from cancer. He was 57 years old. While not a massive star, Taylor Negron also passed away from cancer in 2015. Taylor Negron delivered Spicolli's pizza in *Fast Times at Ridgemont High* and the mail in *Better Off Dead*. He was also 57.

Plenty of the actors and actresses in these films are still active on TV shows and films. They might not have names on the posters, but they're busy. Between movies, you might want to look up their IMDB or Wikipedia entries to see what they've been up to lately. Do this before the lights come down while you're enjoying our intermission mixtapes. When you see their filmography, there's a chance you've been watching them for a while. You might not have recognized them in recent roles because they're a bit older like yourself.

Chances are a few of you have been doing your best to get lost in the giant screen. You imagine you're back at the Crabtree Twin watching the movie for the first time. You want to recapture that feeling and gain a sense of time travel. You want to be able to sense that next to you is your original date at their original age. You won't look to your right because you don't want them to think you're staring at them. You can't break the spell. You want to be able to feel that you haven't grown up or graduated for the next two hours or all day long. We recommend a few more Old Styles to help you drift back in time.

Today's movies are all about the stars proving they can survive graduating from high school. *The Pick-up Artist* lets Robert Downey Jr. play an elite private school teacher that only cares about hooking up Molly Ringwald. *Fresh Horses* gives us a Molly Ringwald as a hooker on the wrong side of the river that strikes a fancy within rich boy Andrew McCarthy. It's a bleaker *Pretty In Pink* which also describes *The Pick-Up Artist*. *St. Elmo's Fire* has a group of friends floundering after graduating from college. Our night ends with *Less Than Zero*. James Spader pimps out Robert Downey Jr. to pay off his cocaine bill as Andrew McCarthy wanders through a lot of Cali parties. All four films will remind you're not enrolled in Shermer High anymore.
.

The Pick-up Artist

September 18, 1987

20th Century Fox

Directed by James Toback

Starring Molly Ringwald, Robert Downey, Dennis Hopper, Danny Aiello, Harvey Keitel, Vanessa L. Williams, Polly Draper, Robert Towne and Lorraine Bracco

Rated PG-13 - 81 minutes

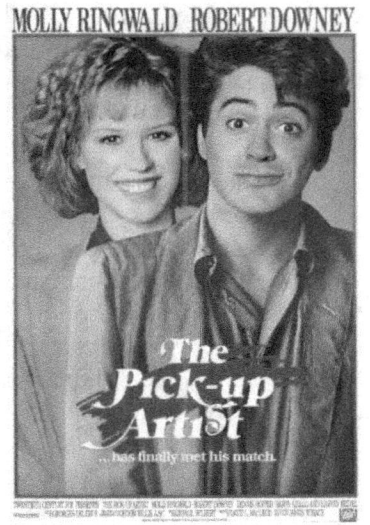

Ever have a weekend where you felt like you were living someone else's life? That's exactly how I felt the time I ended up hanging out with director James Toback at a party in Manhattan.

In order to explain how I ended up at the party, I have to take you back to a time of 56K modems and AOL Instant Messenger. It was a time best known as 1998. I had read producer Jane Hamsher's book about making *Natural Born Killers*. It was a rowdy account of all the weirdness she and her producing partner Don Murphy experienced dealing with Quentin Tarantino and Oliver Stone. But what struck me was her list of bands she liked which reflected my own taste. So as a joke on my Geocities site, I wrote that Jane Hamsher couldn't date me because she'd steal my record collection. One day I received an unexpected email from Jane Hamsher saying it's probably true. Her email account was also on AOL so I sent her an instant message. We ended up having plenty of cool conversations online. Nothing tawdry was exchanged. And I knew she really was Jane when she mailed me a complete set of Alan Moore's *From Hell* graphic novels with the FedEx address being her production office. She was in the process of developing it for a movie. In the middle of our penpal friendship, I found out through a contact in Manhattan that Jane's upcoming film *Permanent Midnight* was getting a premiere in New York City. During an IM chat I played a gambit and mentioned I was going to be in New York City and she mentioned the premiere and asked if I'd like to attend. I jumped at it. I even picked up a Krispy Kreme t-shirt for her since at the time I lived in Winston-Salem, the hometown of the donut chain. She liked their donuts when they were brought on the set.

I stayed in Manhattan at the apartment of my college pal Sidney who was head of publicity for a major record label and whose father was gearing up for a run for president. I was excited to get to see Jane and hopefully be able to make connections for my work in film. A piece of mine had just aired on the Independent Film Channels' *Split Screen* series. It focused on a film school classmate's Oscar winning short documentary about a rural dog catcher. I even landed *The Price Is Right*'s Bob Barker to record a testimonial introduction. Jane was impressed that I'd attracted Bob to the project.

The day before the big premiere, I hung out with John Pierson, the host and producer of *Split Screen* (the series is currently being streamed on the Criterion Channel). As I told him about my excitement about landing an invitation to the premiere party, he let me in on a harsh truth: Jane and Don Murphy were breaking up their partnership. The premiere party had just gone from showbiz frivolity to being invited to a divorce party. At the end of the night, I wouldn't be getting an invite to Hollywood to pitch projects at Jane and Don's office. But I wasn't going to bail because it was a Ben Stiller movie and I liked Jerry Stahl's autobiographical book about how he ended up a heroin junky while working on dumb sitcoms.

Arriving at the big premiere at the movie theater was a rush of

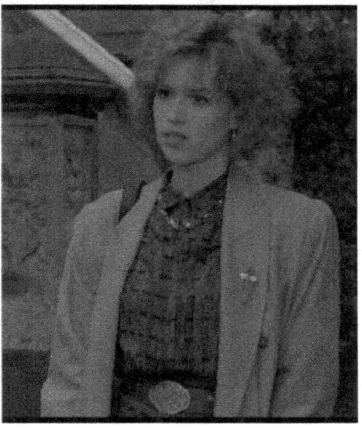

famous faces and flashing bulbs. I ran into *Village Voice* writer Michael Musto who was on the other velvet rope since he was working. I told him how much his La Dolce Musto column mattered to me as a college kid in North Carolina. I even offered him my spare ticket to the after party, but he had another event to cover at that time. While waiting for the theater to open up, I ended up meeting Anne Meara and Jerry Stiller. I had grown up seeing the comedy duo on *Tattletales* and the *Carol Burnett Show*. Anne was so sweet to me as if she was my aunt. I told them how it took me a decade to understand their "gay pandas" joke when they played Chairman Mao and his wife in bed. Jerry was astonished that I remembered the routine. I sat down in my seat and noticed a few other famous faces. I sipped on my soda to make sure I didn't get a hangover before the third reel. I'd had a couple beers on the trip over to settle my nerves before meeting Jane. Things were going great until the projector turned on.

Permanent Midnight the book is a masterpiece. The film was a mess. There were so many cinematic elements on the page that didn't make it on the screen. All the edges in Jerry

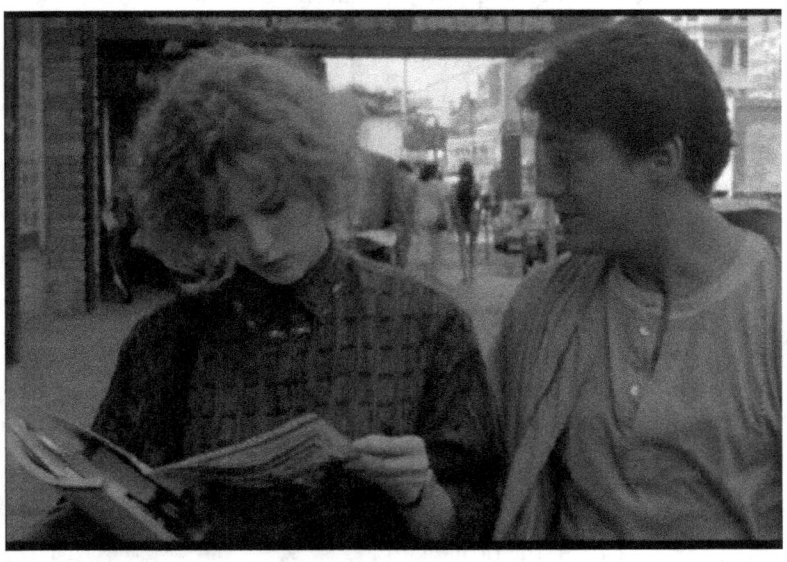

Stahl's self-destructive fall upward had been wrapped in child-proofing foam. At one point the disappointment was too much, I wandered out of the theater. I found myself staring at Sarah Jessica Parker. On a second trip out of the theater for a refill on my soda, I hit the exit door the same time as Ben Stiller. He asked where the restroom was, I told him it was on my way so follow me. The men's room was next to the theater showing *There's Something About Mary*. "Be careful in there," I joked to Stiller. The only thing that kept me watching the film and not theater creeping was the after party. There were buses taking us to the "fun."

The party was at a club that normally charged $10 for a can of Budweiser. That's $16 in today's money. But the studio had an open bar for the premiere. I was ordering up double Jack and Cokes which normally cost the same as monthly rent for a studio apartment in Soho. I felt weird talking to Jerry Stahl after my second drink since I knew he was on the wagon. I told him, "I don't have a drinking problem, I just can't turn down an open bar." He nodded, but I kept my drink hand low. We spoke mostly about his work on the '80s erotic science fiction classic *Cafe Flesh*. He said that actor Andy Nichols who played the sinister MC at the nightclub had just vanished into the Los Angeles underworld and never came back up. Later at the party I watched Elizabeth Hurley and Famke Janssen dancing together, but not in a dirty dancing way. They were like girls at junior high that were sick at how lame the boys danced. Even though I was five feet away from them, when they looked my way I was in an alternate reality. Neither made eye contact with me. Oh well. I was avoiding saying hello to Jane Hamsher since she was dealing with others talking to her. That's when I spotted James Toback standing to the side of the dance floor.

Why would I know what James Toback looked like? *Spy* magazine had done a piece on him and his unrelenting way of sexually propositioning women in Los Angeles and Manhattan. He was like Ugly George without the portable video camera gear. According to the article, he'd use any excuse to talk a woman into hopping into bed. He'd even claim it was a medical condition.

There were plenty of pictures in the article so I knew that it was Toback. So, I went over to say hello. At first, he seemed standoffish. I praised the moment at the end of *Two Girls And A Guy* when Heather Graham wraps herself after Robert Downey Jr and covers his face with her hair. It's like he vanished within him as if she was giving him the insulation to weather all going on within him. Our tone changed. Toback opened up as if we were two people who had just survived a bumpy elevator ride. The conversation at first did center on Robert Downey Jr. I said he has the capability to be the best actor of his generation. Toback didn't fight me. He adored working with Robert. What's interesting is that when *The Pick-up Artist* was coming out, lazy film writers kept suggesting that Downey's character was based on producer Warren Beatty. But Downey was playing Toback in his style of just hitting on any woman on the sidewalk. Toback was excited to share that Downey was going to be in his film that was about getting ready to hit production. He let me know that in one scene, Downey was going to hit on Mike Tyson and Tyson didn't know this was going to happen before the cameras rolled. He wanted a natural reaction. This was a shocker. I insisted he inform the crew before the scene of the immediate fire exits in case Tyson explodes. He didn't think Tyson would go that far in a reaction. You can see the finished scene in *Black and White*.

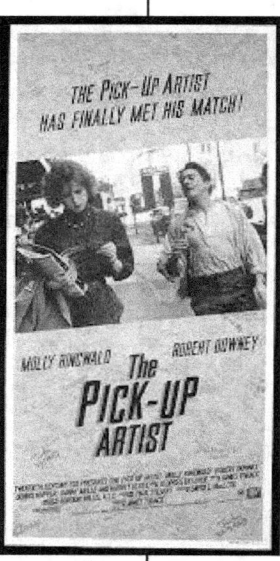

During our chat, I spotted a famous face and instinctively reacted. The Razzie Award winning star of *Ghosts Can't Do It* stormed into the bar. For just pure goofiness, I stepped forward and stuck out my hand. He shook it. "Love yer hotels, buddy!" I shouted in a pathetic Texas accent at Donald Trump over the music. His handshake was like holding a rotting fish. Earlier in the day I had stumbled into a Barnes and Noble and found Jackie Chan signing

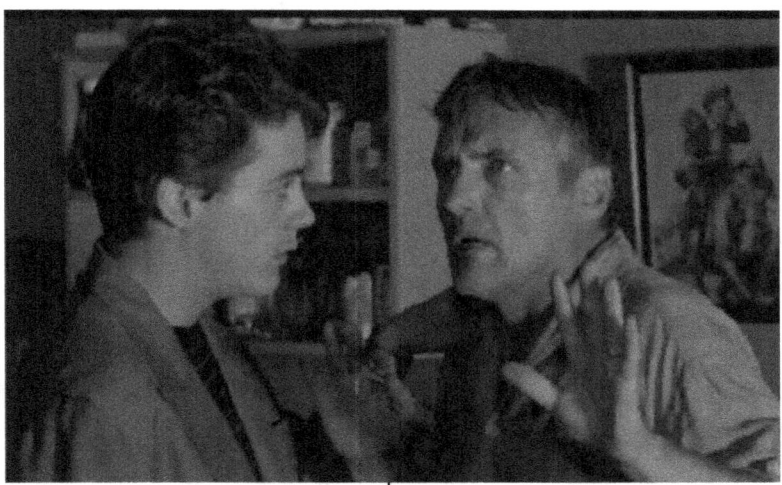

his autobiography. Jackie knew how to shake my hand so I knew he was Jackie Chan. Trump's handshake equaled touching the paw of a sock monkey with a combover. He mumbled something and walked away. I turned back to find Toback howling. "Do you know what you did?"
"I shook Donald Trump's hand," I replied.
"Do you know what you did?" Toback repeated.
"I just shook his hand."
"He's a germaphobe! Look!"
I turned back to see Trump rushing across the bar. His arm dangling in the air and his fingers stretched out as if he'd just touched something that had been in a David Cronenberg film. Toback kept laughing at the sight of the future president fleeing into the men's room.

"I took the subway up here. Who knows what's on my hands?" I declared.

We ended up talking about how Trump at that point was so broke and yet the banks couldn't admit how broke he was because then they'd have to admit the money they'd loaned him was gone. He had pulled off the perfect way to rob a bank.

Around this time our conversation was joined by a writer for AOL's entertainment department. This was when it struck me that I now had the perfect way to introduce myself to Jane Hamsher. I explained to the guy about how Jane and I were AOL chat friends so it only made sense that he'd take my Krispy Kreme t-shirt over to Jane and point me out to her. I didn't even insist he say, "You Got Mail!" He wasn't buying it. Over the course of five minutes, I did my best to hammer into him that it was his corporate responsibility to bring Jane and I together. While I was dealing with his resistance, Toback was smiling at the interaction. The AOL writer was stubborn and not into the fun. He finally said no and stormed off. Toback praised my tenacity. "That was a great scene," the director said.

"But I failed," I admitted.

"It was still entertaining," Toback said. And with that he offered to take the t-shirt over and introduce me to Jane. And he did. And after I thanked him and began chatting with Jane, Toback wandered off.

She sort of introduced me to Don Murphy and he gave me a sneer since he knew I was one of Jane's friends. It was a divorce party. There would be no invitation to his half of the production company. Oddly enough years later, I got into a flame war with Don Murphy on a website's comment section. So happy I don't have to feel obligated to him for a big break. I kept up my online friendship with Jane for a bit more, but she would soon get out of producing movies and focus on political activities. We lost touch, but it was so nice that we met that evening.

The next morning on my long drive back to film school in Winston-Salem, I realized that I had completely screwed up by not giving James Toback my name, phone number or an AOL email address. It hurt even more later when I discovered that even though Toback was a screenwriter, he liked a lot of improvisation in his films and working with non-actors. I had impressed him with Trump and the AOL writer. I could have weaseled my way into a small part in *Black and White* and starred with Ben Stiller and Robert Downey Jr. Oh well. Oddly enough, one of my film school classmates was Danny McBride. He ended up in *Tropic Thunder* with Ben Stiller and Robert Downey Jr. Strange to think I experienced a weekend in Danny's future life.

SOUNDTRACK NOTES: *The Pick-Up Artist* didn't seem to have an original soundtrack album released when the movie came out. Nearly 20 years later, composer George Delerue's score was released on a CD along with the score of *Sherlock Holmes in New York*. Later it would be re-issued with Delerue's 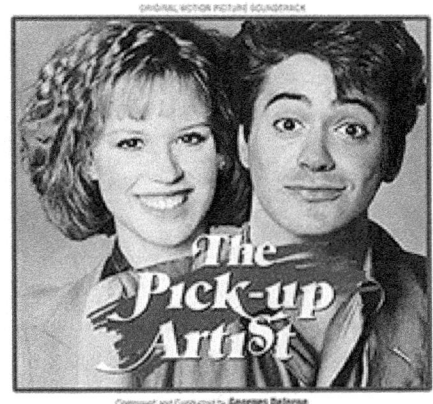 score of *Rapture*. If you don't remember much of the orchestra, it's because Toback went heavy with songs which didn't make it on an album. "Da Doo Ron Ron" by the Crystals with Phil Spector producing sets the pounding tone and wall of sound. You are ready for Robert Downey Jr. to not back down from hitting on women. Phil Spector gets another two songs on the screen with Darlene Love's "Wait Til' My Bobby Gets Home" and The Ronette's "(The Best Part of) Breakin' Up." In one of the strange things, Stevie Wonder wrote and played all the instruments on "The Pickup Artist" yet has Keith John sing the song. All the music isn't old. The Beastie Boys' "She's Crafty" blasts as Downey stalks Molly Ringwald to her apartment in Coney Island. LaVert's "Casanova" brings on the seductive New Jack Swing. This jam is still right when you're ready to make your move.

Fresh Horses

November 18, 1988

Columbia Pictures

Directed by David Anspaugh

Starring **Molly Ringwald, Andrew McCarthy, Patti D'Arbanville, Ben Stiller, Leon Russom, Molly Hagan** *and* **Viggo Mortensen**

Rated PG-13 - 103 minutes

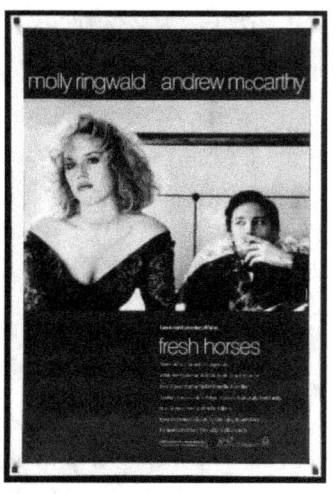

I hope Andrew McCarthy doesn't take this as a slam, but not once in the '80s did I hear anyone say, "Do you want to see the new Andrew McCarthy film at the Imperial 4?" McCarthy was a rather unassuming superstar of the time. Even with his name on the poster and his face in the trailer, you'd sit down in the theater and during the film's opening credits, you'd lean over and tell your date, "Andrew McCarthy is in this too?" He just didn't overwhelm viewers of the time with his image and persona like Tom Cruise, Molly Ringwald or Judd Nelson.

Think I'm making this up? When you bought the all-day pass for this Sunday's lineup: Did you call this "Andrew McCarthy Night?" Or have you just sat down in the theater and noticed that we're showing an Andrew McCarthy Triple Feature? Was your focus on the bookend of Robert Downey Jr. movies? Were you eager to see Molly Ringwald as Dennis Hopper's daughter and a country gal? Or were you thrilled to finally see *St. Elmo's Fire* on the big screen? It's perfectly fine to admit that Andrew McCarthy wasn't on your mind until this moment.

When you describe an '80s film starring Andrew McCarthy, you don't feel the obligation to mention his name until the second sentence.

Think of all the Andrew McCarthy movies you've seen here and his two monster hits after he left the Brat Pack universe. He didn't get between the camera and the concept. *Class* was about a mother who sleeps with her son's high school roommate. *Pretty In Pink* was about an artsy girl who chooses between her quirky friend and a rich boy. *St. Elmo's Fire* was about a group of friends who can't cope with life after college in Georgetown. *Less Than Zero* is about a group of friends who can't cope with life after high school in Los Angeles. *Mannequin* is about a store mannequin that comes alive. *Weekend At Bernie's* is about a boss who becomes dead and employees that make him look alive. You're under no obligation to start off with Andrew McCarthy's name at the beginning of the logline. Attempt to describe an Andrew McCarthy film without mentioning Andrew McCarthy and you will easily succeed. The marketing focus of *Fresh Horses* was Molly Ringwald playing what might be hooker and not Andrew McCarthy as a conflicted rich boy. That's not to say that McCarthy is forgettable. But he didn't get between the viewer and the core reason to buy a ticket. This also meant that people didn't avoid buying a ticket to a movie if they noticed Andrew McCarthy on the poster.

There were a few critics who felt that McCarthy was rather disposable as an actor. As if all the young actors of this era were interchangeable and parts were determined by a massive game of musical chairs to a Wang Chung soundtrack. But don't be fooled by this attitude. Andrew McCarthy brought more to the screen than impeccable '80s hair, a naive charm and boyish enthusiasm.

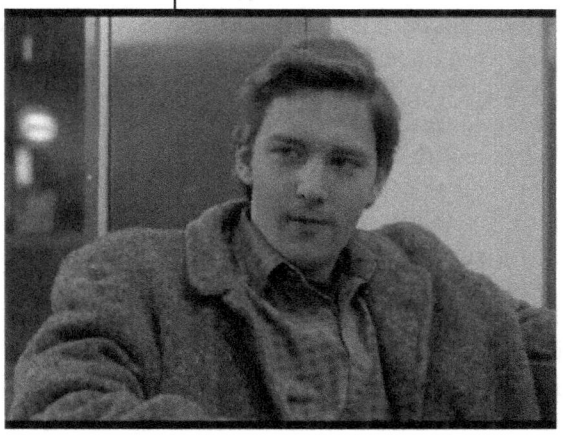

McCarthy was deceptive. He disappeared into a character and yet the character didn't alter his identity afterward. If you were the kind of person that screamed out at celebrities passing you on the moving sidewalk at the airport, what would you yell at Andrew McCarthy? Would you scream: Jonathan Ogner! Kevin Dolenz! Blane McDonough! Clay Easton! Matt Larkin! Or just stick with Andrew McCarthy!!! Although you might yell out "Where's Bernie?" Ultimately you have a good feeling seeing Andrew McCarthy.

Those who thought Andrew McCarthy could easily be replaced by any of his co-stars are wrong. However, Andrew McCarthy could replace his co-stars without an issue. When it comes to *Class*, he would have been a perfect Squire Franklin Burroughs IV. But Rob Lowe couldn't have pulled off Jonathan Ogner. Lowe lacked that puppy eyed sweetness that made you view Jonathan as someone swept up in a sex and booze whirlwind. If Lowe had hooked up with McCarthy's mother, it would be so slimy and leery like a Penthouse Forum letter. The same is true for *St. Elmo's Fire*. He could have played Rob Lowe's irresponsible man-child, Emilo's Woody Allen worshipping waiter/lawyer or Judd Nelson's jerkish political operative. But none of that trio could have pulled off sleeping with Ally Sheedy and looking hurt when it doesn't turn into his dream romance. You'd imagine those other three merely notching their bedpost and taking aim at Demi Moore. In *Pretty in Pink*, McCarthy could have stiffened up to achieve Steff, but there's no way James Spader would have been accepted as Blane. Would you believe James Spader would buy a Steve Lawrence record and listen to it thinking it was cool because Molly Ringwald recommended it? Likewise, in *Less Than Zero*, McCarthy could have gone emotionally cold to play the drug dealing Rip. But Spader wouldn't be believable as Clay and neither would Robert Downey Jr. at that point in his career. You can't buy that either actor would be looking out for his friends except to screw them over even harder the second time around. There's no way Ben Stiller could make us believe he'd leave his fiancé for a maybe-hooker if roles were swapped

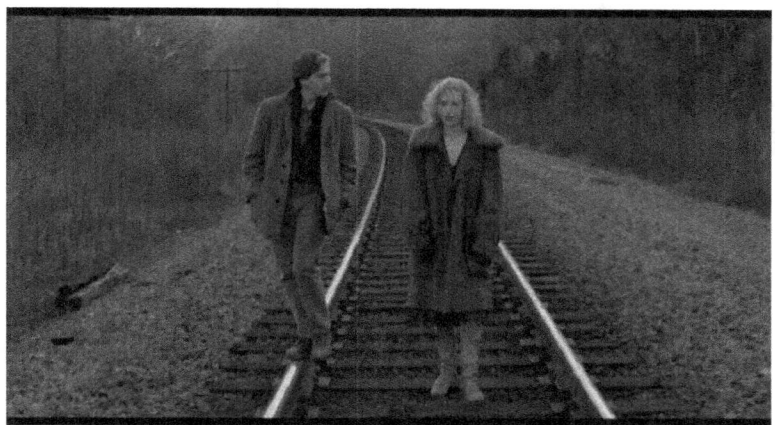

in *Fresh Horses*. He'd probably figure out an arrangement and live a double life. Andrew McCarthy wouldn't want to play Stiller's character since it's pretty insignificant of a role.

Andrew McCarthy was the umami of '80s actors. He brought a new taste to the screen. Viewers didn't hate him for his character's actions like they did James Spader, Rob Lowe and Judd Nelson. Director's must have loved the fact that they had a performer who could do the unspeakable without being immediately viewed as a creep. Even John Cusack couldn't pull off what McCarthy could do with a character. He had that umami factor that none of the other Brat Pack actors could offer audiences. This is why Andrew McCarthy became an '80s icon without overwhelming us.

During an interview by Andrew Goldman in the *New York Observer* back in 1999, Andrew McCarthy was not happy being lumped in with the Brat Pack. He hated the misconception that it really existed as a social unit like Frank Sinatra or Bogart's previous packs. He didn't party with his *St. Elmo*'s castmates. He didn't even have their phone numbers. He hadn't even met Anthony Michael Hall at this point. Not sure if he's met him since then. But it wasn't like there was a clubhouse or even a secret VIP room at the Hard Rock Cafe. What burned McCarthy most was in the original Brat pack article Emilio Estevez slams him as doubting he'll have much of a career. There was probably a massive amount of jealousy between him and the other male actors from *St. Elmo's Fire*. Why? Because Andrew McCarthy arrived as a star. His other co-stars had spent time as child actors taking bit parts in movies and TV shows before they got their names at the top of the credit roll. Andrew McCarthy's family wasn't in showbusiness to hook him up with a gig. Andrew McCarthy showed up to audition for *Class* and walked away with his first movie role, his name in a star credit spot and the focus of the movie poster since he's only wearing a tie while playing footsie with Jaqueline Bisset. Rob Lowe had been plunking away for a few years and had to share equal status with an overnight sensation. All of them dreamed that they'd get the big break like McCarthy. John Cusack was stuck in the minor role of a cigarette swallowing classmate in *Class*. He had to work his way up through three films before becoming the star of *The Sure Thing*. McCarthy took the express elevator to the top of stardom and got to make out with Jacqueline Bisset on that ride. Why did McCarthy get cast in *Class*? I have no solid idea, but I have a bit of theory what made him stick out at the cattle call. When you see him in *Class*, you'll be struck at how he looks like a teenage David Hemmings. The English actor had always had a bit of a following in Hollywood after great performances in Michelangelo Antonioni's *Blowup* and Dario Argento's *Deep Red*. What casting director wouldn't have their eyes opened wide when a young Hemmings enters the room? That's just my theory. Although McCarthy might clear it up when he releases his autobiography *Brat: An '80s Story* in 2021. And you might run into

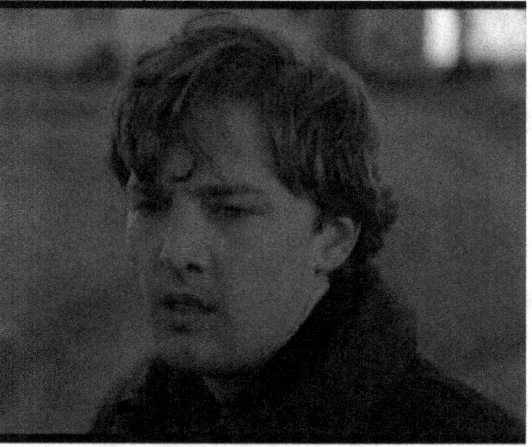

McCarthy at the airport. Beside directing TV shows including episodes of *Orange Is the New Black*, McCarthy is an editor-at-large at *National Geographic Traveler*. He wrote the book *The Longest Way Home: One Man's Quest for the Courage to Settle Down*. Be prepared to see him on the moving sidewalk when making your flight connection.

The ultimate way to describe Andrew McCarthy is to remember the last time you flipped through the shoebox that contains your old Instamatic photos from the '80s. You spotted a slightly familiar person next to you in a party shot. You remember him as a nice enough guy even though he slept with your mom, stole your girlfriend, had revenge sex with your fiancé, dumped your sister for a hooker and caused you to relapse. But all and all, he's a nice enough guy. Such was the deceptive edamame charm of Andrew McCarthy in the '80s.

SOUNDTRACK NOTES: Turns out there was no official soundtrack to *Fresh Horses*. There was no perfect cassette to play while crossing over the river to that party house in Kentucky. There were enough fine tracks that could have 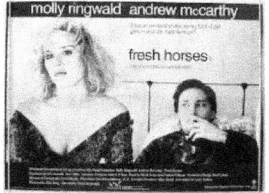 compiled a decent album. College rockers The BoDeans warn us to "Don't Be Lonely." Dwight Yoakam gives a little geography with "South of Cincinnati." Timothy B Schmit performs "Into The Night" while waiting for The Eagles to reunite. Starship picks up your hopes with "It's Not Over Til It's Over." And we get a rockin' number from that Little Ol' Band From Texas with ZZ Top's "Blue Jean Blues." Louise Goffin contributes "Bridge of Sighs." She was part of the *Fast Times at Ridgemont High* soundtrack. One of the most interesting things is three songs by ragtime pianist Jules Ruben including "Play It Again Jules," "Misty Day" and "Shear Music." All are perfect songs for calling off your engagement.

St Elmo's Fire

June 28, 1985

Columbia Pictures

Directed by Joel Schumacher

Starring **Emilio Estevez, Judd Nelson, Rob Lowe, Andrew McCarthy, Demi Moore, Ally Sheedy, Mare Winningham, Andie MacDowell & Jenny Wright**

Rated R - 110 minutes

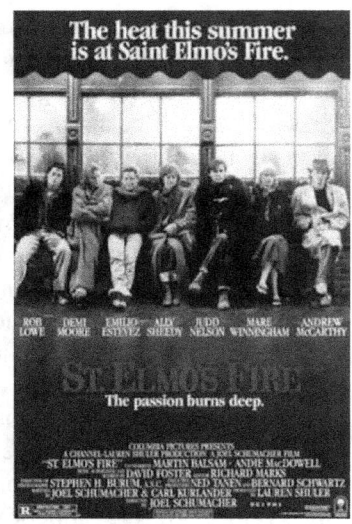

Before *The Avengers*, we had *St. Elmo's Fire*.

People were excited in the summer of 1985 when the cast members of *Class*, *The Breakfast Club* and *No Small Affair* united for an epic adventure as they battled the ultimate villain of teenage years: Adulthood.

Barely four months before, Emilio Estevez, Ally Sheedy and Judd Nelson were enduring Saturday detention in Shermer High. Even after they were forced to write that essay about "Who you think you are," the trio were blaming others for their lack of responsibility. *St. Elmo's Fire* had them still struggling to find an answer. After four years of Georgetown University, the trio are rather aimless and quite ruthless in the adult world. They were joined by three other teen flick idols. Rob Lowe and Andrew McCarthy seemed like the self-entitled schmucks that graduated from the snobby prep school in *Class*. Rob was avoiding responsibility with drunk driving, sax playing and no consequences attitude. Andrew still had issues getting laid and feeling like a fraud. Demi Moore remained a rocking chick although now stuck with a day job instead of nightly gigs at the club.

Along with the six teen flick all-stars, Mare Winningham was part of the cast. I don't

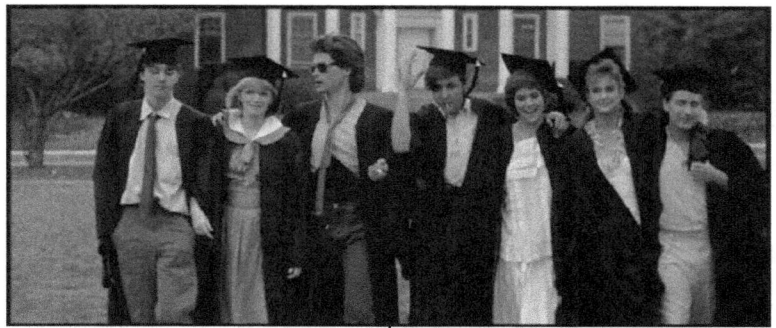

mean to make the Oscar nominated actress sound like an afterthought, but she really wasn't part of the teen flick scene. She had won an Emmy for a TV movie. She'd guest starred on *James At 15, Police Woman* and *Starsky and Hutch*. But as far as film went, at this point she had roles in Paul Simon's *One Trick Pony* and *Threshold* with Jeff Goldblum and Donald Sutherland. She hadn't enrolled in an '80s cinematic high school. Since this was the time before the internet and smartphones, most kids in the theater had no clue where Mare came from. Many people assumed she was the Molly Ringwald stand-in since her character was daddy's princess and she had a crush on the bad boy like Claire Standish at the end of *The Breakfast Club*. But *St. Elmo's Fire* was being developed by Joel Schumacher long before *The Breakfast Club* so this is just a case of character coincidence.

Now you may wonder why Molly Ringwald and Anthony Michael Hall didn't end up in the film with their fictional classmates. Turns out they really were of high school age when making *Breakfast Club*. They wouldn't be old enough to get served mugs of beer at St. Elmo's. The other three Shermer students were old enough to be defending their doctoral thesis projects at college when they were serving high school detention. What about the other familiar faces that weren't at the reserved table? Jon Cryer was still rather unknown with *O.C. and Stiggs* still trapped in the MGM vault. James Spader was just getting a name for himself with *Tuff Turf* and *New Kids* being released this year. John Cusack was off making *The Sure Thing* and *Better Off Dead*. Oddly enough Brat Packer

Robert Downey Jr was not considered for the film although he'd go on to be in *The Avengers* films. He was busy yanking down the gym shorts of Anthony Michael Hall in *Weird Science*.

Getting *St. Elmo's Fire* off the ground wasn't an easy process. When Schumacher was shopping the project, the studios weren't marveling at the package. Let's face the fact that a year before the movie opened, none of the eventual cast were box office stars. All the studio executives had to deal with was the pitch and what was written in the screenplay. Schumacher admitted, "A lot of people turned down the script" in Susannah Gora's book *You Couldn't Ignore Me If You Tried* (2010). The director recounted how the head of one studio described the main characters as "the most loathsome humans he had ever read on the page." That studio executive was so right.

I still remember walking out of a screening of *St. Elmo's Fire* opening week with a group of college newspaper pals and someone said, "Are we going to be that horrible when we graduate?" Nobody in the group wanted to emulate anyone in the film. Nobody was eager to hit the mall to dress like Georgetown Yuppies in training. This was also the first time we considered liking Woody Allen might be a bad thing. Although the movie did lead to people reciting the lines from when Judd and Ally bust up their record collection which was still on vinyl at the time. Except the record collection would include The Butthole Surfers, Throbbing Gristle and Raffi.

If a serial killer showed up with a chainsaw in *St. Elmo's Fire* and started lopping their heads off, your first response isn't "What the Hell?" You'd be hollering at the screen, "About time!!!" But there would be no Jason, Michael or Freddy claiming victims. You want them to suffer consequences for their life choices. So why wasn't there a serial killer in the script? First off, studios in the '80s didn't want to make serial killer films where every character is so deserving of being chopped into little pieces. Hollywood doesn't want to make a film where the audience would boo if there's a final girl. By the end of the film even sweet Wendy Beamish (Mare Winningham's character) wore out her welcome when she kept going back to Billy Hicks (Rob Lowe). Not one character deserved to survive this nightmare. The second reason was someone must have thought they could have made a sequel and maybe teenagers would buy another ticket if they believed there'd be a blood drenched massacre at St. Elmo's bar. I was expecting such a disturbing fate when the movie came out.

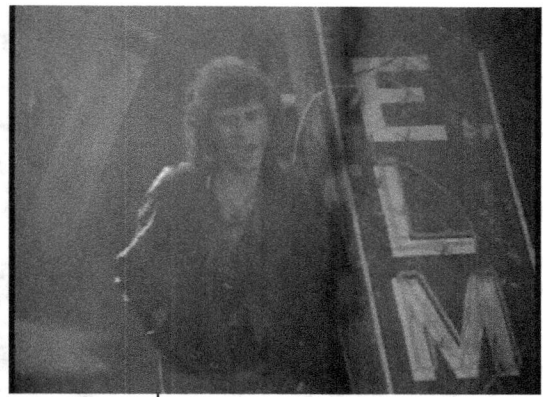

One of the big places that created buzz for *St. Elmo's Fire* was MTV. The channel was all about teenagers and a key to getting kids hyped up for the film. Thus, John Parr's theme song "St. Elmo's Fire (Man In Motion)" was being played every other hour with Mark Goodman, Alan Hunter and Martha Quinn reminding us the film was coming to select theaters. While the video got butts in those select seats, it confused me into thinking this was going to be a teen Irwin Allen disaster film. I expected *The Towering Inferno* at P.D. McSwingers bar. Why? Because the rock video featured the famous cast roaming around the smoldering ruins of the St. Elmo's bar set as Parr sings about feeling St. Elmo's Fire burning within him. (We'll be playing the video before the film so don't be late to your seat.) Maybe the video was a clue that all seven of the friends had perished in the fire and John Parr was the Angel of Death collecting their insignificant souls. For nearly two hours, I waited for the giant fire at the bar that the gang might not survive. I wanted to see Judd Nelson running around with his arms blazing. I imagined Emilo Estevez beating the flames off Demi Moore's cocktail dress. I wanted to find out that Andrew McCarthy was the pyro, but everyone forgives him because he's Andrew McCarthy. I wanted to witness Rob Lowe melt like that Gestapo agent in

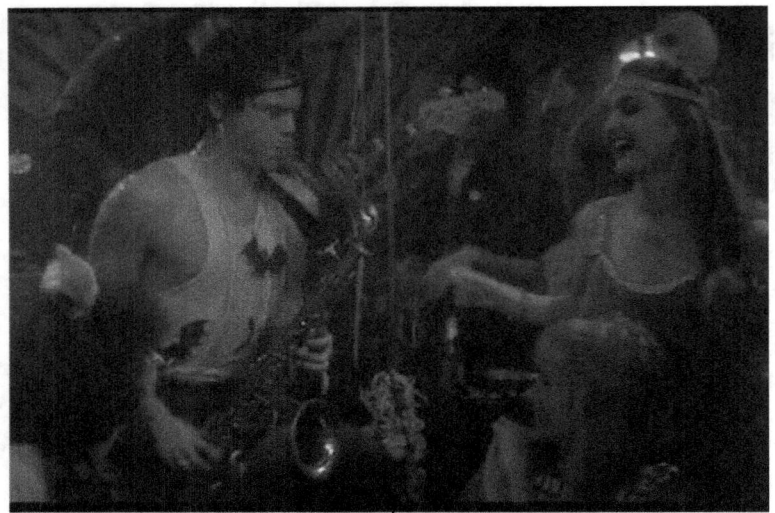

Raiders of the Lost Ark. But there would be no fern bar inferno. When the end credits rolled, I wanted to run up to the projection booth to find out what happened to the real ending. I felt cheated out of my imagined redemption slaughter. How could these seven vile college friends still be lurking amongst us? Why didn't we see any comeuppance? Where's my fiery tragic ending?

The film's ending did prove to be tragic for hundreds of people. How could this be? Why wasn't there a massive protest? Because the victims were saxophonists. Major bands from around the world came together in London, Philadelphia and other locations to be a part of Live Aid on July 13, 1985. If you sat at home and watched MTV all day, you saw dozens of memorable performances in support of feeding the starving people of Ethiopia. Many of the bands that day featured saxophonists with big time solos including Men at Work, INXS, The Style Council, Spandau Ballet, Sade, Sting, Bryan Ferry, David Bowie, George Thorogood and the Destroyers, and Hall & Oates. The sax solo was a mainstay of early '80s New Wave culture and a few weeks after Live Aid, the sax vanished from rock bands. By the late '80s, rarely did a person hold a saxophone in the band photo. Even established bands would just work out a way to play that sax solo on the synthesizer to save a seat on the tour bus. The new bands discarded the instrument completely as a viable part of their sound. 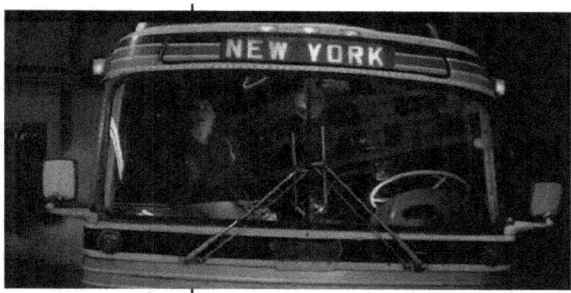 Since the invention of rock and roll, the saxophone was that instrument that brought spiced up rock music with a sensual nature. Think of Bobby Keys' sax solos on Rolling Stones tunes. But no more. Saxophonists found there was no future for them once they stopped playing in the college marching band. What possibly could have happened to make it so the only saxophonist left standing was Clarence Clemons of Bruce Springsteen's E Street Band?

Billy Hicks happened. Rob Lowe played Billy as a saxophonist who was an absolute disaster in Billy Hixx And The New Breed. He had to be the center of attention no matter what anyone else in the band wanted to do. He wasn't even the singer. His main role in the band was dry hump the audience during a solo, shake his hair sweat on the ladies and beat up his baby mama's date.

Seemed like the only place he could get booked was St. Elmo's. They weren't touring anytime soon. Billy was a nightmare and not a stellar bandmate. At the end of the film, he announces he's leaving town and heading up to New York City to join any band that will take him. "If I can find someone who's fool enough to let me play my sax," Bill cockily declared. As he stood on the bus with the New York destination sign lit, you could hear every musician in the greater Manhattan area decide they would never have a saxophonist in their band for fear that it was the "real" Billy Hicks. And once New York City closed their doors to saxophonists, other cities with bus terminals closed their rock band memberships for fear that Billy would sneak into their practice rooms and recording sessions.

And sadly, few people at the

time noticed how the saxophone had vanished from American Top 40. There were now guitar and synthesizer solos to fill the gap. Eventually we'd get the guest rapper solo. The saxophonists would have to retreat to the world of light jazz and fight Kenny G. for record sales. Billy Hicks was responsible for the Great '80s Saxophone Slaughter and he never suffered any consequences like pretty much everything in his life.

If Hollywood ever remakes or produces the long-delayed sequel to St Elmo's Fire, I better hear a chainsaw at the end of the trailer.

SOUNDTRACK NOTES: John Parr's "St. Elmo's Fire" made zero sense since as we learn from the film what St. Elmo's fire means, there's no way it burns inside you. But this didn't matter to listeners who elevated the song to number 1 on Billboard. Oddly enough while the song featured a trombone and a trumpet, there was no 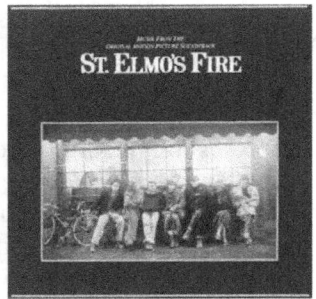 saxophone. Billy Hicks was already making the instrument unpopular. "Love Theme from St. Elmo's Fire" hit 15 on the chart. Although this is confusing since was there any real love between the characters? They should have called this "The Pity Fuck Theme from St. Elmo's Fire" or "The Revenge Fuck Theme from St. Elmo's Fire" or even "The Will You Give Me Money If We Fuck Theme from St. Elmo's Fire." But "Love?" That's a nasty big word for an emotion that wasn't really happening in the film between these seven horrible friends. Other songs featured two vocalists without their famous bands. Fee Waybill does "Saved" without The Tubes. Jon Anderson said no to the reunited Yes and solo recorded "This Time It Was Really Right" solo. Rocker Billy Squier's "Shake Down" doesn't quite shake the image of him prancing around in the video for "Rock Me Tonite." Most of the record is David Foster's instrumental compositions that sound perfect for antiquing in Georgetown. Foster sneaks his old band Airplay onto the vinyl with "Stressed Out (Close to the Edge)."

Less Than Zero

November 6, 1987

20th Century Fox

Directed by Marek Kanievska

Starring **Andrew McCarthy, Jami Gertz, Robert Downey Jr, James Spader, Nicholas Pryor, Tony Bill, Sarah Buxton, Lisanne Falk, Michael Greene, Anthony Kiedis, Flea and Brad Pitt**

Rated PG-13 - 103 minutes

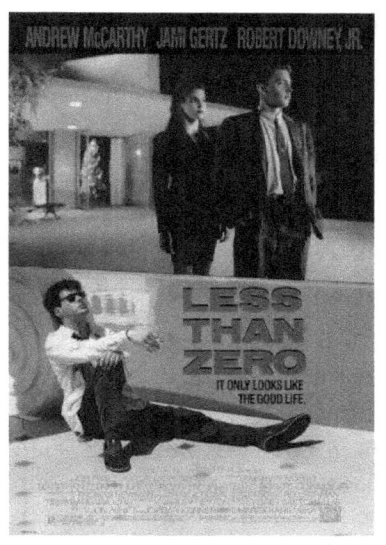

We talked quite a bit about the Brat Pack. But do you remember the Literary Brat Pack? Are you thinking the Brat Pack wrote novels? This is slightly true. Ally Sheedy had her children's book *She Was Nice to Mice* published in 1975 when she was just 13. Ally was not one of the members of the Literary Brat Pack. Neither were any of the other actors who would come out with tell all autobiographies. The Literary Brat Pack was coined and corralled in 1987 thanks to an article in the *Village Voice* that bundled together a group of young writers whose first novels were receiving a bit of buzz.

In the '80s, America was aching for a new pack of writers to promote. In literature class you'd learn about the Romantics, the Lost Generation, the Algonquin Round Table and the Beat Generation. But then what? There were superstar authors in the '70s, but they didn't seem too eager to be shoved in a box and given a nickname. Quite a few of them would probably have gotten into fist fights inside that box. Then in 1987 a plucky writer at the *Village Voice* discovered the new literary group and gave them a slightly familiar nickname. Thus the Literary

Brat Pack united whether they wanted it or not.

Who were a part of the new breed of writers that were going to set Waldenbooks and B. Dalton on fire at your nearest mall? There are arguments as to who really was considered part of the group. But most lists include the Big Three names.

The first out of the box was Jay McInerney. His *Bright Lights, Big City* was about a fact checker at a magazine who snorts lots of cocaine, stays up all night at discos, screws up his work, gets his ass fired and, in the end, eats bread. Oddly enough Jay McInerney worked at the *New Yorker* magazine as a fact checker and found himself fired after a few months. We can find no verification that McInerney ate bread so it might not be a cleverly disguised autobiography. His book was released as part of Vintage Contemporaries, a new line of trade paperback books that Random House launched to attract younger readers who didn't want the burden of hardback novels in their delicate hands. So McInerney's debut work got an extra buzz since it was part of the debut of this new wave of marketing fiction.

The second name mentioned was Tama Janowitz with *Slaves of New York*. She wasn't exactly a new novelist since her novel *American Dad* had come out and vanished without much impact in 1981. Her follow up novel was rejected by the publisher. She did find success writing short stories that ended up in the

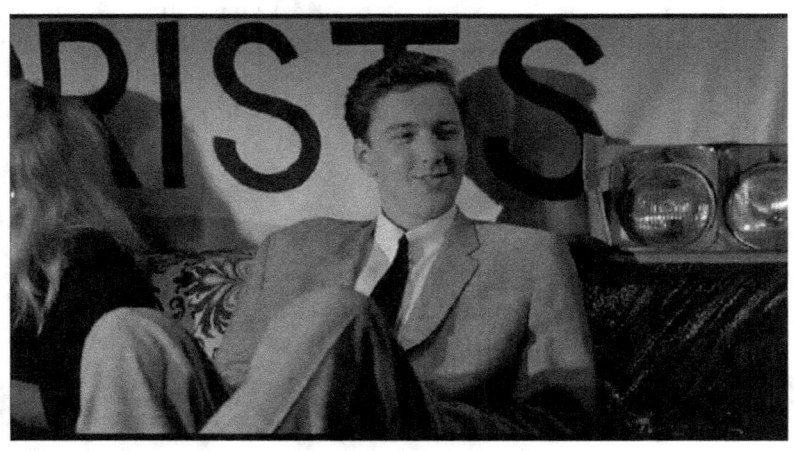

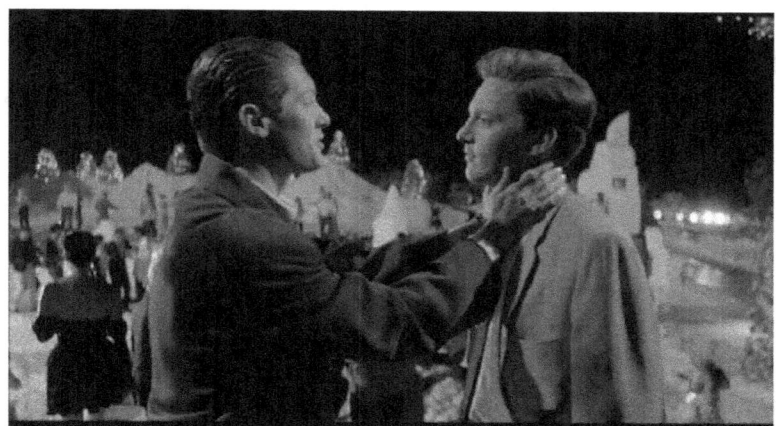

New Yorker including what became the title story in *The Slaves of New York*. She was all about the artsy life in New York City since she was part of Andy Warhol's final entourage before his death in 1987. She quickly turned her literary fame into commercial dollars as a spokesperson for Amaretto liqueur. The magazine ads featured her with her piles of hair looking literary near books or just scribbling on paper with the catchy phrase, "Amaretto di Janowitz." Critics viewed her as a commercial sell out. Those with a bit of sense understood that living in New York City was expensive. You don't say no to free money or complimentary booze. It was advertising that would get your name and face in magazines all over the place. Publicity for novelists was a rare thing if your name wasn't Stephen King.

The final angle of the core Literary Brat Pack triangle was Bret Easton Ellis. He was the true youth of the group and the only one from the West coast. Ellis grew up in Sherman Oaks, California. That's right, he got to hang out at the Galleria like the kids from *Fast Times At Ridgemont High* and the victims of *Chopping Mall*. He did end up in the Northeast like his other two Literary Brat Pack compatriots. He wrote *Less Than Zero* as part of his creative writing studies at Bennington College in Vermont. What is Bennington College? Back in the '80s, I found myself at a frat party on the Duke campus because a pal didn't want to pay for beer. The frat bros began circling us since we didn't look like we truly belonged. A few months before my friend Todd had almost got into a fight at a different frat until his date told the Greek dorks that he really was Peter Buck. Todd looked nothing like the guitarist of R.E.M., but the frat dudes bought the story and took photos with him. As I was being eyed, I didn't want to fake being Mike Mills of R.E.M. The band was getting their videos in rotation on MTV so they might notice the difference. So instead coming clean that I was a student at N.C. State, I lied about being on break from Bennington. They chilled out immediately. Why? Because in the mid-80s, Bennington was the most expensive college in America. Even more frightening was the Vermont liberal arts school didn't believe in grades or course credits at the time. If you didn't graduate with a degree, you walked away with nothing to transfer to Duke. In the frat boys' eyes, I was an academic daredevil and had parents with money to burn. I continued to drink for free.

Bret didn't need to worry about his bar tab since *Less Than Zero* sold over 50,000 copies during its hardback release in 1985. The book was about a rich kid heading back to Los Angeles for his Christmas break from a preppy New Hampshire college. The character does drugs, has sex with either gender and realizes most of his friends are soulless, junkies, hookers, soulless junky hookers or dealers. He reflects upon a poster for Elvis Costello's *Trust* album cover. Then he flies back to New Hampshire for spring semester. Since his character went to school in New Hampshire instead of Vermont, *Less Than Zero* might not be a cleverly concealed autobiography.

As much as the three writers over the decades have tried to distance themselves from each other and the literary Brat Pack tag, they were connected. They were photographed at the same party in the '80s. Their biggest connection is that all of them at this high point in their career were represented by literary agent Amanda "Binky" Urban at ICM. And before that gig, Binky was a General Manager at the *Village Voice* which ended up promoting her clients as "The Literary Brat Pack." Coincidence?

There were other writers who got lumped into the Literary Brat Pack because in the world of books, anything to get your name out in the public is a

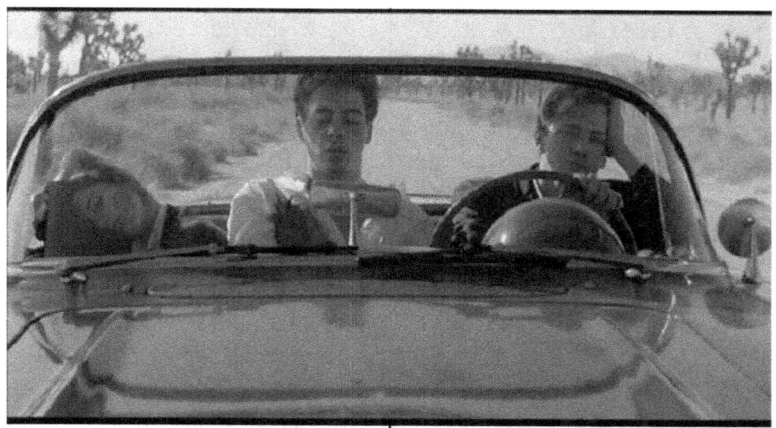

good thing since publicity budgets for a novel are rather limited. Literary agent tried to get their client stuck on the list. Novelists need attention. It is easier to list the writers of the '80s that weren't considered part of the Literary Brat Pack: Stephen King, Steve Erickson, Kurt Vonnegut and Kathy Acker. Among the authors that were frequently mentioned as part of the outer circle were Jill Eisenstadt, Mark Lindquist. Susan Minot, Donna Tartt, Peter Farrelly and David Leavitt. For those of you curious, Peter Farrelly is the guy who along with his brother Bobby wrote and directed *There's Something About Mary* with Ben Stiller and the remake of *The Heartbreak Kid* with Stiller and my old classmate Danny McBride. He would not direct the theatrical adaptation of his novel *Outside Providence* that came out in 1999.

All three of the core members of the Literary Brat Pack found themselves dealing with filmmakers when it came to their breakthrough books. This is exactly how McInerney was there for the birth of the Brat Pack. In the original *New York* magazine article, the hot new author was partying with the actors since they were interested in being part of the *Bright Lights, Big City* movie. At the time Joel Schumacher was attached to direct with Tom Cruise as the troubled fact checker and Judd Nelson, Rob Lowe and Emilio Estevez as part of his partying world. Perhaps Demi Moore and Ally Sheedy would also be back. No news if Andrew McCarthy was interested although he could have played the rabid ferret if necessary. It was going to be *St. Elmo's Fire 2*. Until it wasn't. After Schumacher and Tom Cruise ankled the film, the Brat Packers fled the project. It fell into the lap of Michael J. Fox who was superhot from *Back to the Future*. But the material had to be watered down since Fox wasn't quite the guy who could do loads of drugs and get out of control like his character in *Class of 1984*. He was a likeable star with fans now. It did end with him eating bread. The film didn't make *Back to the Future* bucks or *Teen Wolf* cash.

Janowitz had a more prestigious art house experience as Merchant Ivory productions made *Slaves of New York*. She was dealing with the classy tandem of producer Ismail Merchant and director James Ivory that gave us *A Room With A View* and *Howard's End*. Janowitz adapted her stories into a bit of a narrative about Eleanor (Bernadette Peters) being stuck in a bad relationship with an artist. She can't break up with him because she doesn't want to lose their downtown apartment. The film is a fun look at the Manhattan art scene in the '80s. But the movie was a box office bust and died quickly on the art house circuit.

Which brings us to what happened when Hollywood turned *Less Than Zero* into the Literary Brat Pack meets the Brat Pack. When 20th Century Fox started to adapt the book to the screen, they realized there was a problem at its core. Clay, the student back in Los Angeles was not a studio approved character. He did lots of drugs.

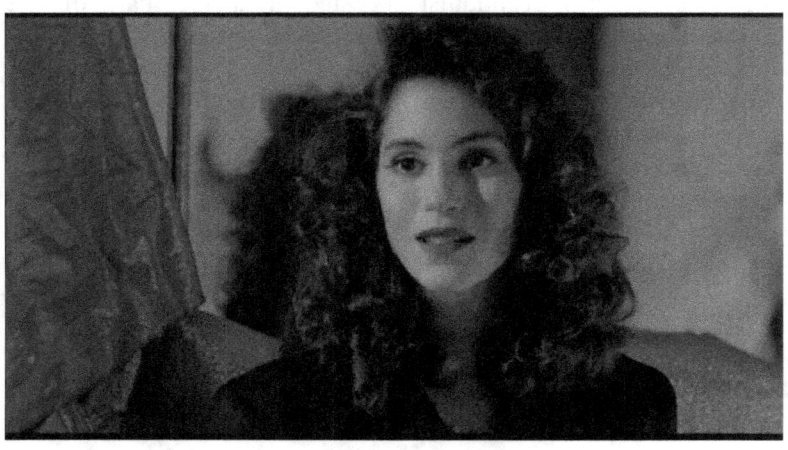

He was bisexual. He barely registered any emotion even when finding out his drug dealer has a teenage girl held hostage as a sex slave in his bedroom. This would be like a major studio making a movie out of an unenthusiastic *Penthouse Forum* letter. The studio wanted to exploit the title, but not the debauchery in the pages between the covers. So the studio gave it the same treatment as when James Bond's producer made *Moonraker* and *Octopussy*: Just use a few names and the title. In order to make Clay a bit more likeable, they cast Mr. Likeable: Andrew McCarthy. They created a plot where he returns to Los Angeles for Christmas so he can save his girlfriend (*Sixteen Candles* & *The Lost Boys*' Jami Gertz) and best friend (Robert Downey Jr) from the decadent and deadly life represented by drug dealing James Spader. If you liked the book, you won't recognize the movie. The oddest part of the film is how drug dealer James Spader gives a $50,000 line of cocaine credit to Robert Downey Jr. When Downey can't pay up the money, Spader forces his *Tuff Turf* pal into gay prostitution. How much money was Spader charging guys who wanted sexual favors from future Tony Stark? Downey was going to be on his knees for years to pay off all the blow that went up his nose. Spader seems like a pretty bad small business owner. I pondered how much cocaine did Robert Downey Jr buy with his credit line. Was it the size of a five-pound sack of sugar or just a pint-sized baggy? I wrote to the Twitter account of screenwriter Harley Peyton.

He tweeted back, "The usual 80s movie weight." Well, there you have it.

The Literary Brat Pack quickly lost its luster thanks to their next novels being rather disappointing and their movies not selling tickets to teens or the art house. Bret Easton Elis had a massive payday in the '90s with the controversial *American Psycho* which was adapted to a movie with Christian Bale. McInerney and Janowitz never came close to their initial burst of '80s fame. All that's left of this era are faded Page 6 photos of the authors at parties and a dog-eared spoof of a yellow Cliff's Notes by *Spy Magazine* that summarizes all the Literary Brat Pack books during their glory days.
.

SOUNDTRACK NOTES: Def Jam records went full force on the original soundtrack album. This is where LL Cool J's "Going Back to Cali" came from. This is the track to jam on your Walkman as you're descending into LAX or even the Bob Hope airport in Burbank. The Bangles rock up Simon and Garfunkel's "Hazy Shade of Winter." Although they snip out the 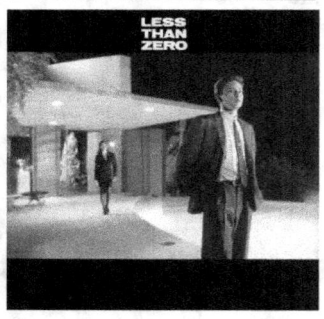 line about vodka. The record label didn't want them talking about booze. Slayer gives their version of "In-A-Gadda-Da-Vida" that doesn't last the entire side of an album like the original by Iron Butterfly. Poison covers Kiss' "Rock and Roll All Nite." Public Enemy gets wicked with "Bring the Noise." Not only does Glenn Danzig do "You and Me (Less than Zero)," but he sticks around to co-write "Life Fades Away" with Roy Orbison. The soundtrack album is perfect music to accompany your friend working off his $50,000 drug debt.

Monday - May 25 (Memorial Day)

River's Edge 4:00 p.m.
The Rachel Papers 7:00 p.m.
Say Anything... 9:00 p.m.

Ione Skye: The '80s Supernova Sweetheart

She appeared out of nowhere in 1987 and shined so brightly in 1989. During this short course of time Ione Skye captured the fancy of many with her smart and precious characters.

Where did she come from? The simple answer is England. But her life was not a low profile start like many of her thespian peers. She's the daughter of English folk rock superstar Donovan and American model Enid Karl. Her father's big hits were "Mellow Yellow," "Catch the Wind," and "Jennifer Juniper." Your mother probably played them in the station wagon while driving you to soccer practice. Ione's mom might not have played them since she left the singer before Ione's birth. She moved back to America and Ione grew up in California where she became friends with Moon Unit Zappa, the singer of "Valley Girl." During an interview with *People* magazine in 1987, Ione said she never had any contact with her famous father.

Unlike other kids who dreamed of being an actress and did hundreds of auditions, Ione Skye lucked into her first major role. She had posed with her older brother Donavan Leitch for a fashion piece in the *L.A. Weekly*. Her brother had already appeared in the earth-shattering dance epic *Breakin' 2: Electric Boogaloo*. Later in the decade, he'd end up in the remake of *The Blob* and

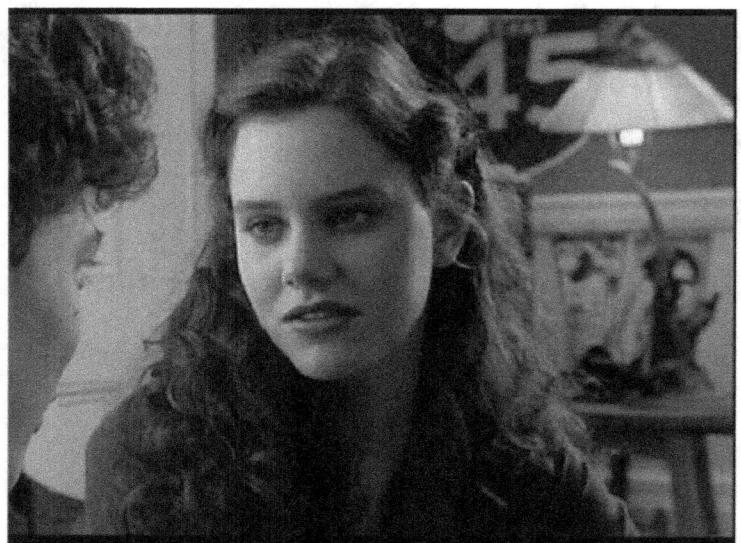

Glory with Matthew Broderick. The fashion layout was supposed to be a promotional tool for his career. Instead, director Tim Hunter saw the photos in the entertainment weekly and had her contacted to see if she wanted to audition for *River's Edge*. Ione didn't let the director down. Her role as Clarissa gave a bit of shine in the bleak high school tale of murder and silence among a group of students. In any other teen flick, her and co-star Keanu Reeves would have been the most dazzling and beautiful Prom Queen and King. Since they were in a movie that opened with a classmate's naked corpse down by the river, it's not good to think about beautiful things. Even with the dark and nihilistic tone of the film, people couldn't help having a crush on her character. Her long curly black hair and off-white cable knit sweater stuck out from a greasy world of denim and leather. *River's Edge* received critical acclaim during its theatrical release with Ione Skye getting pegged as the hot new star.

Clarissa led to even more work for Ione Skye. She had parts in *A Night in the Life of Jimmy Reardon* with River Phoenix, the science fiction tale *Stranded* with Maureen O'Sullivan (*Tarzan and His Mate*) and the miniseries *Napoleon and Josephine: A Love*

Story with Jacqueline Bisset (*Class*). Ione was so busy that she had to drop out of high school.

In 1989, Ione had the amazing back-to-back roles in *The Rachel Papers* and *Say Anything*. Viewers enjoyed her performances without having to feel repulsed by the subject of teen homicide. Both movies were about young men wanting to be her characters' lovers. This was something many of the viewers in the audience could understand. Although Lloyd Dobler (John Cusack) in *Say Anything* was a bit more noble in his intentions than Charles Highway in *The Rachel Papers*. Highway is a bit of an English cad trying to lure her away from James Spader. Lloyd is just a goofy American with dreams of Mixed Martial Arts fame in an era where UFC wasn't a big sport. What is interesting is that the end of *Say Anything* features Ione's character leaving for England and *The Rachel Papers* has her in England. We're running the films opposite how they came out so no one gets confused and ponders how during the transatlantic journey John Cusack turned into James Spader.

You might have anticipated Ione Skye being a massive star in the '90s with such a career arc. But as quickly as she arrived, her name vanished from the marquees. Now this isn't turning into a tragic "True Story" biography. Nor will this piece turn into an investigative search for Ione Skye. Her career doesn't appear to have been derailed and destroyed after she fought off the sexual advances of a creepy studio executive or agent. Her profile lowered because she just wanted to enjoy life and love. She had fallen hard for Ad-Rock (Adam Horovitz) of the Beastie Boys. She was having more fun being with him and the band. She enjoyed being on the tour bus and not stuck inside a Star Waggon waiting for a PA to say the set had been lit. Their relationship was the primary focus of her life. Eventually the two would marry (they divorced in 1999).

We always have to remember that being a leading actor means a lot more than showing up on the set at call time. You're responsible for all the publicity that builds hype and sells tickets. You have to do the TV talk show circuit as well as all the magazine interviews and fashion layouts. If you get big enough, you have to start developing your own projects. There's a lot of stuff that must be tended to that doesn't happen in front of the cameras. It's rather overwhelming for someone whose big break was helping her brother out with a fashion shoot. This leads quite a few up-and-coming actors to flee Hollywood for a different life. Although instead of stepping away, she just stepped back.

There's a telling quote from an interview with *People* (August 3, 1987) after *River's Edge* had come out. She said, "If all this stopped. I could slip back into the way I was. I'd miss acting, but I wouldn't be wrecked." Ione figured out how to have the star element stop without losing the acting. She focused on life and took smaller parts. She started with Alison Anders' *Gas Food Lodging* where she was the troublesome older sister with less screen time than Fairuza Balk. She's been in *Wayne's World, Guncrazy* (with Drew Barrymore), *But I'm A Cheerleader, Fever Pitch, Zodiac* and dozens of TV shows including *Arrested Development*. Far as her life on the other side of the camera, Ione Skye is a mother, a painter and wrote the kids book *My Yiddish Vacation*. You can find her work at https://www.ioneskyepaintings.com/

Tonight, we remember the three biggest roles for Ione Skye when she was the Sweetheart Supernova of the '80s.

River's Edge

May 8, 1987

Island Pictures

Directed by Tim Hunter

Starring Crispin Glover, Keanu Reeves, Ione Skye, Daniel Roebuck, Dennis Hopper, Joshua John Miller, Roxana Zal, Josh Richman, Phillip Brock, Richard Richcreek & Taylor Negron

Rated R - 100 minutes

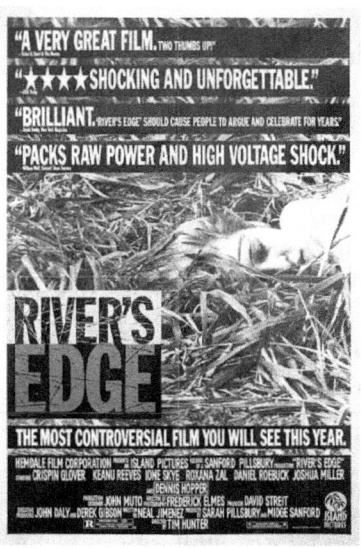

Normally when discussing *River's Edge*, it turns into a discourse about poverty, drugs and nihilism in American youth. "What's wrong with the kids?" types the concerned critic. How does a society end up with a teenager that kills and his friends do not want to narc him out? Where did this attitude in the youth come from? The answer was being projected in the neighboring theaters at the cineplex. There were two other films about kids that kill featuring actors that have appeared in our festival.

Already playing in the cineplex was Oliver Stone's *Platoon* when *River's Edge* was added to the marquee in the spring of 1987. The movie about Charlie Sheen (*Ferris Bueller's Day Off*) dealing with life in Vietnam had just won the Oscar for Best Picture. A few weeks later Stanley Kubrick's *Full Metal Jacket* deployed with Matthew Modine (*Private School* & *Vision Quest*) surviving Marine boot camp and Vietnam during the Tet Offensive. Both films were about young men learning what it takes to be a soldier in a warzone where every day can be your last alive. And part of their job was to make someone else's life their last day alive. Modine's Private Joker is taught how to be a killer at Parris Island. During training, Gunnery Sergeant Hartman declares, "Your rifle is only a tool. It is a hard heart that kills. If your killer instincts are not clean and strong you will hesitate at the moment of truth. You will not kill. You will become dead marines." He learns how to harden his heart so that when the moment of truth arrives during the Tet Offensive in Vietnam, he won't be a dead Marine. Private Joker also learned what it's like to keep silent from authority and not report things like the night they have a blanket party for Private Gomer Pyle. Charlie Sheen's Private First Class Chris Taylor is transformed during his time fighting in Vietnam and it wasn't exactly for the better. Both men came of age in a world where randomly firing an automatic rifle at a crowd of strangers wasn't completely considered a bad thing. While the Vietnam War was long over by the '80s, teenagers still had a fear of being unwillingly dragged into the next major conflict.

The military draft came to an end in 1973 when the Secretary of Defense announced the military would be all volunteer in the wake of the signing of the Paris Peace Accords that were supposed to bring peace to a divided Vietnam. There was relief in the teenagers of America knowing their birthdays would no longer be used against them for a draft lottery. Presidential Gerald Ford scrapped making men register for the draft in 1975. And the relief lasted until 1980. What happened? After the Soviet Union invaded Afghanistan on Christmas Eve of 1979, President Jimmy Carter took several steps to show his displeasure without launching a direct attack at the cold war foe. There were several sanctions

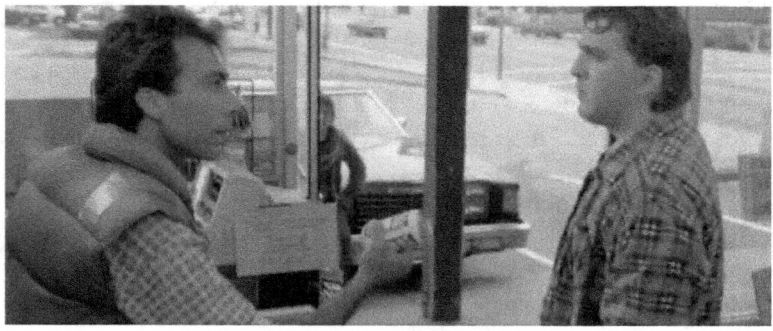

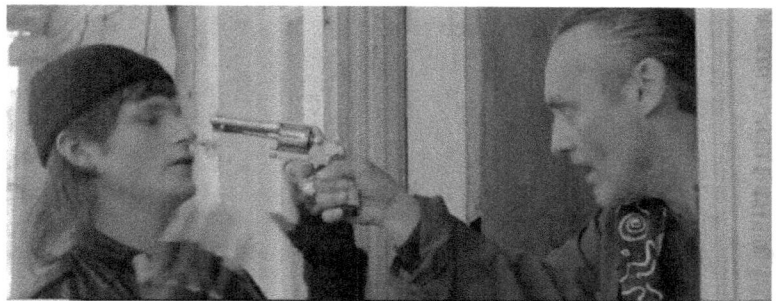

instituted. The biggest global action was to unite other countries into boycotting the 1980 Olympics scheduled for Moscow. The games were still held, but who cared how commie countries did against themselves? One of Carter's saber-rattling actions got the attention of the youth of America. In order to show this country may eventually go to war with the Commie USSR, Carter signed the Registration Under the Military Selective Service Act on July 2, 1980. All males born on or after 1960 had to march down to the post office and register for the selective service. This was met with quite a bit of resistance. Republican presidential candidate Ronald Reagan swore he would eliminate the Selective Service if he won the election. This move swung a bit of youth vote to Reagan and he won in a landslide that November. And then Reagan decided to keep the Selective Service. He also blackmailed into existence a national drinking age of 21 by withholding highway funds to states that think 18-year-olds should have an Old Style. You want to know why the teenagers of America hated Reagan; these two backstabbing actions were it. The young men of America were back to being denied booze and being forced to sign up for the military. And if you tried to protest by not signing up, you could spend six years in prison and be fined up to $10,000. I didn't know anyone who had enough cash to fight the government. Off to the post office I went to fill out a postcard and pray for peace until I'm middle aged.

The only good part was during the '80s there weren't prolonged wars that needed the Selective Service to be converted into a military draft. Even though 241 U.S. Servicemen died in a suicide bomber's truck attack in Beirut, Lebanon, Reagan chose to withdraw rather than elevate the U.S. presence. The invasion of Grenada was a four-day affair in 1983. The Panama invasion was also a rather short event at the end of 1989 under President George Bush (the H.W. came later). This was a bit of a relief for those of us who had registered and feared having their life turned upside down if the Department of Defense decided to start picking out ping pong balls to build up troop numbers. Although the recruiters for the volunteer army were as insistent as a timeshare salesman as they beat the bushes for volunteers.

Towards the end of high school, an army recruiter showed up at career day. He had found out that my father was a West Pointer and received a Bronze Star for his actions during the Tet Offensive in Vietnam. The guy must have thought he'd lined up a pigeon to beef up his quota of recruits for the month. At the time, I had a classmate who was getting hassled by a Navy recruiter who was calling his house more than his girlfriend. I didn't want this guy bothering me like a college coach eager to land a four-star quarterback. After he gave me a short pitch, he asked if I was interested in a military career like my father. "I'm a self-starter," I told him. "I don't like being told when it's time to kill." He stared at me as if I was joking. I stared back and didn't crack a smile. He immediately started talking to a student walking past the table and ignored me. I moved on with the good feeling that I wasn't his target anymore. In all honesty, the only three people I was prepared to kill during my college years were Johnny Walker, Jim Beam and Jack Daniels.

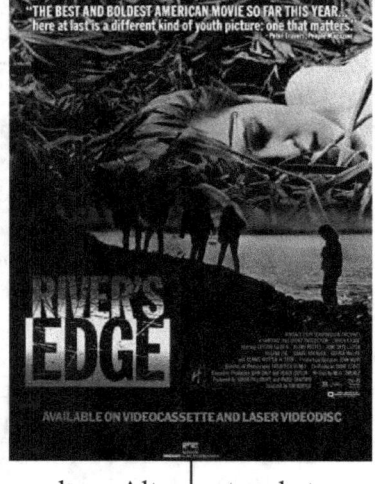

The army recruiters had a better place to find their future service members than my school. While they weren't in the film, you could sense they were lurking around the high school from 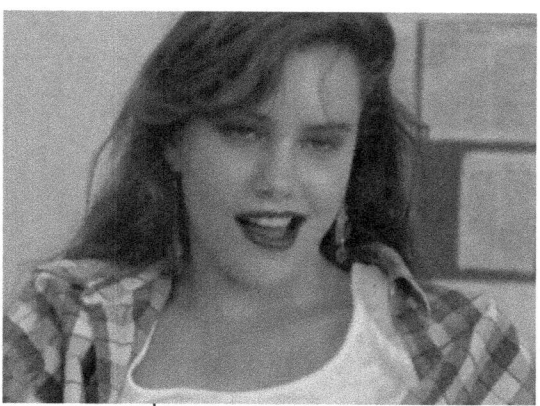 *River's Edge*. They thrived in communities where the only hope for a better life was enlisting in the military or receiving an athletic scholarship. If you didn't have a jump shot, you might as well practice lacing up combat boots. The military was ready to pitch the promise of seeing the world, learning a trade and earning a scholarship for college education. They did have better fringe benefits than working at the convenience store with about the same chances of taking a bullet on the job. Think of how many life stories feature the speaker declaring how when they were growing up in their dangerous neighborhood, they had only three choices: the grave, prison or the army. They enlisted and found their true calling in life.

While movie critics were shocked at the behavior of the kids from *River's Edge*, there's got to be a few military recruiters who viewed the high schoolers as displaying a lot of potential in the infantry or as a marine. The students understood how to keep a secret and stay loyal to their unit. They weren't squeamish around a dead body. Most importantly their blood flowed through a hard heart. These were the kids with those special traits that the military-industrial complex craved for in the volunteer fighting force. They were ready to leave high school and serve Uncle Sam. There was nothing wrong with the kids if you had the right job for them...and they weren't all self-starters.

SOUNDTRACK NOTES: The record album didn't hold back the nature of the movie with the cover declaring, "The Soundtrack Album to The Most Controversial Film of the Year." You're not going to read that on the soundtrack to *The Care Bears Movie*. The folks at Enigma Records put together 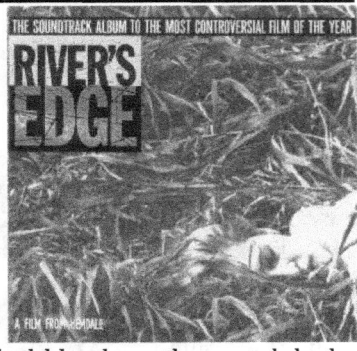 the songs for *River's Edge* didn't hold back on the metal darkness. The movie that scared your parents featured the music that frightened your parents. There are four tracks from Slayer, a thrash metal band that didn't mind putting Satan and the occult on their album covers with titles such as *Hell Awaits, Reign in Blood, South of Heaven* and *God Hates Us All*. On this record we get "Die By the Sword," "Captor of Sin," "Evil Has No Boundaries" and "Tormentor." There's also Hallows Eve's "Lethal Tendencies," Fates Warning's "Kyrie Eleison" and Agent Orange's "Fire In the Rain." This truly was a cassette you'd pop into the car stereo when you were up to no good. Even now you'd look fearsome blasting this music while waiting in line at your kids' carpool lane. These aren't the poppy songs your local Big '80s music channel put in rotation. Oddly enough things went South for Enigma Records when they attempted to push a comeback for former *Partridge Family* teen heartthrob David Cassidy. Guess Satan wasn't pleased.

The Rachel Papers

May 12, 1989

United Artists

Directed by Damian Harris

Starring **Dexter Fletcher, Ione Skye, Jonathan Pryce, James Spader, Bill Paterson, Jared Harris, Lesley Sharp, Claire Skinner & Michael Gambon**

Rated R - 94 minutes

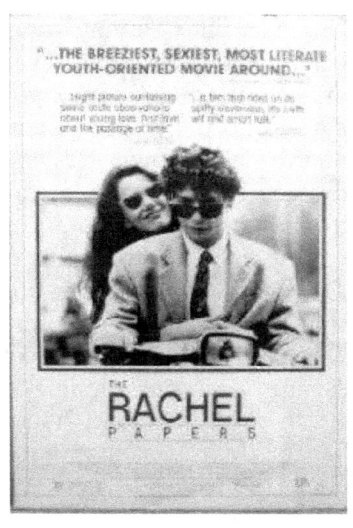

The Art House was a cinematic palace of wonder in the '80s, but you might not have known it until you matured. As a high schooler, you never asked your parents to take you to Cambridge to see *The Tin Drum* at the Orson Welles Cinema. You were too busy plotting how to get into see *The Empire Strikes Back* for the fifth time at the Showcase Cinemas in Dedham. Even if you asked your mom to drop you off at the Orson Welles, she'd think there's something extra disturbing about the foreign film with subtitles since when was the last time you wanted to "read a movie." You were only able to pass English Literature with the assistance of Classics Illustrated comic books. You might as well have asked her to drop you off in the Combat Zone to see *Sexus* at the Pilgrim Theatre. You could claim you have a book report on Henry Miller due on Monday morning. But all this didn't matter. You wanted to see Luke get his hand cut off by his father one more time so you could brag about it during homeroom.

This attitude changed when you arrived at college and the allure of the local art house took hold. There's a desire when you're away from your parents to appear a touch more educated and sophisticated. You wanted to show that level of maturity that might fool a bartender into serving you a beer without asking for your driver's license. Or trick your date into not recognizing you're only a lowly freshman dweeb. There were two ways to approach this upping your education beyond the syllabus. The hard way was to constantly read a lot of fancy worded books and quote Jacques Derrida, Simone de Beauvoir and Arthur Schopenhauer during conversations about the nature of man. The easy way was to run down to the Art House Cinema so during a house party later in the night you can say, "Guess what I saw at...." Even a three-hour movie was faster than digesting Friedrich Nietzsche's *Beyond Good and Evil*. And in the movie, there was a chance of nudity.

Finding the local art house could be a bit tricky. They were the ones who always had a tiny advertisement in the newspaper while the major studios would take over an entire page to let you know Burt Reynolds was back as the Bandit. If you picked up your area's alternative weekly, the local reviewer would rave for inches about the latest film playing the art house. You knew a bit about what was playing on the screen. The chances of nudity kept your attention when your eyes grew tired of reading subtitles. The trouble began when you wanted to figure out how to get to the theater.

Most of the theaters were not ornate palaces in the poshest of commercial districts like your local Opera house. There was no opulence of lush carpets, velvet curtains and shining brass doors. They were rather old and dumpy because art

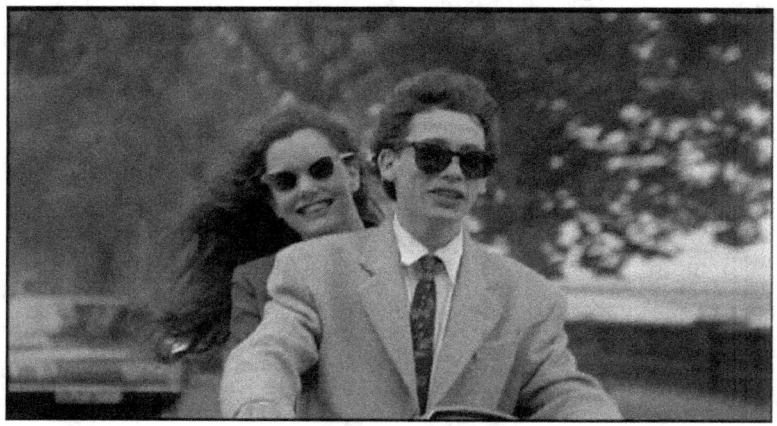

house movies didn't quite pack in the crowds like *Smokey and the Bandit II*. In Raleigh, the Colony Theater was in a rundown strip mall that was a bit of a drive from my college. The space had formerly been a Jerry Lewis Cinema in the '70s. Yes, Jerry Lewis had his own theater chain that was supposed to only book family films of G and PG ratings. Shockingly enough, the concept was a failure. But the abandoned theaters across the country were given new life offering up either second run films for a buck, porn flicks or converted to art houses. The Colony had '70s shag carpet tacked to the walls to help the acoustics that stayed up for decades. The Rialto Theatre was a bit closer to campus and lacked the tacky nature of Jerry Lewis. The theater opened back in 1942 when movies were a major community activity. Even forty years later the building felt like a place to congregate instead of lurk anonymously in order to theater creep past the ushers.

The first thing you'd experience is people hanging out under the marquee smoking. But instead of Lucky Strikes, they were puffing on clove cigarettes. Your nose let you know this was going to be a different experience than the Cineplex 6. Because there wasn't a big lobby and only a single screen, you'd have to wait under outside on the sidewalk for the earlier screening to let out. This was good because it gave you a few extra minutes to see if there's a familiar face from school mingling near you. It could be someone you've been meaning to meet. Waiting for

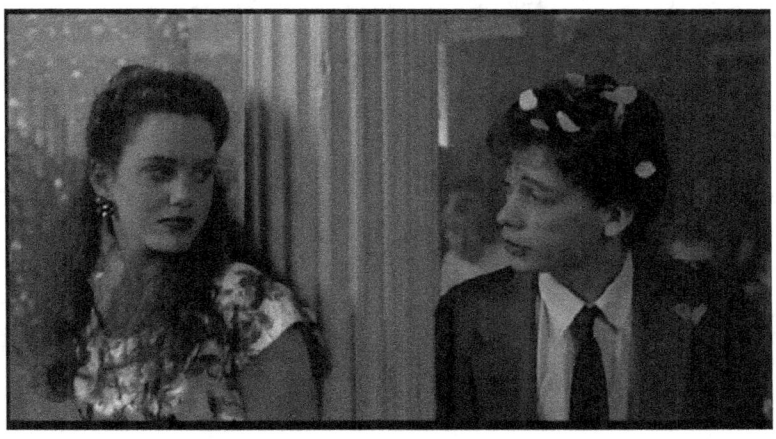

the doors to open gave you a chance to break the ice by asking them about the film instead of dropping the usual "What's your major" line. If the conversation went well, the doors would open and they'd be cool if you'd sit next to them instead of finding a seat by yourself. But before the seat, you'd want a snack. The biggest difference between the Art House and a Cineplex 20 was found at the concession stand. The art houses near me offered freshly popped popcorn. You could hear the corn kernels explode into the fluffy white goodness. They were still warm in the tub. The dark secret of the cineplex is that the employees pop the corn from Monday through Thursday, shovel the popcorn into big green garbage bags and stash them into a utility closet. When the weekend arrived, they just dumped it out into your medium tub. You've been eating days old trash popcorn at the Cineplex 20. Another special touch was the art house would remind you that you were getting authentic butter poured on your popcorn. The Cineplex 20 would squish out an unknown chemical from a dispenser legally required to declare its contents as "Golden Flavoring." This ooze might have been a failed attempt at creating Interferon. Real butter did have its own issue. You have to be ready to eat all the popcorn at a good pace. Why? Because if there's too much butter poured into the tub, it will congeal and your fingers won't like what it touches when it gets close to the bottom.

The candy selection at both places might seem to be the same with theater size boxes of Milk Duds, Lemonheads, Sno-Caps, Goobers, Raisinets, Dots, Junior Mints, Hot Tamales, Mike and Ike M&Ms. But the Art House offered the most precious chocolate bar known to mankind. Amongst the domestic sugary riff raff was a

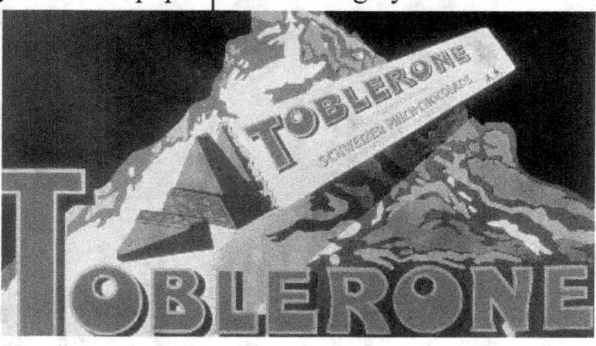

pleasure imported from Europe like the movie you had bought a ticket to see. The rectangular boxes gave way to the triangular joy of Toblerone. This Swiss milk chocolate with honey and bits of almond nougat was so much more decadent on the tongue. You'd slide the Toblerone out of the box and pop off the squished chocolate pyramid of sweetness from the conjoined pieces. It felt so esoteric. This was elevated viewing.

Back in the '80s, an art house theater provided a variety of films to attract an audience that wasn't up for the latest mindless entertainment from Hollywood. They booked international films that had subtitles if they weren't from England or Australia. Although sometimes the Commonwealth flicks needed subtitles with translations for the slang and the exchange rate for when they mentioned money. How much was a British Pound?

This was a time of true independent film distributors. The American indie films were a bit edgier and grainier with unfamiliar faces. They weren't out to attract everybody into the theater with that special crowd-pleasing formula. *My Dinner with Andre, Stranger Than Paradise* and *The Stepfather* weren't filled with car chases, explosions and big stars slumming it for a shot at an Oscar. Later we'd end up with the "Dependies" when Disney snagged Miramax, Warner nabbed New Line and the other major studios created their "Indie studio" for their Oscar bait productions.

There was also a bit of classic Hollywood revival when the art house would dedicate a week to the icons including James Dean, Humphrey Bogart, Marilyn Monroe and Alfred Hitchcock.

The revival house aspect started to get dialed back as so many of the classic films found their way onto Beta, VHS, laserdisc and even SelectaVision. Why go to a movie theater to see a film that you could easily rent from Videorama? By the end of the '80s, the only "old" studio film that got played at the Art House was the Friday midnight screening of *The Rocky Horror Picture Show*. That alone kept the teenage crowd coming even if they left a lot of rice and toast in the aisles.

While most of the movies that played at the Art House were adult in nature, teen flicks did occasionally pop up on the screen. Bill Forsyth's *Gregory's Girl* was a hit with the tale of a boy dealing with a girl who wants to play on his school's soccer team. I didn't actually see it in the theater since by the time my cousin Bill and I made it to the downtown theater, we were late. Although we did see another artsy teen flick in Éric Rohmer's *Pauline at the Beach* instead. That was about a teenage girl going to a beach in France with her older cousin. It was not one of those European bikini tops optional beaches we'd read about in *Playboy*. Julian Temple's *Absolute Beginners* gave us a taste of what it was like when the teenage explosion hit London in the early '60s. The film didn't linger long in the Art House as much as David Bowie's great theme song lasted on MTV.

One of the big things to remember about the Art House was the importance of seeing the film on opening weekend. Since the ones in my area had one or two screens, rarely did a film last longer than two weeks on the marquee. Merchant Ivory's *Room With A View* stuck around all summer in 1986, but that was a major exception for the times. Unlike the Cineplex 20 that could shuffle a Hollywood mega-production into a smaller screening room, an art film that tanked on Friday was in the cans and waiting for UPS to pick up on Thursday night. Such was the case for *The Rachel Papers* at my local art house. Even with the promise of Ione Skye romping around London, it didn't catch fire like *Say Anything* that came out around the same time. Why was it a bust? Perhaps part of it was the lack of a serious following for Martin Amis' novel from 1973. Those that were fans of the novel may have been outraged how the film altered the plot by having

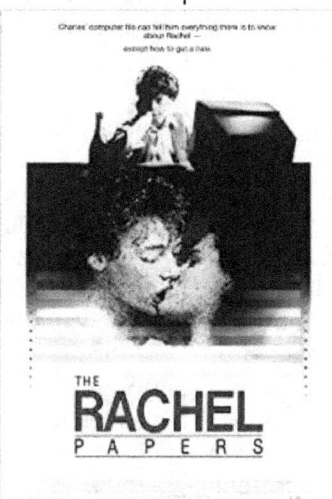

Charles Highway (Dexter Fletcher) type on a computer instead of always scribble in a notebook. If you're wondering what happened to Dexter Fletcher, he's become a bigtime director. He took over the Oscar winning Queen biopic *Bohemian Rhapsody* when Bryan Singer had to leave because of "issues" and completely directed *Rocketman* about Elton John. His upcoming *Sherlock Holmes 3* with Robert Downey Jr will not be playing at your nearby Art House theatre.

SOUNDTRACK NOTES: There appears to be no official soundtrack release for *The Rachel Papers*. This is a shame since there's plenty of English pop songs in the movie. Ex-member of Squeeze and British TV host Jools Holland con- 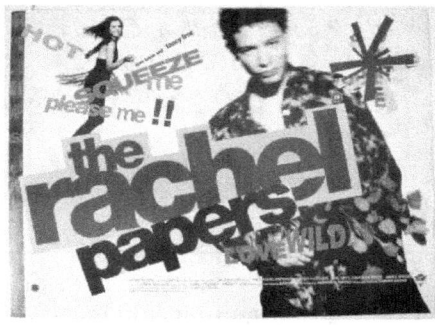 tributes "We're Through" and "Tongues in the Woods." His old Squeeze mates Chris Difford and Glenn Tilbrook use their duo project Difford & Tilbrook on "Within These Walls Of Without You" and "Simple Words." This is kind of confusing because by the time the movie came out, Difford and Tilbrook had reformed Squeeze for a few years. Ex-Bananarama singer Siobhan Fahey new band Shakespeares Sister provided the tracks "Electric Moon" and "You Made Me." The Godfather of House Music, Frankie Knuckles crushes it on "Tears." There are a few recognizable American voices with Michelle Shocked's "Graffiti Limbo," Los Lobos "Anselma" and Willy DeVille's "Assassin of Love." This would have been a great album to play while offering James Spader's girlfriend a segment of Toblerone?

Say Anything...

April 15, 1989

20*th* Century Fox

Directed by Cameron Crowe

Starring **John Cusack,** Ione Skye, John Mahoney, Lili Taylor, Polly Platt, Bebe Neuwirth, Pamela Adlon, Chynna Phillips, Jeremy Piven, Eric Stoltz, Philip Baker Hall, & Joan Cusack

Rated PG-13 - 100 minutes

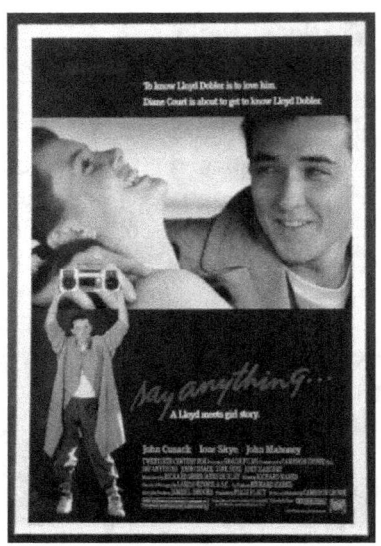

In the early morning light, Lloyd Dobler (John Cusack) pulled onto a park's dirt road, held a boombox over his head and played Peter Gabriel. He hoped that a slumbering Diane Court (Ione Skye) would wake and hear this grand gesture. Would she remember what they did the last time they were together and "In Your Eyes" played? Could Peter Gabriel bring them back together?

In a strange way, this moment is both powerful and lazy. What had happened to wooing culture in the '80s? This would be like Christian holding Cyrano de Bergerac on his shoulders in a chicken-fighting position and Roxanne thinking everything the long-nosed guy said were Christian's sentiments. Judging from Lloyd's earlier card to Diane after their intimate moment, he needed Peter Gabriel's help. And let's not forget how the only creative artist in the film is Corey (Lila Taylor) who wrote 63 songs about how Joe was so horrible to her when they dated. "They're all about pain," she declared. By the way, as a Joe Corey, *Say Anything...* is strange since Corey is singing about Joe. It's like Writer-Director Cameron Crowe had seen me on CBS'

48 Hours episode talking about NC State's Jim Valvano in 1988 and decided to split my name in half. But enough about me. Let's get back to Lloyd and his boombox.

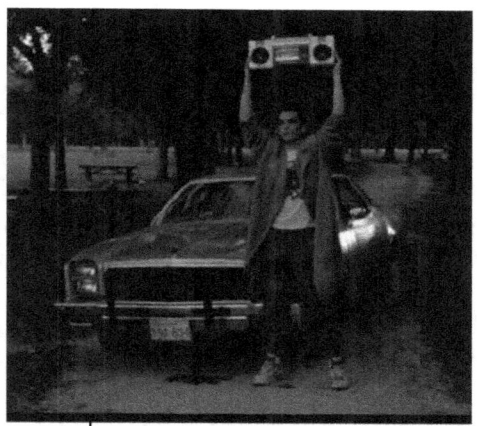

I won't spoil what happens when Lloyd puts down his boombox, but the memory he wants to inspire brings up plenty of questions. You might want to stop reading here if you haven't seen more than the trailer for *Say Anything*... Although why not read on since it's not exactly a shocking twist. You can read this now or wait 100 minutes to pick up the conversation. Just don't track me down after the screening and scream that I ruined it all for you. This is your choice: Proceed or dogear the page.

Are we all good? Let's get back to what led to Lloyd standing with his boombox. Why did he pick Peter Gabriel's "In Your Eyes?" Because a few days before when Lloyd and Diane went all the way in the backseat of his car, Peter Gabriel was singing during their post coital confessions. The song was the perfect aftercare. Still there are so many questions about this moment. Did Lloyd have the radio going in his car while he was in the backseat with Diane? Or Was he using his boombox to make sure the battery didn't drain? Was radio or boombox tuned into a radio station, playing the album or using a special mixtape?

There's no real visual clue such as a close up of the glowing car radio or the cassette twirling in the boombox. The headlights are off on Lloyd's car and there's no dashboard glow in the establishing shot. Seems like Lloyd didn't leave anything running as he parked near the ocean for the perfect view of nature while he's in the backseat with Diane Court. There's a serious chance that Lloyd went with the boombox to make sure the car battery didn't die. He didn't need to explain to anyone why they needed a jump in such a remote spot. Judging from how he and Diane take up the entire back seat with the blanket, the boombox had to be in the front seat.

Was the boombox on a radio station? Peter Gabriel's "In Your Eyes" peaked as a single in the Fall of 1986 after the *So* record came out in May. Lloyd and Diane had their precious moment in the Summer of 1988. If a radio station was playing the song, it would be considered an "oldie" in the rotation list. What if the DJ cued up one of the major summer songs? There could have been a tenderness if the needle dropped on Cheap Trick's "The Flame" or even Poison's "Every Rose has Its Thorn." But there were a lot more songs that would have destroyed the moment. You think anyone got laid to Bobby McFarrin's "Don't Worry Be Happy?" How good would Diane feel undressing to "I Hate Myself For Loving You" by Joan Jett and the Blackhearts? Lloyd might have appealed to her nerdy side with The KLF's "Doctorin' The Tardis," but it lacks the slow romantic jam quality. A massive hit that summer of DJ Jazzy Jeff and the Fresh Prince's "Parents Just Don't Understand." Sure, the lyrics might be expressing the sentiments of Mr. Court toward Lloyd, but would Diane want to feel Lloyd's hand on her naked butt while Will Smith rapped about Bowser and Sha Na Na? We won't even discuss what a train wreck this scene could have been if a demo by the Cherry Poppin' Daddies had come over the airwaves. The strangest and greatest thing that could have been found on the dial was Billy Ocean's "Get Out of My Dreams and Into My Car." For the love scene, this would have been too on the nail for Lloyd's finally getting buck wild with Diane. Imagine later when Lloyd stands with the boombox over his head and unleashes Billy Ocean's musical demand on Diane's window. He really would have come off as a stalker even with such an upbeat number blasting away in the A.M. haze. We will experiment with these tunes and that scene before the film starts.

Judging from what would have been played on a radio station influenced by MTV's hottest hits playlist, chances are Lloyd had his boombox switched to the tape mode. Which leads to our next question of whether he was playing the store-bought cassette of Peter Gabriel's *So*. For those who remember pre-recorded cassettes, they had two sides. "In Her Eyes" might be in the middle of your mom's CD or the album's digital playlist. But on a cassette, it's the first song on the second side. That means one of two things: Mixed Martial Arts maniac Lloyd Dobler couldn't last five minutes and 27 seconds with Diane Court or his boombox had an auto-cassette flip feature. If he started with side one, that means he was able to maintain a romantic mood through "Sledgehammer." Unless maybe Diane was begging for Lloyd to drive her to Pound Town. I'm not even sure if you can truly have sex with "Don't Give Up" with guest vocals from Kate Bush. The song is so weepy. It's like trying to get romantic while one of those commercials about donating to save starving puppies plays in the background.

This is why I'm convinced that Lloyd Dobler created a mixtape of songs he wanted playing the first time he got freaky with Diane Court. Back in the '80s, my old dorm pal Stan wrote "Bone MixTape" on the tape label of the cassette he played when he lured his date back into his dorm room. He refused to tell us his playlist. But judging from the noises, it was a recipe for success. This inspired us to concoct our own Bone MixTape using tunes that leaked from his room while the sock was on the doorknob. We also added our own songs that we'd hear and

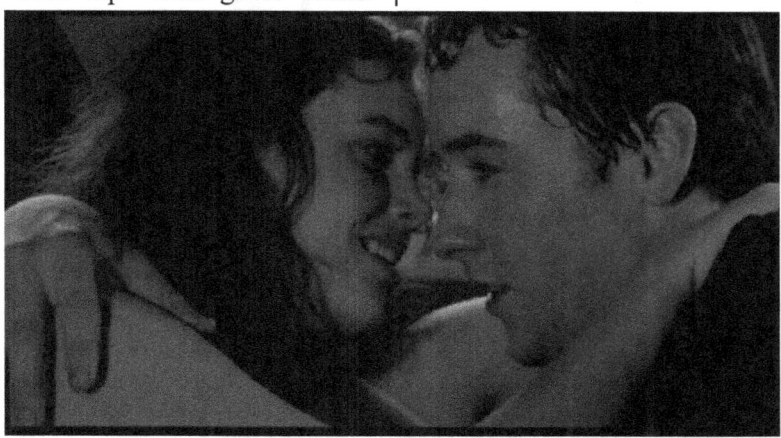

say, "Damn, I want that playing while I'm getting lucky." What was the key to this magical magnetic tape? A lot of time the music had what was considered the right beat for the downstroke loving motion. You needed a beat that worked for thrusting and not just a bunch of mushy ballads from Air Supply and Little River Band. The perfect song has always mattered for the moment. During a dance at junior high, you'd wait for the DJ to play the perfect song so you could approach the most approachable girl. Just the right beat so you could get close to her and not move like you're suffering an epileptic fit, but not slow enough that you'd blanket her immediately. No need to scare her away until the third dance. When you could legally get into strip clubs, you'd wait for the perfect song before begging the stripper to give you a table dance. What song could that be? Anything by Metallica since halfway through their marathon anthems, the stripper's mail will be forwarded to

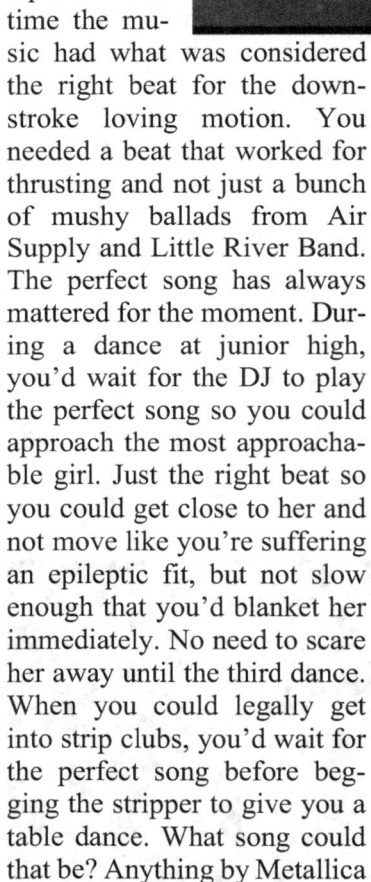

the table. After the bachelor party, you'd crave that special song for the first dance from your first wedding which is never Metallica's "Sad But True."

While we don't see him make the Bone MixTape in the movie, the fact that Lloyd picked out a perfect location, made sure the backset of the car wasn't covered in his mother and siblings' clothes and even remembered to bring a blanket showed he was prepared for more than just another friendly drive. Further proof that Lloyd was capable of striking a Bone MixTape is a deleted scene where he gives Diane a "Cool English Road Tape" after she decides to go to England. Lloyd probably spent more time picking out tracks for Diane than preparing for his next big bout in the ring. He probably calculated things so as "In Your Eyes" comes up, he'd start his countdown to ecstasy. Diane would always remember being in his arms and hearing Peter Gabriel confess that her eyes made him complete. What woman isn't going to think this isn't the most wonderful first sexual encounter ever? It was the perfect way to stick the landing. You didn't need to make a seductive mixtape if you owned a CD of Roxy Music's *Avalon*. When the prog rock gods released *Avalon* in May of 1982, they had created the most seductive and suave album ever. This was aural Spanish Fly. You didn't want the vinyl album or even the cassette tape for fear of flipping the sides. You didn't want to interrupt the 37 minutes and 31 seconds of music made to melt your clothes off as you go from sofa to waterbed. There was no "Sledgehammer" or "Big Time" to ruin the romantic flow. If Lloyd had pressed play on *Avalon*, movie theaters across the country would be turned into carnal orgies. But he stuck with a differnt prog rocker in Peter Gabriel.

What I've done is merely speculate what happened on the screen between Lloyd, Diane and the boombox. What's the real story? Turns out both scenes were a case of "We'll Fix It In Post." No music was playing in the car when Cusack and Skye delivered their post-coital lines. According to Cameron Crowe on the commentary track, he had written in the script that Billy Idol's "To Be A Lover" would be playing. This seems like an awkward song for a first hook up since it mostly features Billy repeating, "Forgot to be a lover." Nothing like starting a romantic relationship with an original UK punker expressing regrets. Cameron admitted he quickly jettisoned that request during production. Diane Court might have gone to third base on Billy's "Flesh For Fantasy."

There was music coming out of the boombox as Lloyd held it over his head, but it was also not Peter Gabriel. What cassette was turning when he pressed play? On the commentary track, Cusack said he chose Fishbone's "Turn The Other Way." The rather apocalyptic tinged lyrics of the song might have the neighbors calling the police with the fear that Lloyd had hung himself in the park. These two scenes were on course to be absolute trainwrecks until someone suggested "In Your Eyes." Watching in the audience, we all know what's being communicated when Lloyd holds that boombox and makes a plaintive plea with "In Your Eyes" to a distant Diane. The music has been connected with a moment between the once happy couple. The song has a transportive effect that makes us think of them in that car when things were so perfect.

We should all have those transportive songs that take us back to a moment in the '80s when things felt just right. For me, whenever I hear The Pet Shop's "West End Girls," my mind wanders back to the time my student newspaper went down to Atlanta in an RV to play in a basketball tournament featuring other college periodicals. We camped out on the floor of a Georgia Tech student's rental home. We won the title and I became legendary for fighting a Daily Tarheel player that tried to throw an elbow at me. After the party, I ended up hanging out with Lynn. She was one of the housemates. We laid on the floor, leaned against the sofa and quietly talked as others slumbered around us. She told me about growing up a Baptist minister's daughter, her love of skeet shooting and job at an art gallery. As we kept talking, MTV was playing on a small television. It felt like every thirty minutes, Nina Blackwood or J.J. Jackson would introduce The Pet Shop Boys' "West End Girls." Nothing happened between us like Lloyd and Diane. Lynn did invite me to sleep in her room, but it was nearly time to load up the RV and head back to Raleigh. I stayed put. I feared nobody would think of looking for me in her bedroom and they'd just leave without me. We said goodbye, she went off to sleep in her bed and away I eventually went. I never found myself back in Atlanta. I never called or wrote her. I didn't even try to get a long-distance dedication out of Casey Kasem of American Top 40.

Sometimes when I'm pushing

a shopping cart in the grocery store, I hear "West End Girls." I think of that moment in time. I wonder what Lynn thinks about when she hears "West End Girls" while pushing a shopping cart around a Piggly Wiggly supermarket. Does she remember the goofy college kid who laid next to her on the floor that night? Does she wish I had stayed in touch? Does she imagine my life? Does she wish she'd used her shotgun on me? Or does she just think, "MTV used to play this song every hour in the '80s" and investigate the best head of cabbage in the bin. If MTV had been playing Peter Gabriel's "In Your Eyes" video all night long, I know Lynn would merely remember Lloyd Dobler holding his boombox.

SOUNDTRACK NOTES: The original soundtrack cassette does not qualify as a Bone MixTape. It's all over the place musically although probably what a teenager in Seattle would play on their boombox. Things start off with Nancy Wilson of Heart doing "All For Love." At this time, Nancy Wilson had gone from being 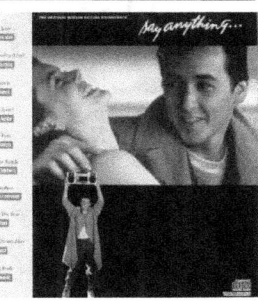 the lady flirting with Pirate Brad in *Fast Times At Ridgemont High* to writer-director's Cameron Crowe's wife. Living Colour's big hit "Cult of Personality" gets released with a live version. Guitar ace Joe Satriani overwhelms the frets for "One Big Rush." Remember when we joked about Cheap Trick's "The Flame?" Turns out "You Want It" made it on the soundtrack. The Red Hot Chili Peppers appropriately play "Taste The Pain." In case you want to dub a Lloyd Dobler inspired Bone MixTape, they included Peter Gabriel's "In Your Eyes" with Youssou N'Dour supplying his Senegalese vocal smoothness on the backing vocals. Giving a dance floor tinge, there's Depeche Mode's "Stripped." Proving it's an '80s cool soundtrack, we are given The Replacements' "Within Your Reach." Since John Cusack wanted them in the film, there's Fishbone's "Skankin' To the Beat." Things wrap up with the unlisted "Lloyd Dobler Rap." This would snap your Bone MixTape.

HONOR ROLL

Curtis Armstrong
Risky Business
Better Off Dead
One Crazy Summer

Matthew Broderick
Ferris Bueller's Day Off

Nicholas Cage
Fast Times At Ridgemont High
Valley Girl

Phoebe Cates
Fast Times At Ridgemont High
Private School

Tom Cruise
Losin' It
Risky Business

Jon Cryer
No Small Affair
O.C. and Stiggs
Pretty In Pink

John Cusack
Class
Sixteen Candles
The Sure Thing
Better Off Dead
One Crazy Summer
Say Anything....

E.G. Daily
Valley Girl
No Small Affair
Better Off Dead

Robert Downey Jr.
Weird Science
The Pick-up Artist
Less Than Zero

Emilio Estevez
The Breakfast Club
St. Elmo's Fire

Jami Gertz
Sixteen Candles
The Lost Boys
Less Than Zero

Crispin Glover
My Tutor
River's Edge

Jennifer Grey
Red Dawn
Ferris Bueller's Day Off

Anthony Michael Hall
Sixteen Candles
The Breakfast Club
Weird Science

Dennis Hopper
O.C. and Stiggs
River's Edge
The Pick-up Artist

Rob Lowe
Class
St. Elmo's Fire
Youngblood

Andrew McCarthy
Class
St. Elmo's Fire
Pretty In Pink
Less Than Zero
Fresh Horses

Matthew Modine
Private School
Vision Quest

Demi Moore
No Small Affair
St. Elmo's Fire
One Crazy Summer

Taylor Negron
Fast Times At Ridgemont High
Better Off Dead
One Crazy Summer
River's Edge

Judd Nelson
The Breakfast Club
St. Elmo's Fire

Keanu Reeves
Youngblood
River's Edge

Molly Ringwald
Sixteen Candles
The Breakfast Club
Pretty In Pink
The Pick-up Artist
Fresh Horses

Robert Romanus
Foxes
Fast Times At Ridgemont High

Alan Ruck
Class
Ferris Bueller's Day Off

Michael Schoeffling
Sixteen Candles
Vision Quest

Ally Sheedy
The Breakfast Club
St. Elmo's Fire

Charlie Sheen
Red Dawn
Ferris Bueller's Day Off

Ione Skye
River's Edge
The Rachel Papers
Say Anything...

Harry Dean Stanton
Red Dawn
Pretty In Pink

Eric Stoltz
Fast Times At Ridgemont High
Some Kind of Wonderful
Say Anything...

James Spader
Pretty in Pink
Less Than Zero
The Rachel Papers

Patrick Swayze
Red Dawn
Youngblood

Lea Thompson
Red Dawn
Some Kind of Wonderful

Ray Walston
Fast Times At Ridgemont High
Private School
O.C. and Stiggs

Forest Whitaker
Fast Times At Ridgemont High
Vision Quest

Daphne Zuniga
Vision Quest
The Sure Thing

The 2020
'80s Teen Flick Festival
is dedicated
to the memory of
Taylor Negron
(1957 - 2015)

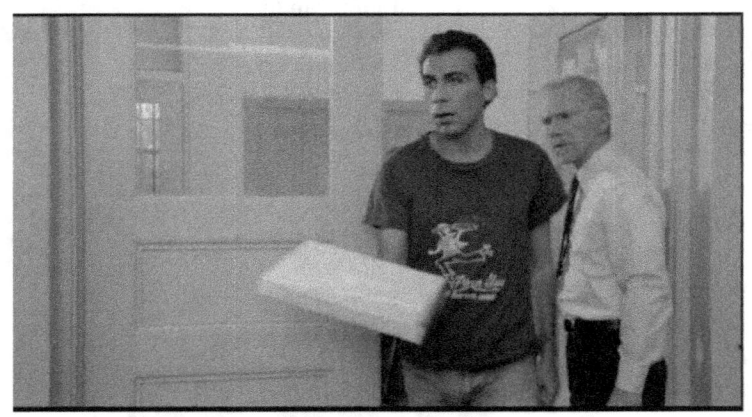

He always delivered.

See Taylor Negron in
Fast Times At Ridgemont High,
Better Off Dead,
One Crazy Summer & *River's Edge*